Durkheim and the I

Also by Steven Lukes

Emile Durkheim: His Life and Work
Individualism
Power: A Radical View
Marxism and Morality
The Curious Enlightenment of Professor Caritat: A Novel of Ideas
Moral Relativism

Also by Andrew Scull

Decarceration
Museums of Madness: The Social Organization of Insanity in
    Nineteenth-Century England
Madhouses, Mad-doctors and Madmen: The Social History of Psychiatry
    in the Victorian Era
Social Control and the State (with Stanley Cohen)
Social Order/Mental Disorder: Anglo-American Psychiatry in Historical
    Perspective
The Asylum as Utopia
The Most Solitary of Afflictions: Madness and Society in Britain,
    1700–1900
Masters of Bedlam: The Transformation of the Mad-doctoring Trade
    (with Nicholas Hervey and Charlotte MacKenzie)
Undertaker of the Mind
Patrons and Customers of the Mad Trade: The Management of Lunacy
    in Eighteenth-Century London
Madhouse: A Tragic Tale of Megalomania and Modern Medicine
The Insanity of Place/The Place of Insanity
Hysteria
Madness: A Very Short Introduction

Durkheim and the Law

Second Edition

Edited By

Steven Lukes

Professor of Sociology, New York University

and

Andrew Scull

Distinguished Professor of Sociology,
University of California

First published 1983 by Martin Robertson & Company
Reprinted 1984 by Basil Blackwell Publishers

Second edition published 2013 by
PALGRAVE MACMILLAN

Palgrave Macmillan in the UK is an imprint of Macmillan Publishers Limited, registered in England, company number 785998, of Houndmills, Basingstoke, Hampshire RG21 6XS.

Palgrave Macmillan is the global academic imprint of the above companies and has companies and representatives throughout the world.

Palgrave® and Macmillan® are registered trademarks in the United States, the United Kingdom, Europe and other countries

ISBN 978–1–137–35240–8 hardback
ISBN 978–1–137–03181–5 paperback

This book is printed on paper suitable for recycling and made from fully managed and sustained forest sources. Logging, pulping and manufacturing processes are expected to conform to the environmental regulations of the country of origin.

A catalogue record for this book is available from the British Library.

A catalog record for this book is available from the Library of Congress.

Printed and bound in the UK by Charlesworth Press, Wakefield

Contents

List of Sources

CHAPTER 1: The Durkheimian View of Morality and Law

Durkheim, Review of Neukamp's 'The Historical Development of Legal Constraint' ('Das Zwangsmoment im Recht in entwicklungsgeschichtlicher Bedeutung') in *L'Année sociologique*, vol. 3 (1900), pp. 324–5, translated by Andrew Scull.

Durkheim, Review of Lévy-Bruhl's *Morality and the Science of Morals* (*La Morale et la science des moeurs*) in *L'Année sociologique*, vol. 7 (1904), pp. 380–4, translated by Andrew Scull.

Durkheim, 'Moral and Juridical Systems' ('Systèmes juridiques et moraux') in *L'Année sociologique*, vol. 11 (1910), pp. 286–8, translated by Andrew Scull.

Durkheim, 'Criminal Sociology and Moral Statistics' ('Sociologie criminelle et statistique morale') in *L'Année sociologique*, vol. 4 (1901), pp. 433–6, translated by Andrew Scull.

CHAPTER 2: Law as an Index of Social Solidarity

Durkheim (2013) *The Division of Labour in Society* Steven Lukes (ed.), Basingstoke, Palgrave Macmillan: pp. 51–6.

CHAPTER 3: From Repressive to Restitutive Law

Durkheim (2013) *The Division of Labour,* op. cit., pp. 57–63, 64–5, 88–91, 226–8.

CHAPTER 4: The Evolution of Punishment

Durkheim 'Two Laws of Penal Evolution' ('Deux lois de l'évolution pénale'), *L'Année sociologique* 4 (1901), pp. 65–95, translated by T. Anthony Jones and Andrew Scull, first appearing in *Economy and Society* 2 (3) (August 1973). It is reprinted here in slightly amended form.

CHAPTER 5: Crime and Punishment

Durkheim (2013) *The Division of Labour*, op. cit., pp. 67–74, 83–4.
Durkheim (2013) *The Rules of Sociological Method and Selected Texts on Sociology and its Method* Steven Lukes (ed.), Basingstoke: Palgrave Macmillan: pp. 60–4.
Gabriel Tarde, 'Criminality and Social Health' ('Criminalité et santé sociale') *Revue philosophique* 39 (1895), pp. 148–62, translated by Andrew Scull.
Durkheim, 'Crime and Social Health' ('Crime et santé sociale'), *Revue philosophique* 39 (1895), pp. 518–23, translated by Andrew Scull.

CHAPTER 6: The Legal Prohibition of Suicide

Durkheim, *On Suicide* (translated by Robin Buss), Penguin Books: Harmondsworth and New York, 2006, pp. 362–75.

CHAPTER 7: The Moral Foundations of Modern Law: Individualism

Durkheim, 'Individualism and the Intellectuals' ('L'Individualisme et les intellectuels'), *Revue bleue*, 4th series 10 (1898) pp. 7–13, translated by Steven Lukes.

CHAPTER 8: The Origins of Law

Durkheim, Review of Richard's 'Essay on the Origin of the Idea of Law' ('Essai sur L'origine de L'idée de droit') in *Revue philosophique* 35 (1893), pp. 290–6, translated by Andrew Scull
Durkheim, Review of Kulischer's 'Research on Primitive Penal Law' ('Untersuchungen über das primitive Strafrecht'), *Zeitschrifc für vergleichende Recluswissenschaft*, XVI (1904) Bd., 1–11, pp. 1–22. In *L'Annee sociologique* 8, pp. 460–3. Translated by Steven Lukes and W. D. Halls.

CHAPTER 9: The Basis and Evolution of Contract

Durkheim, *The Division of Labour in Society*, op. cit., pp. 159–70, 177–9.

From Durkheim, *Leçons de sociologie: physique des moeurs et du droit.*
Foreword by H. N. Kubali; Introduction by G. Davy. Istanbul:
L'Université d'Istanbul, Publications de l'Université, Faculté du Droit
no. 111 and Paris: Presses Universitaires de France, 1950, pp. 206–59,
translated by Raphaelle Thery.

Preface

The law was a central topic of innovative thinking by Emile Durkheim, yielding concepts and insights that have had a long-lasting and continuing influence on subsequent scholarship. This is a revised and expanded edition of a book we originally published in 1983. In the original edition, we gathered together key passages from his major works and posthumously published lectures, a seminal essay about legal evolution and newly translated book reviews from his remarkable co-edited journal, *L'Année sociologique,* as well as making available in English for the first time his celebrated debate with Gabriel Tarde over his provocative theory of crime and punishment. The aim of bringing these texts together was to help the reader to obtain a comprehensive view of Durkheim's distinctive contribution to the sociology of law.

This new considerably expanded and revised edition seeks to further that aim by adding to these original texts some further examples of Durkheim's thinking on the sociology of law. We have taken the opportunity to amend some of the translations of materials we originally reprinted, where this provided for a more accurate rendering of particular texts. To the materials we began with we have added several revealing further reviews and notes from the *Année,* as well as a major essay occasioned by the Dreyfus Affair. This essay, 'Individualism and the Intellectuals', was a polemical intervention into one of the most fraught political conflicts of the *fin de siècle* and was influential at the time. For present purposes, however, we contend that it has a more enduring importance for understanding Durkheim's ideas, prompting him to engage in some extremely provocative extensions and clarifications of his thoughts about the links between law, morality and social cohesion in modern complex, heterogeneous societies.

Revisiting this territory together has given us the opportunity to revise and expand our earlier introduction. We have incorporated further reflections on the continuing importance of Durkheim's ideas for the contemporary sociology of law, crime and punishment. Some of these were stimulated by responses to the original edition of this book, and others by scholarship that has appeared since its publication – a variety of work that has caused us to rethink as well as to clarify some of our original arguments. At our publisher's suggestion, we have also included as part of this new edition a set of short introductions to each of the nine chapters of the

book. These aim to provide non-sociological readers, and readers encoun-
tering Durkheim for the first time, with some additional background
knowledge about both the man himself and the Durkheimian school of
sociology. These introductory passages also seek to make clear the place
each of the reprinted texts occupied in the evolution of Durkheim's thinking on legal matters.

   Obviously, Durkheim's work continues to stimulate and engage us, as it
does so many others, and we hope this new edition will contribute to a
broader appreciation of his contributions to the sociology of law, and of
the centrality of law and morality to his thinking about society.

STEVEN LUKES
ANDREW SCULL

Acknowledgements

It has been a great pleasure for both of us to have had the chance to work together again on this considerably revised and enlarged second edition of *Durkheim and the Law,* after an interval of almost three decades. On this occasion, we have had the inestimable advantage of the internet, which has greatly facilitated our collaborative work, living as we do some 3,000 miles apart. We are grateful to Frances Arnold of Palgrave Macmillan for her interest in and support for this project, and for soliciting a number of penetrating reviews of our original manuscript. Two of those anonymous reviewers, in particular, made some extremely helpful suggestions about how to strengthen the book, and we are greatly in their debt. We should also like to acknowledge David Garland's very close and generous reading of our introduction to the volume as a whole, which substantially improved the text.

Editors' Introduction to the Second Edition

Like other great sociologists Emile Durkheim addressed questions that, according to C. Wright Mills, typify the sociological imagination. Among these questions are: What is the structure of this society as a whole? What are its essential components and how are they related to one another? How does it differ from other varieties of social order? Where does the society stand in human history? What are the mechanisms by which it is changing? And how are we to understand the connections between 'personal troubles' that beset the individual 'within the range of his immediate relations with others' and 'the public issues of social structure' (Mills 1959: 6–8)?

Durkheim addressed such questions across a wide range of sociological fields, and his distinctive answers remain of compelling interest, even – perhaps especially – where we are led to qualify and criticize them. In these answers the law has a very central place. His first major work, *The Division of Labour in Society*, contrasts the 'organic solidarity' of modern, industrialized societies, consisting in ever-growing interdependence and functional differentiation of roles, with the 'mechanical solidarity' of clan-based and ancient, pre-industrial societies, unified by segmental structures composed of similar component units. The growing division of labour constituted the great transformation from homogeneity to heterogeneity and from collectivism to individualism, accompanying increasing volume and density of populations and involving the growth of cities and markets. The law both reflected and regulated this transformation. It was, he thought, an external index registering the nature of social solidarity: hence his early thesis that pre-modern societies were characterized by penal or 'repressive' law and modern societies based on the division of labour by 'restitutive law' of which the central example is contract.

Organic solidarity could, however, also take pathological, or 'abnormal', forms, when, because of 'unjust contracts', it involved exploitation, or when, because of insufficient regulation, it led to *anomie*, or normlessness, whose victims are afflicted by an obsessive acquisitive drive. He was responding in this instance to the final question in the first paragraph above, which he explored further in his famous work *Suicide*. Here *anomie*, the 'malady of infinite aspiration' (which was manifest in both economic and sexual relations), together with what he called 'egoism', or

1

social isolation, are presented as distinctive pathologies of contemporary capitalist societies. The remedy, he thought, lay in legal reforms: in regulating contracts to render them more just; and in the development of secondary occupational associations, composed of workers and employers, with their own means of normative self-regulation. These would mediate between the individual and an interventionist state, which had a special responsibility to impose rules of justice on economic exchanges, to ensure that 'each is treated as he deserves, that he is freed of all unjust and humiliating dependence, that he is joined to his fellows and to the group without abandoning his personality to them' (Durkheim 1950: 87). Durkheim's writings on the family, the incest taboo, on divorce and on property also focus on the law, which he always saw as the entry point into the study of the messier subject matter of social norms, customs and practices.

In the mid-1890s Durkheim's thought took an interesting turn towards the study of religion, which in his great work *The Elementary Forms of Religious Life* he came to define as '*a unified system of beliefs and practices relative to sacred things, that is to say, things set apart and forbidden—beliefs and practices which unite into one single moral community called a Church, all those who adhere to them*' (Durkheim 1995: 44). Notice that on this definition there can be 'secular religions', such as what he called the 'religion of individualism', which he saw as the unifying ideology of his own society, the French Third Republic. Reflection on religion thus understood led him to an ever-deeper set of reflections on the criminal law. The link between the two lay in what he came to call '*représentations collectives*' – collective beliefs and sentiments which crime violates and punishment re-animates. This led him to his paradoxical thesis that crime is a normal phenomenon, even a factor in social health, provided its incidence lies within 'normal' limits, by eliciting punitive reactions on the part of authorities, reactions that would express and thereby reinforce what is central, even 'sacred', within prevailing morality. The seeming relativism of this view was, however, mitigated by his idea that crime can also be a force for moral innovation, when the violation of anachronistic norms and values that are incompatible with society's 'conditions of existence' is the harbinger of an emergent moral code. These claims about crime and punishment led to an acrimonious debate with the magistrate and criminologist, Gabriel Tarde, with views sharply opposed to his, which we reprint in Chapter 5.

This view of punishment echoes Durkheim's earlier 'index thesis', for he saw the form of punishment, and thus the sanctions of the criminal law, as symbolic: as expressing and serving to reinforce prevalent *représentations collectives*. And so he supplemented his earlier account of legal evolution, from repressive to restitutive law, with a further thesis concerning the evolution of punishment. The earlier account had suggested that penal law had progressively declined with the recession of mechanical and the advance of organic solidarity. He now argued that punishment becomes milder as one goes from less to more advanced societies, consisting increasingly of the deprivation of liberty. The central idea here was that in so-called 'less advanced' societies, crimes largely took the form of sacrilege against 'collective things', offending sentiments directed towards transcendent and superhuman beings and inspiring reverential fear. In modern societies, by contrast, typical crimes were offences against the new locus of 'the sacred', namely, the human person, injuring only individuals – offences such as murder, theft, violence and frauds of all kinds. As crime became more human and less religious, he ingeniously argued, punishment became generally less severe, for the intriguing reason that there is 'a real and irremediable contradiction in avenging the offended human dignity of the victim by violating that of the criminal' (this vol.: 98). Since this antinomy could not be removed, it could only be alleviated by alleviating the punishment as far as possible. Needless to say, this account of penal evolution has been widely and hotly contested, but, as we shall suggest, that discussion has been of real value for the understanding of punishment in our own time.

Much of Durkheim's writings about law, as well as those of his followers, has relevance for our own time. We here single out two grand themes that are central and fundamental today. These can, we suggest, be brought under two broad headings that correspond to the two phases of his thinking just outlined: namely, his account of the relations between law and social solidarity and his account of the symbolic dimension of the criminal law.

It was in the mid-eighteenth century that the idea of 'natural order' entered the field of political economy – the notion, in Bernard Harcourt's words, that 'economic exchange constitutes a system that autonomously can achieve equilibrium without government intervention or outside interference'. This notion 'made possible the belief in self-adjusting and self-sustaining markets' and enabled 'our contemporary perception of modern markets as free' (Harcourt 2011: 26). It was Durkheim, we contend, who provided the most compelling because the most far-reaching critique of that perception.

He developed that critique (see the extract from *The Division of Labour* reproduced in Chapter 9) in opposition to Herbert Spencer's then influential articulation of that perception. Durkheim's central insight is succinctly captured in Talcott Parsons's phrase 'the non-contractual element in the contract'. Spencer's picture of social order in modern industrial societies was of a natural, pre-social order from which social order would supposedly result. But this would not be genuine social order, since, Durkheim argued:

> social solidarity would be nothing more than the spontaneous agreement between individual interests, an agreement of which contracts are the natural

expression. The type of social relations would be the economic relationship, freed from all regulation, and as it emerges from the entirely free initiative of the parties concerned. In short, society would be no more than the establishment of relationships between individuals exchanging the products of their labour, and without any social influence, properly so termed, intervening to regulate that exchange. (This vol.: 182)

Such a society would be unstable, since 'every harmony of interests conceals a latent conflict, or one that is simply deferred' (185). Besides, in any case, the trend in industrial societies was towards ever more extensive public regulation of private contractual relations, so that '[w]henever a contract exists, it is submitted to a regulatory force that is imposed by society and not by individuals; it is a force that becomes ever more weighty and complex' (188). The role of society, he wrote, is not merely to ensure the contracts are carried out. It also has to determine 'in what conditions they are capable of being executed and, if the need arise, restore them to their normal form. Agreement between the parties concerned cannot make a clause fair which of itself is unfair. There are rules of justice that social justice must prevent being violated, even if a clause has been agreed by the parties concerned.' (191) Moreover, the 'rules of professional morality and law' play the same role, maintaining 'a network of obligations from which we have no right to disengage ourselves.' We are, however, ever more dependent on the state, for the 'points where we come into contact with it are multiplied, as well as the occasions when it is charged with reminding us of the sentiment of our common solidarity' (193).

There are two separable ideas here concerning the law and market-based exchange. The first is that the law serves to *constitute* market relations. It does so, for instance, by allocating property rights and by providing the techniques or instruments required to make markets work, through contract and tort law. Durkheim, however, went further than this, arguing, as Prosser puts it, that law and regulation generally 'provide the essential social underpinning of mutual trust and expectation which is necessary for markets to function' (Prosser 2006: 382). The second idea – of considerable contemporary relevance – is that Durkheim's conception of social solidarity can provide a rationale for regulating markets, and indeed for determining where market exchange is appropriate and where it is not. Such a rationale, unlike the usual case for regulating markets in terms of market failure, does not embody the default assumption that market allocation is best, unless shown otherwise, and directly raises the question of the ways in which market exchange can corrode and fragment social solidarity.

This points to a further respect in which this aspect of Durkheim's thought about law and regulation is relevant to our times: namely, his very conception of social solidarity. Cotterrell has rightly observed that for Durkheim and some writers in a renewed Durkheimian tradition, a pressing issue is how to symbolize social unity and create for modern complex societies a moral framework in which regulation is effective, and the regulated are able, in some way, to participate as moral actors in a solidary society which is more than an economic free for all. (Cotterrell 1991:936)

Durkheim's distinctive way of addressing this issue can be read as a significant contribution to the ramifying debates among political philosophers since the publication of John Rawls's *A Theory of Justice* about principles that are to define a 'well-ordered society' that is both liberal and socially cohesive. His view is distinctive in combining strongly defended features of both liberal and communitarian perspectives. This can be seen in his remarkable essay 'Individualism and the Intellectuals', reprinted in Chapter 7, written at white heat in the midst of the Dreyfus Affair. Here Durkheim argued that central liberal principles expressing respect for individual dignity, notably the protections of basic individual rights, are inseparably part of the 'religion of individualism', which has 'penetrated our institutions and our customs' and 'become the sole link which binds us one to another'. Thus, he wrote, 'the individualist, who defends the rights of the individual, defends at the same time the vital interests of society' (this vol.: 154, 160).

The second grand theme of Durkheim's work that is central and fundamental to our time relates to his later preoccupation with religion: namely, his focus on the symbolic dimension of the law, and in particular the criminal law. This has generated both disagreement and alternative developments from his central ideas. We turn to the discussion of this theme later in the course of this introduction, and, in particular, in its concluding section.

The Development of Durkheim's Ideas about Law

Law was, then, a topic of central interest to Durkheim, as it was to several of his followers. In his first major work, *The Division of Labour in Society*, as we have briefly indicated, Durkheim in effect advanced three bold and striking theses about law. The first was what we can call 'the index thesis': that law should be conceived as an 'external' index which 'symbolizes' the nature of social solidarity (this vol.: 57) – of which there were two broad types: 'mechanical solidarity', typical of simpler, relatively homogeneous pre-modern societies and 'organic solidarity', typical of more complex, differentiated and organized modern societies. The second was the thesis concerning law's evolution, summarized in Table 1, according to which societies developed from less to more advanced forms, from an all-encompassing religiosity to modern secularism, and from collectivism to individualism, alongside an overall shift from a predominantly

Table 1   Mechanical and organic solidarity

	Mechanical solidarity based on resemblances (predominant in less advanced societies)	*Organic solidarity* based on division of labour (predominant in more advanced societies)
(1) Morphological (structural) basis	Segmental type (first clan-based, later territorial) Little interdependence (social bonds relatively weak Relatively low volume of population Relatively low material and moral density	Organized type (fusion of markets and growth of cities) Much interdependence (social bonds relatively strong Relatively high volume of population Relatively high material and moral density
(2) Type of norms (typified by law)	Rules with repressive sanctions Prevalence of penal law	Rules with restitutory sanctions Prevalence of cooperative law (civil, commercial, procedural, administrative and constitutional law)
(3a) Formal features of *conscience collective*	High volume High intensity High determinateness Collective authority absolute	Low volume Low intensity Low determinateness More room for individual initiative and reflection
(3b) Content of *conscience collective*	Highly religious Transcendental (superior to human interests and beyond discussion Attaching supreme value to society and interests of society as a whole	Increasingly secular Human-oriented (concerned with human interests and open to discussion) Attaching supreme value to individual dignity, equality of opportunity, work ethic and social justice
	Concrete and specific	Abstract and general

Source: Lukes, *Emile Durkheim: His Life and Work*, p. 158.

penal law with 'repressive organized sanctions' to a prevalence of 'civil law, commercial law, procedural law, administrative and constitutional law' with 'purely restitutive' sanctions (60–1). The third thesis concerned law's functioning, above all in the context of crime and punishment, claiming that crime is a violation and punishment an expression of collective sentiments, and that punishment's 'real function is to maintain inviolate the cohesion of a society by sustaining the common consciousness in all its vigour' (113).

These theses were fundamental to Durkheim's early work but they raised deep and difficult theoretical and conceptual problems with which he later tried to grapple. In later writings, moving in important ways away from his earlier formulations, he eventually developed a more complex approach to understanding the relationship between law and morality, as part of a general attempt to move beyond the problems associated with the notion that modern societies were characterized by organic forms of social solidarity. Central to his thinking was a Durkheimian analysis of the development of individualism as a core element of modernity, a value system rooted in what was most characteristic of developed societies, and one that took on some of the characteristics of a religion. The interrelations of law, morality and individualism lie at the heart of this emerging perspective, which saw Durkheim pre-occupied with the role of these factors in creating symbols of social unity that reined in the tendency of modern societies to dissolve into an economic free-for-all. Freedom, for Durkheim, was the very opposite of anarchy. It could manifest itself only in the context of regulation. Liberty, he memorably wrote (Durkheim 1961: 54) 'is the fruit of regulation'.

This paradoxical claim expresses an insight central to his discussion of *anomie* in *Suicide* (Durkheim 1951), and developed further in 'Individualism and the Intellectuals' (reproduced in Chapter 7), and in his lectures on Moral Education. As he put it in those lectures, 'Morality... is basically a discipline. All discipline has a double objective: to promote a certain regularity in people's conduct, and to provide them with determinate goals that at the same time limit their horizons. Discipline promotes a preference for the customary, and it imposes restrictions' (Durkheim 1961: 47). Only in the context of limits can human beings achieve happiness and fulfilment, and regulation thus 'deserves to be cherished' (Durkheim: 1961: 54). In their absence, existential terror beckons, as nothing in our nature serves to moderate or contain our passions, to curtail our desires, or to allow us to restrain ourselves. Emancipation and freedom, even for individuals, require self-mastery and self-control: 'Like everything else,' Durkheim insisted, 'man is a limited being: he is part of a whole. Physically, he is part of the universe; morally, he is part of society. Hence, he cannot, without violating his nature, try to supersede the limits imposed on every hand.' (Durkheim 1961: 51) Discipline is thus not regrettable or a necessary evil. Rather, gratification of our desires requires that they be held within some bounds. Social constraint is vital to a satisfying existence, even in contemporary society.

Yet under modern conditions, with society constantly in a state of flux and change, discipline can no longer involve 'a blind and slavish submission' to rigid rules (Durkheim 1961: 52). Necessarily, morality has to incorporate elements of reflection, and to be subject to criticism, so as to be flexible enough to change gradually, even while simultaneously retaining the authority, the ability to constrain, that Durkheim saw as the most central feature of *la morale*. Thus the problem of order in modern complex societies was, in essence, one of creating, to quote Roger Cotterrell (1991: 943), 'a moral framework in which regulation is effective and the regulated are able, in some way, to participate as moral actors in a solidary society…'. As various forms of traditional discipline weaken with the advance of modernity, social conditions 'may easily give rise to a spirit of anarchy… a common aversion to anything smacking of regulation' (Durkheim 1961: 54). That road leads, in Durkheim's view, to chaos, the breakdown of social order, the complete loss of liberty as we lose the capacity to govern ourselves. And if we are to avoid this fate, law and legal regulation will necessarily occupy centre stage.

We might even say, moving beyond the three hypotheses about law he had propounded in his earlier work, and that we have outlined above, that Durkheim in this later work put forward a fourth provocative hypothesis which is really an extension of the third) about law's place in society: law, he contended, functions indispensably 'as an instrument and expression of community and social solidarity, given the diverse modern milieus of modern societies' (Cotterrell 1991: 943); its rituals, its interventions, its occasions for debating and authoritatively resolving moral issues, and ultimately its invocation of penal force, all serve to reaffirm and to reinforce the sorts of flexible yet firm regulation essential to the preservation of social order. Even under modern conditions of existence, deviance threatens to demoralize society, for such violations of societal norms, left unpunished, sharply call moral authority into question, indeed will eventually cause it to collapse. Or as Durkheim (1961: 167) himself put it, in *Moral Education*, 'punishment does not give [moral] discipline its authority, but it prevents discipline from losing its authority, which infractions, if they went unpunished, would progressively erode'. Our commitment to the moral order, our sense of its power to constrain and to order our existence, and thus our very ability to trust others – the foundation of the complex relations that make up modern society – are at stake: 'the law that has been violated must somehow bear witness that despite appearances it remains always itself, that it has lost none of its force or authority despite the act which repudiated it. In other words, it must assert itself in the face of the violation and react in such a way as to demonstrate a strength proportionate to that of the attack against it. Punishment is nothing but this meaningful demonstration ... the palpable symbol through which an inner state is represented; it is a notation, a language ... which ... expresses the feeling inspired by the disapproved behaviour' (Durkheim 1961: 166, 176).

Both Durkheim's early theses about law and its evolution, and his later attempt to resolve the difficulties they raised, have been influential among his followers and raise important questions for the sociology of law. Among modern sociologists, particularly in the English-speaking world, it was the three earlier claims that long received the most attention, and for a time were broadly influential. Yet they were vulnerable to important criticisms, as we shall spell out in the discussion which follows, and as Durkheim implicitly acknowledged by grappling with a more complex account of law's place in modern societies in his later lectures and writings. Partly because those ideas were advanced in less than obvious places – a polemical essay written as an intervention into the Dreyfus affair; a series of essays ostensibly about the sociology of education and the moral upbringing of children; a review in the *Année sociologique* of Lucien Lévy-Bruhl's *La Morale et la science des mœurs* – it is only in more recent decades that Durkheim's later reflections on law and modern societies have begun to attract sustained attention, most notably, as we shall see, in the innovative and probing work on the problem of penality in the late twentieth and early twenty-first centuries that has appeared over the last quarter-century.

Characteristically, though his thinking on the sociology of law evolved in other respects, Durkheim never ceased to see law *systematically*: 'the diverse juridical phenomena,' he wrote, 'are not isolated from one another; rather there are between them all manner of connections and they are linked with one another in such a way as to form, in each society, an *ensemble* which has its own unity and individuality' (Durkheim and Fauconnet 1903). He devoted a special section of his journal, the *Année sociologique* (twelve volumes, 1898–1913), to 'the analysis of works where the law of a society or social type is studied in its entirety', and always in such a way as to reveal principles of social organization and collective thinking. Similarly, he pursued his evolutionary inquiries, particularly into the law against suicide (Durkheim 1951) and into the development of punishment (Durkheim 1901b) and of property rights and contract (Durkheim 1957).

These inquiries gained an added dimension after Durkheim's turn from 1895 onwards, towards the study of religion and the ethnography of 'primitive' societies, which was governed by his preoccupation with the religious origins of all social phenomena.[1] In line with this, in 1896, Durkheim's nephew, Marcel Mauss, published his seminal article 'La Religion et les origines du droit pénal', in which he advocated studying the origins of law through the use of ethnographic data.[2] This approach strongly influenced other Durkheimian works in this field, notably Paul

Fauconnet's (1920) study of penal responsibility, Georges Davy's (1922) study of the potlatch and the origins of contractual obligation, the writings of Paul Huvelin (1907) on magic and the law, and Emmanuel Lévy's (1899) work on responsibility and contract. Finally, Durkheim stated his distinctive theory of crime and punishment in such a striking way that, as we have noted, he provoked a most interesting and illuminating debate with Gabriel Tarde, of which more below.

The *study* of law, then, was central to the Durkheimian enterprise. As he claimed in 1900, 'Instead of treating sociology *in genere*, we have always concerned ourselves systematically with a clearly delimited order of facts: save for necessary excursions into field adjacent to those which we were exploring, we have always been occupied only with legal or moral rules, studied in terms of their genesis and development' (Durkheim 1900: 648). Legal practices, institutions and systems were, for him, social facts (Durkheim and Fauconnet 1903; Durkheim 2013b, Ch.1) revealing wider social developments and processes, and eminently worthy of study in their own right, both historically, in the quest for their 'origins' and sociologically, in the examination of their functioning. Two sections of the *Année* (the introductions to which we include here) were devoted to these tasks: that on 'Legal and Moral Sociology' mainly to the former; that on 'Criminal Sociology and Moral Statistics' to the latter. A mass of contemporary work was analysed in these sections, to which over half (24) of the Durkheimians contributed (Vogt 1983).[3] Taken together with the original works mentioned in the previous paragraph, this represents a substantial and distinctive contribution to the sociology of law.

What, then, was distinctive about the Durkheimian view of the law – on what did it focus, and what did it neglect? What is its lasting contribution, in light of the contemporary study of law and legal phenomena? In offering some answers to these questions, we shall first consider Durkheim's own writings on law, gathered here (in Chapters 2 to 4), on the three initial theses indicated above and on Durkheim's attempt to resolve the problems they raise.

The Durkheimian View of Law

We should first note that the object of the *sociologie du droit* or *sociologie juridique* was, indeed, *droit* and that this is only imperfectly translatable as 'law'. As H.L.A. Hart (1955: 442) has written, *droit,* along with the German *Recht* and the Italian *diritto*

> seems to English jurists to hover uncertainly between law and morals, but they do in fact mark off an area of morality (the morality of law) which has special characteristics. It is occupied by the concepts of justice, fairness, rights and

obligations (if this last is not used as it is by many moral philosophers as an obscuring general label to cover every action that we ought to do or forbear from doing). (Hart 1955: 178)

This linguistic fact combined with Durkheim's lifelong preoccupation with morality and its scientific study (to which *The Division of Labour* was intended to contribute) to focus his attention upon the linkages, analogies and parallels between legal and moral rules. He tended to see law as derivative from and expressive of a society's morality. 'Moral ideas,' he wrote, 'are the soul (*l'âme*) of the law' (Durkheim 1987: 150). Indeed, one way to state the central thesis of *The Division of Labour*, of a great transition from mechanical to organic solidarity, is in the form of a three-fold claim: that the integrative functions once performed by 'common ideas and sentiments' were now, in industrial societies, increasingly performed by new social institutions and relations, among them economic ones; that since 'social solidarity is a wholly moral phenomenon' (Durkheim 2013a: 52), this social change involved a major change in morality; and that this was best observed through observing changes in the law. But, as we shall see, this last claim was at the heart of the difficulties his early thesis posed.

In his early work Durkheim not only linked law and morality in these ways, he also focused on certain aspects of law, above all its constraining or what has been called its 'negative, obligatory and prohibitive aspects' (Vogt 1983: 180). One general reason for this can be traced back to the very definition (in his *Rules of Sociological Method* of 1895) of social facts, of which he saw legal rules as paradigmatic, in terms of normative *constraint*, controlling, giving direction and setting limits to individual action. Laws *command*, and are a pre-eminent demonstration of Durkheim's favourite theme, the force and power of the social: 'the individual finds himself in the presence of a force which dominates him and to which he must bow' (Durkheim 2013b: 97). Hence his particular focus on the sanction, which he defined as 'the consequence of an act that does not result from the content of that act, but from the violation by that act of a pre-established rule' (Durkheim 1974: 43) and in the study of penal law. After the mid-1890s his view of social facts broadened; he came to stress their power of attraction, attaching individuals, through allegiance and commitment, to social goals and values.

He distinguished law from morality by pointing to its 'organized' rather than 'diffuse' character and its dependence upon specific persons or agencies who interpret legal rules and apply sanctions according to recognized procedures. He always tended, however, to regard these persons and institutions as in turn embodying and applying '*représentations collectives*', collective beliefs and sentiments of 'society' as a whole; he never treated them as having distinct interests and goals that might conflict both with one another and with the wider social consensus. Vogt (1983: 183) is right to notice that Durkheim and the Durkheimians 'had a (largely unwitting) tendency to be 'statist' in their definition of law', but we should further note that the Durkheimian view of the state was as 'a special organ whose responsibility it is to work out certain representations which hold good for the collectivity. These representations are distinguished from the other collective representations by their higher degree of consciousness and reflection' (Durkheim 1957: 50). Only once, and briefly, did Durkheim attempt to come to terms with the independent role of political action and political structures: in 'Two Laws of Penal Evolution', he allows that governmental authoritarianism could influence the intensity of punishment, but he saw this as secondary to the influence of social-structural factors and without wider implications. So he did not investigate further the impact upon the functioning of law of politics, or even that of legislators, judges, the police and the courts.

In short, Durkheim's distinctive view of law focused upon its links with morality, deriving from it and expressing it, initially upon its constraining or negative aspects, and upon its organized character, but without examining the independent explanatory role of the actors and institutions that combine to influence, create, interpret and apply it. Max Weber's emphasis on the impact on the law of the specialist bearers of legal tradition and their characteristic modes of recruitment and training, his lengthy examination of the relationships between law and the economy (Weber 1978: Vol. 1, Part 2, Ch. 1; and Vol. 2, Ch. 8), are all domains of inquiry which are not merely absent from the Durkheimian corpus, but are indeed fundamentally incompatible with Durkheim's most basic meta-theoretical assumptions.

Assessing Durkheim's Sociology of Law

Law and social solidarity

The most general line of criticism of Durkheim's view of law has been that it is remarkably narrowly focused. In taking social solidarity to be 'a completely moral phenomenon', and the law to be an 'external index which symbolized it', he closed off a number of important sociological questions about law.

First, there are, it is true, significant links between morality and law: laws *often* reflect moral beliefs and sentiments and can serve to revive and reinforce them; and there is *often* a moral commitment to conform to what the law enjoins. Durkheim, however, wanted to go further than this. He recognized that 'social relationships can be forged without necessarily taking on a legal form' (this vol.: 58) but then hastened to assure us that this is essentially irrelevant for sociological analysis, since '*normally* customs are not opposed to law; on the contrary they form the basis for it' (58). Deviations from this state of affairs are no more than temporary (and 'pathological') aberrations. Since custom is 'secondary' and law 'essential' to the constitution of social solidarity, law may be safely treated as an undistorted reflection of society's collective morality:

> social life, wherever it becomes lasting, inevitably tends to assume a definite form and become organized. Law is nothing more than the most stable and precise element in this very organization. Life in general within a society cannot enlarge in scope without legal activity similarly increasing in a corresponding fashion. Thus we may be sure to find reflected in the law all the essential varieties of social solidarity. (57–8)

For all Durkheim's dialectical skill, this whole line of argument rests exclusively on *a priori* assertion. He begs, in a characteristically Durkheimian fashion (Needham 1963: xv), the very question at issue, and at once seeks to distract attention from this manoeuvre by proceeding directly to an empirical analysis of the changing forms of social solidarity as reflected in the legal system. Nor does his subsequent work on law bring any modification of this basic assumption.

Thus, as Vogt (1983: 184) has well said, the Durkheimians 'slighted the importance of conflict: between moral principles, between laws, and ... between legal and moral rules'. This was an underlying feature of Durkheim's thought as a whole: he assumed that 'normally' the elements of a social order were integrated and 'solidary' and he saw conflict as pathological and transitory. He was certainly aware of such conflicts: witness his comments (at the end of Chapter 9 of this volume) on class exploitation and conflict and the injustice (relative to prevailing morality) of inherited property. He also argued, as we shall see, at the time of the Dreyfus Affair that outrages against an individual's rights, such as the court had committed against Dreyfus, could not 'be freely allowed to occur without weakening the sentiments they violate: and as these sentiments are all we have in common, they cannot be weakened without disturbing the cohesion of society' (160). Notwithstanding such periodic acknowledgments, however, he never focused as a sociological analyst upon moral conflicts within societies, or on the various ways in which the law and prevailing morality can come into conflict with each other. This constitutes a crucial and highly damaging deficiency, and yet, as we shall suggest below, to have taken such conflicts seriously would have been to question the basis of the Durkheimian vision of the human sciences, undermining his own way of conceiving 'a sociology that is objective, specific, and methodical' (Durkheim 1913b: 6).

Second, Durkheim's initial focus on the negative or constraining aspects of law, on sanctions and obligations, precluded any systematic inquiry into

its positive or enabling aspects, as a set of procedural rules, permitting
individuals and groups to act in certain ways, and constitutive rules, defining practices and relationships (for example, drawing up a will or forming
a company), and, despite the subsequent broadening of his conception of
social facts and morality, he never explored these aspects of law (Hart
1961: Chs. v and vi). There is no doubt, however, that these are aspects of
the law which he recognized. Consider his (rather obscure) discussion, not
reproduced here, of the ways in which, as the division of labour, and the
necessary functional interdependence of individuals, grows in societies,
regulative norms (including laws) arise which in turn facilitate the further
growth of the division of labour (Durkheim 1913a, Book III, Ch. 1,
Section III). But it is noteworthy that his interesting discussion of property
and contract law (the latter reprinted as the first part of Chapter 9 below),
focuses entirely on genetic explanations of their obligatory force and not
at all on their enabling consequences. (The characteristic absence of
concern with such matters contrasts sharply – and unfavourably – with
Weber's (1966: passim, esp. 201ff.) rich and detailed discussion of the
influence of legal systems in facilitating or retarding the development of
modern capitalism (see Cartwright and Schwartz 1973).)

Third, as we have already indicated, Durkheim (and the Durkheimians
followed him in this) was curiously blind to the sociologically explanatory significance of *how* law is organized – that is, formulated, interpreted and applied – of the role of the 'intermediaries' between 'society'
and 'its' legal rules and practices. (Again, Weber's approach to these
issues is far more sophisticated and suggestive: compare, for example, his
analysis of the dominant role of the organization of the English legal
profession, in the context of early political centralization, in the preservation and development of a unique common law system of 'a highly
archaic character', in the face of 'the greatest economic transformations'
(Weber 1966: 202; see also Hunt 1978; Trubeck 1972).) For Durkheim,
the State, as the instrument through which collective morality finds
durable expression and the organ 'qualified to think and act instead of
and on behalf of society' (Durkheim 1957: 48), is the agency through
which the 'passionate reaction' of the community finds organized
response (see Clarke 1976). Although, in many instances, within the state
apparatus 'power was held by a privileged class or by special magistrates
... [and] although the feelings of the collectivity are no longer expressed
save through certain intermediaries, it does not follow that these feelings
are no longer of a collective nature just because they are restricted to the
consciousness of a limited number of people' (this vol.: 68). On the
contrary, these 'special officials' constitute the executive committee, not
of a ruling class, but of the moral consensus of the society as a whole; they
are the authorized 'interpreters of its collective sentiments' (68).These
'interpreters' add nothing distinctive in the process of translating 'social

representations' into law. Indeed, Durkheim even wrote that 'a legal rule is what it is and there are no two ways of perceiving it' (Durkheim 2013b: 47) – a claim with which most modern legal scholars would take great issue. As Roger Cotterrell (1999: 33–4) has remarked, Durkheim failed to see law through lawyers' eyes, in terms of the practical problems of interpretation and application that make it hard to treat law as an unproblematic datum.

In mysterious fashion, the law's interpreters constitute 'a mere cipher without effects' (Garland 1983: 53). Thus, as admirably stated by Henri Lévy-Bruhl (1961: 113), the Durkheimians embraced the curious position that 'for the sociologist, the true author of a legal rule' is much less the individual who writes it and much more the 'social group'; the legislator merely 'translates the aspirations' of the social group. It is probably not too much to say that, in making this assumption of 'immediate and unambiguous translatability' (Vogt 1983: 185), Durkheim and the Durkheimians closed off most of the questions that have been central to the modern sociology of law, criminology, and the study of deviance.

The evolution of law

This is not the place to discuss Durkheim's overall evolutionary scheme relating the less advanced to the more advanced societies, though it should be noted that his picture was less simplistic and unilinear than that presented by many other nineteenth-century thinkers. Nor can we discuss here his later assumption that contemporary 'primitive' societies, as observed by travellers, missionaries and ethnographers, embodied both (structural and cultural) simplicity and evolutionary priority, and could thus provide evidence of the 'origins' of social institutions. Nor, again, can we examine Durkheim's grand substantive hypothesis of the great transition from pre-industrial to modern industrial societies consisting in a shift of the principles of social integration from mechanical to organic solidarity. As far as law is concerned, the chief criticism to which his evolutionary thesis has been subject is two-fold: (i) that he vastly over-stated the role of repressive law in pre-industrial societies; and (ii) that, in developing a model of social change that lacks any consideration or 'conception of intermediate stages between primitive and modern society … he misses many of the distinctive features of modern legal evolution' (Hunt 1978: 72–3). Plainly, Durkheim erred in 'crushing all pre-industrial societies into one category' (Clarke 1976: 249). The error was, arguably, a profoundly damaging one, since it left his analysis bereft of more than passing attention to historical developments crucial to the understanding of the nature of modern legal systems. As for his thesis about the changing role of repressive law, let us examine in turn each of the claims he makes.

Pre-industrial societies

Consider first the ethnographic record. According to Durkheim (2013a: 108), 'As far as we can judge of the state of law in very inferior societies, it appears to be entirely repressive.' As Sheleff (1975) has noted, Malinowski's research in the Trobriand Islands (Malinowski 1922) stressed the reciprocity of their social relations and the secular basis of their legal system. Malinowski (1966: 51) himself wrote that these societies 'have a class of obligatory rules, not endowed with any mystical character, not set forth in the name of "God", not enforced by any supernatural sanction, but provided with a purely social binding force'. 'The rules of law,' he wrote, 'stand out from the rest in that they are felt and regarded as the obligations of one person and the rightful claims of another' (Malinowski 1966: 55). Hoebel (1954) argues similarly with regard to the reciprocal and restitutory features of primitive law, as do Gluckman (1955), Bohannan (1957) and others. Schwartz and Miller (1964: 167; but for criticism on the relevance of Schwartz and Miller's indicators to Durkheim's thesis, see Cotterrell 1977), on the basis of a survey of 51 societies, conclude that 'restitutive sanctions – damages and mediation – which Durkheim believes to be associated with an increasing division of labour, are found in many societies that lack even rudimentary specialization'. Indeed, they add that, by stipulating that 'restitutive law exists only with highly complex organizational forms, Durkheim virtually ensured that his thesis would be proven' (Schwartz and Miller 1964:166). In short, it is hard to disagree with Barnes's (1966: 168–9) conclusion that 'the ethnographic evidence shows that, in general, primitive societies are not characterized by repressive laws' and that 'it is governmental action that is typically repressive'.[4] As Barnes (1966: 168–9) further remarks, at this stage, Durkheim 'took his evidence on legal order from Classical Antiquity and early Europe' which perhaps give proof of 'some historical progression of the kind he had in mind'. In order to discover if this is so, we should look more closely at the evidence Durkheim relied upon.

Sheleff has noted that Durkheim appealed to Biblical evidence, arguing that in the Pentateuch there are very few non-repressive laws, and even these 'are not so far remote from the penal law as at first sight one might believe, for they are all marked with a religious character' (Durkheim 1973: 110). This was intended to illustrate the religious basis of the early penal law, oriented to a transcendent power, symbolizing the collectivity. A number of scholars have, however, argued exactly the contrary: that the Torah basically embodied religious and moral exhortations devoid of punitive backing, and existed alongside a legal system distinct from religious affairs and invoking restitution for secular offences (Sheleff 1975, citing the work of Julius Wellhausen, Yehezkel Kaufman and A.S. Diamond).

As for classical antiquity, here too the contrary view to Durkheim's has been maintained, not least by an authority on whom Durkheim himself relies – Sir Henry Sumner Maine. According to Durkheim, restitutive and co-operative law had made its appearance with the Roman Twelve Tables, but penal law still predominated. Maine, however, argued the direct opposite: that 'the penal law of ancient communities is not the Law of Crimes; it is the Law of Wrongs, or, to use the English technical word, of Torts. The person proceeds against the wrong-doer by an ordinary civil action, and receives composition in the shape of money-damages if he succeeds' (Maine 1919:328, cited in Sheleff 1975: 21). According to Maine, repressive, vengeful action on behalf of the community was only taken in exceptional and serious cases. More recently, Diamond has argued that early law accentuated civil law and that it was the criminal law that developed out of the law of tort (Diamond 1971; Sheleff 1975).

The evidence from early modern Europe would also seem directly to contradict Durkheim's thesis. Lenman and Parker (1980) forcefully maintained that the picture of criminal legal practice in early modern Europe was one of the barbarous punishment of certain crimes (witchcraft and heresy, parricide and infanticide, incest and sodomy, arson and murder – that is, homicide done in secret, by stealth or by premeditation) and the composition of others in the form of arbitrated extra-judicial settlements (originating in the blood feud) to pacify the parties to a criminal offence. There were, moreover, wide differences in crime rates between different areas, depending partly on the individual costs of, and community pressures against, reporting offences, and partly on the institutional remedies available. Lenman and Parker (1980: 44) also suggest that the composition system was part of the tradition of 'community law' which, in Durkheim's terms, exalted restitutory justice, and which developed from the laws of the German tribes who invaded the Roman Empire, while 'State law' emphasized punitive justice and was 'rooted, at least in part, in the legal system of the Empire and its Byzantine successor'. Between the tenth and the nineteenth centuries, State law gradually displaced community law throughout Europe, very early in England, with the development of Common Law, later on the Continent, with the reception of Roman Law. Thus, in Anglo-Saxon England, 'local customary legal systems emphasized the settling of disputes though reconciliation rather than through punishment' (Dubow 1974:9), a pattern that was reversed as, from the time of Henry II onwards, the 'common law' of the State replaced the legal systems of local feudal authorities, and offences previously treated as civil wrongs were redefined as assaults on the public authority of the State (Dubow 1974: 2). There seems often (as in seventeenth-century France) to have been a significant difference in the clientele and social functions of the two systems: compensation to resolve conflicts between social equals and communal neighbours, summary state justice for the control of the poor.

With the encroachment of State law, a number of inter-related changes occurred. As the criminal law shifted from the private to the public domain, the range of actions subject to criminal sanctions expanded, stretching to include prohibitions which 'had no basis in customary law and, in many instances, were opposed to long-standing traditions' (Dubow 1974: 3). The State's developing monopoly of legitimate violence increasingly undermined the threat of the blood feud and other forms of private violence, on which local settlement of wrongs through restitution ultimately depended (Dubow 1974: 6–7), and thus contributed to an expansion of the role of the punitive state courts. With the professionalization of judicial administration, prosecutions became easier and convictions more likely. Above all, in the Age of Revolution, the criminal court became more punitive, the duties of the more numerous law enforcement agents were likewise more wide-ranging, and 'the State's control over the everyday life of its subjects, through its machinery of law, grew ever closer'. In short, 'the model of European criminal law and its evolution constructed by Durkheim will have to be abandoned' (Lenman and Parker 1980: 15).

Industrial societies

As for the picture in 'advanced' or industrial societies, Durkheim's thesis of declining repressive law in the face of the advance of restitutive law has been no less subject to criticism. Thus Lenman and Parker (1980: 44) point to the new concern with reformation in the nineteenth century:

> The penitentiary system of the nineteenth century was ... significantly different from the secular restitutive justice of early modern society. Instead of readjusting social relationships, if necessary, by financial compensation, and showing little interest in the personalities involved, the penitentiary sought to reconstruct personalities. Furthermore, the norms for reconstruction were laid down by the State. Early modern ecclesiastical tribunals applied Christian norms in a similar way, but even they had looked for a public reconciliation between parties or individual wrong-doers and the community they lived in; the modern State with its monopoly of criminal processes is at once impersonal and, in theory, infinitely demanding.

More generally, Durkheim seems systematically to have understated the repressive aspects of modern law, and in a number of ways. First, there is the punitive dimension of civil law: for not only the criminal but all legal provisions are backed by the enforcement apparatus of the State (as in contempt of court) employing a system of penalties. Often, indeed, the sanctions of the civil law are highly punitive and can be more so than those of the criminal law, and in various ways that are worthy of further investigation (Sheleff 1975: 35). Financially, for example, civil penalties are often far more onerous than fines. Civil punishments may include prohibitions against gaining a livelihood in specified ways, and their terms may be so severe as to cause bankruptcy and wrenching social and economic losses, not to mention having drastic effects on the social reputations and identities of those subject to them.

Second, however, there is the nature of the modern criminal law itself, and notably its tendency to expand its range of application into new areas – such as weights and measures, the details of trade and financial transactions, criminal trespass and, in Britain, trade union legislation – and sometimes for progressive and humanitarian reasons, as with environmental and consumer protection legislation. Sometimes (and this contradicts a further aspect of Durkheim's argument), it does so by stressing vicarious liability and thus collective, and not individual, responsibility. In non-liberal states, of course, such expansion has often embraced individual, private life and the economic sphere, where according to Durkheim organic solidarity should reign: consider the South African pass laws under the apartheid regime and former communist states' penalties for economic crimes and 'thought crimes'. Furthermore, as students of deviance and above all the so-called labelling theorists have stressed, the nature and depth of 'repression' in both civil and criminal law is greater and more complex than may appear on the surface, involving stigmatization and the exclusion of alien elements in a process that can itself be understood in a quasi-Durkheimian manner as a way of reaffirming the collective identity of the in-group (Sheleff 1875; Thompson 1982: 90).

There is, of course, much more to say on all these matters (see Cotterrell 1977, Diamond 1971, Cartwright 1973, Merton 1934; Baxi 1974; Schwartz 1974; Clifford-Vaughan and Scotford-Morton 1967; Calavita *et al.* 1991; Lanza-Kaduce *et al.* 1979; Turkel 1979; Wimberley 1973), but enough perhaps has been said here to indicate how one writer can have come to the dramatic conclusion that, as against Durkheim's evolutionary hypothesis of repression giving way to restitution, 'a strong argument could be made for the contrary proposition that the development of law has been from a basically restitutive model to a repressive mode' (Sheleff 1975: 20; see also Sheleff 1997).

The reader will doubtless make up his or her own mind about Durkheim's particular evolutionary hypotheses concerning the law on suicide and the development of punishment, property and contract. They are all to some degree independent of the master hypothesis just considered, and of the criticisms of it that we have outlined. Here we shall merely refer to one study bearing on Durkheim's account of penal evolution. According to Durkheim, punishment in general has grown less severe as societies advance in concentration and complexity, though this tendency is counteracted by the independent, contingent and transitory effects of political authoritarianism; and, as collective religiosity declines and individualism progresses, the deprivation of liberty, in the form of incarceration, increasingly becomes the normal mode of social control (see Tiryakian 1964). Surveying data from some 48 societies, Spitzer (1975: 631) argued, on the contrary, that

> The severity of punishment does not decrease as societies grow more concentrated and complex. On the contrary, greater punitiveness is associated with higher levels of structural differentiation. (2) While variations in political structure are related to punitive intensity, these variations are neither historically contingent, nor idiosyncratic. (3) Although the 'religiosity' of deviance is correlated with punitiveness, collective crimes are more common in complex than in simple societies. (4) Controls involving social and geographic segregation are not represented by incarceration alone and are not peculiar to advanced societies (e.g., banishment and punitive slavery).

On the other hand, one can say that here, as in the thesis of evolution from repression to restitution, a series of macro-connections is boldly postulated, whose refinement, and indeed refutation, can represent a significant advance in the sociological understanding of law. As is the case elsewhere in Durkheim's work, empirical truth, or even plausibility, is not necessarily the most relevant test of his theories' fruitfulness.

One can further argue, as Cotterrell (1999: 85, 86, 90) does, that there is a difficulty that besets anyone in confronting Durkheim's thesis with evidence from legal history, since that thesis was 'not intended as a survey of legal history' and 'his concepts specify social conditions rather than legal ideas' and his 'legal categories are not designed to correlate with juristic classifications of law'. Perhaps, rather, Durkheim's legal evolution thesis should be read as a 'philosophical device ... for conceptualizing fundamental moral conditions of society. It is a means of depicting graphically Durkheim's ideas about the kinds of moral bonds that can provide social cohesion in different kinds of society' (Cotterrell 1999:91).

Crime and punishment

We turn next to the assessment of Durkheim's third thesis – his theory of crime and punishment, and in particular his idea that crime 'is a factor in public health, an integrative element in any healthy society', and indeed, 'indispensable to the normal evolution of morality and law' (this vol.: 114, 116).

Durkheim's theory of crime and punishment is a somewhat complex affair, open to telling criticisms at a number of points, not all of which are destructive and some of which are a challenge to further specification and elaboration (see Chazel 1991; Cochez 2004; Smith 2003; Garland 2006; Deflem 2008). As we show in the introduction to Chapter 5, this incorporated three distinct claims: the *functional to integration claim* – that both crime and punishment are together functional to social integration insofar as crime elicits punishment which in turn reaffirms and reinforces collective beliefs and sentiments and, thus, social solidarity; the *counter-factual claim* – that a certain level of crime is normal and a crime-free society impossible, since, if all existing crime were to disappear, society would reinvent further crimes; and the *functional to change claim* – that crime (though not in this case punishment) can serve to bring about moral change as a harbinger of an emergent morality.

It is, however, the first, *functional to integration claim*, which Tarde did not address, that both constitutes Durkheim's distinctive contribution and has been most controversial. It is, in fact, a venerable idea, or rather set of ideas which need to be unpacked. In a much-discussed article, 'Social Solidarity and the Enforcement of Morals', H. L. A. Hart (1968) closely examined what he took to be Durkheim's claim – that punishing what common morality condemns is necessary for a society's continued existence (see Lukes and Prabhat 2012). Hart argued that if this is not to be a simple tautology, identifying society with its shared morality, it can be read in three different ways. One is as the *classical thesis*, found in Plato and Aristotle, that the law be used to punish vice and promote moral virtue, where these are given by a uniquely true or correct set of principles, accessed through reason or revelation. A second is as the *conservative thesis* that 'society has a right to enforce its morality by law because the majority have a right to follow their own moral convictions that their moral environment is a thing of value to be defended from change' (Hart 1968: 4). The third is an empirical claim, but for this we would, first, need to be more precise about which parts of a society's moral code (assuming – a large assumption that Durkheim never questioned – that it has a single overall moral code) are essential for the existence of a society and which are not. Secondly, we would need criteria to establish the existence of a single recognized morality and its central core, and thirdly, we would also need an empirically testable account of what would constitute disintegration. Hart offered a number of suggestions as how to satisfy these needs, but commented on 'the massive difficulties of establishing the causal connections in question and establishing the relevant macroscopic generalizations across cases'. His conclusion was one of scepticism concerning what he called 'the disintegration thesis'. His article was written in the context of a British debate in the 1960s with Lord Devlin (1965; see also Moberly 1968: esp. Ch. 8) about whether homosexual acts between consenting adults should remain criminalized and he straightforwardly embraced the counter-thesis that permissiveness and moral pluralism in this domain are likely to be compatible with social integration.

Hart's scepticism is understandable and yet his argument and his conclusion warrant a second look. His characterization of Durkheim as an exponent of the 'disintegration thesis' is something of a caricature, relying on a very selective reading of his early writings. Hart's counter-thesis, focused as it was on the sphere of sexual morals, was, indeed, convincing, and has been amply confirmed by history, and yet Durkheim's view of the relation between punishment and core moral norms remains compelling in ways that Hart did not see. As we shall argue in the next section of this Introduction, his account of the moral foundations of modern law advances the idea that there are core moral norms that have penetrated the life and institutions of plural and diverse modern societies, norms which, in the absence of legal enforcement, may lose their core status, leading to a kind of moral unravelling.

The attentive reader will have noted that there appears to be some conflict between Durkheim's claim that punishment, in the form of penal or repressive law, is supposed to decline with industrialization and the progress of societies, and his claim that some level of crime and punishment is normal for every society. To this problem there are two answers (which in turn only raise further questions). First, he did not suppose that punishment could decline to vanishing point, but rather that it would become less severe and change its character in the face of modern social conditions and, above all, the modern 'religion of individualism'. Second, in any case, his views about the role of collective beliefs and sentiments and the relation to social solidarity changed after writing *The Division of Labour*. In that work he suggested that 'organic solidarity' and the morality associated with it, might take on a co-operative, reciprocal, restitutive form – one that could not require penal enforcement. But, as we shall now argue, this was an incoherent position. His account of organic solidarity was incompatible with his view of morality.

The moral foundations of modern law

Three ideas are fundamental to Durkheim's conception of morality. The first is that moral behaviour is disinterested: that it is motivated by concerns other than an individual's self-interest. Morality, he wrote, 'begins where disinterestedness and devotion begin' (Durkheim 1974: 52). The second is that moral disinterestedness always has a social origin: that we think and act morally in ways shaped by 'society'. Thus 'disinterestedness only makes sense when that to which we subordinate ourselves has a higher moral value than we have as individuals. I only know of one being that has a richer and more complex reality than our own, and that is the collectivity' (Durkheim 1974: 52). And the third is that that origin – what counts as the collectivity or 'society' – is a moving target. It is never precisely identified: its scope can vary from the narrow circle of the nuclear family to the all-encompassing wider society of the nation state. He never doubted that, although our moral life has multiple sources, the latter was the main shaping source of modern morality. 'We cannot aspire,' he wrote (Durkheim 1974: 61), 'to a morality other than that which is related to the state of our society.' He also assumed that morality was unitary, issuing in a single and unifying moral system or code for any given society, though he speculated that morality in modern societies (and in particular the French moral code) incorporated elements of an emergent trans-national and incipiently universal morality.

Now, given this conception of morality, his account of organic solidarity in *The Division of Labour* posed a serious problem. For, according to that account, as the shared beliefs, understandings and sentiments of the *conscience commune* recede, or common consciousness, life, as Cotterrell puts it, is 'varied and the role and positions that people occupy become increasingly specialized or distinct' so that 'the dominant form of solidarity in complex societies … arises through the effective integration of different social groups, reflecting different life experiences and values' (Cotterrell 1999: 28). The principal mechanism for achieving this integration, or co-ordination, is through contracts between individuals or collectivities, between workers and employers, professionals and their clients, between companies and generally between sellers and buyers of goods and services, each pursuing their respective interests. But this account of organic solidarity as functional interdependence is purely instrumental: it lacks a moral dimension – in Durkheim's sense of 'moral' (hence his acknowledgement that the rules that regulate it 'do not form part of the common consciousness'). Contracts create and maintain reciprocal obligations between interested parties, but they leave no place for disinterestedness: they do not render the contracting partners any less interest-driven. Consider, for example, the labour contract. In *The Division of Labour*, Durkheim argued that organic solidarity, when functioning 'normally', is supposed to render capital–labour relations more just. However, as he acknowledged in the chapter on 'The Forced Division of Labour', pervasive inequality and exploitation and thus 'unjust contracts' exist in advanced industrial societies. Where, then, does the impulse towards greater justice come from? His difficulty in answering this is what led him from 1895 onwards to revise his view of the shrinking *conscience collective* and to turn his attention to the changing content and character of shared beliefs and sentiments – he now used the terminology of *représentations collectives* – and thus to the distinctive nature of the evolving morality of modern industrial societies.

Thus he came to think that the modern morality of individualism and distributive justice involves not the abandonment but the transformation of collective beliefs and sentiments, whose need for penal reaffirmation and reinforcement survives (see Joas 1993).The key text for examining this modification of his thinking is his remarkable article 'Individualism and the Intellectuals' (see Chapter 7). As well as this article, Durkheim also published at this time two much shorter pieces, on anti-semitism (Durkheim 2008) and militarism, which supplement its concern: namely, how to restore social solidarity in a fractured modern society. As he put it in the first of these essays, 'the religion of the individual can ... allow itself to be flouted without resistance, on penalty of ruining its credit; since it is the sole link that binds us to one another, such a weakening cannot take place without the onset of social dissolution' (this vol.: 160).

As we explain in the introduction to Chapter 7, 'Individualism and the Intellectuals' was written to counter the anti-Dreyfusard attack on intellectuals, who had been accused by their right-wing critics of 'obstinately refus[ing] to bend their logic before the word of an army general' in the name of 'individualism'. To Ferdinand Brunetière's argument that the unity, indeed the very survival, of the French nation, was being threatened by their campaign for one individual's rights, Durkheim countered that it was individualism that was 'henceforth the only system of beliefs which could ensure the moral unity of the country' Durkheim's article is high-octane, written in the heat of political battle, but it articulates very clearly the thinking about law and morality in modern societies that pervades his post-1895 writings (see Vogt 1993; Joas 2008). Its argument can be briefly summarized.

Modern industrial society, Durkheim argued, like all societies, needs a religion, in the sense of a system of collective beliefs and practices that have special authority. Individualism is such a religion, deriving historically from Christianity, in which the human person becomes its sacred focus: it has 'penetrated our institutions and our customs' and become 'part of our whole life' (154), so that it was the anti-Dreyfusards who, by attacking it, were threatening the nation with moral anarchy. Durkheim drew a sharp contrast between 'the narrow utilitarianism and utilitarian egoism of Spencer' and the economists' reducing 'society to nothing more than a vast apparatus of production and exchange' and the individualism he was seeking to describe. This was the individualism of 'Kant and Rousseau, that of the spiritualists, that which the Declaration of the Rights of Man, sought, more or less successfully, to translate into formulae, that which is currently taught in our schools and which has become the basis of our moral catechism' (153). It is egalitarian, since 'the only ways of acting that are moral are those which are fitting for all men equally, that is to say, which are implied in the notion of man in general' (153–4). It was not 'the glorification of the self but of the individual in general' (156). Thus

the human person, whose definition serves as the touchstone according to which good must be distinguished from evil, is considered as sacred, in what one might call the ritual sense of the word. It has something of the transcendental majesty which the churches of all times have given to their Gods. It is conceived as being invested with that mysterious property which creates an empty space around holy objects, which keeps them away from profane contacts and which draws them away from ordinary life. And it is exactly this feature that induces the respect of which it is the object. Whoever makes an attempt on a man's life, on a man's liberty, on a man's honour inspires us with a feeling of horror, in every way analogous to that which the believer experiences when he sees his idol profaned. Such a morality is therefore not simply a hygienic discipline or a wise principle of economy. It is a religion of which man is both believer and God. (This vol.: 154)

Individualism thus understood has as its motive force 'not egoism but sympathy for all that is human, a wider pity for all sufferings, for all human miseries, a more ardent desire to combat and alleviate them, a greater thirst for justice'. It is 'cult of man' that has 'for its first dogma the autonomy of reason' and for its first rite 'freedom of thought'. It is, moreover, henceforth the only system of beliefs which can ensure the moral unity of the country. For with ever-greater social complexity and diversity, traditions and practices adapt to social change by becoming ever more plastic and unstable: social and cultural differentiation has developed almost to a point at which the members of a single society retain only their humanity in common. Society was evolving, he wrote, towards a state in which the members of a single group will have nothing in common among themselves except their humanity, except the constitutive attributes of the human person in general. Thus the 'idea of the human person', given different emphases in accordance with the diversity of national temperaments, is 'the only idea which would be retained, immutable and impersonal, above the changing tides of particular individual opinions' (158). This Durkheimian approach is very much the reasoning offered today for a universal human rights law project (see Lukes 2006; Cotterrell 2010).

In Durkheim's distinctive approach to morality and the law, outrages against the human person or against the rights of the individual, he wrote:

> cannot rest unpunished without putting national existence in jeopardy. It is indeed impossible that they should be freely allowed to occur without weakening the sentiments that they violate, and as these sentiments are all that we still have in common, they cannot be weakened without disturbing the cohesion of society. A religion which tolerates acts of sacrilege abdicates any sway over men's minds. The religion of the individual can therefore allow itself to be flouted without resistance, only on penalty of ruining its credibility; since it is the only link which binds us to one another, such a weakening cannot take place without the onset of social dissolution. Thus the individualist, who defends the rights of the individual, defends at the same time the vital interests of society; for he is preventing the criminal impoverishment of the final reserve of collective ideas and sentiments that constitutes the very soul of the nation. (160)

And it is on these grounds that, in his short contemporary article about anti-semitism, Durkheim (2008) called for repression of all incitement of hatred of citizens against one another. Such punishment, he recognized, would not by itself change people's minds, but it could strengthen and reinvigorate public revulsion against such incitement. It is a plausible and interesting line of argument, and indeed something like this change in cultural attitudes seems to have been fostered by America's civil rights reforms, in the 1960s and later. The legal changes these statutes and associated court decisions embodied appear over time to have changed, not just behaviours, but underlying belief structures and the boundaries of acceptable belief and discourse (Skrentny 2004).

In *Suicide* (first published in 1897) Durkheim offered a similar reason for why legal and other kinds of intervention are required in order to prevent suicides: the human person – the individual in general – is sacred and has to be preserved. Durkheim connected suicide to the conceptual structure of morality. He observed that by claiming that the abnormal increase in suicides is symptomatic of a moral evil, we are 'far from thinking to reduce it to some superficial ill which may be conjured away by soft words' (Durkheim 1951: 387). He distinguished a greater harm to society from the smaller harm to the individual. Thus:

> It is said that the man who kills himself injures only himself and that society has no cause to intervene, by virtue of the old axiom: *Volenti non fit injuria.* This is not so. Society is harmed, because the feeling on which its most respected moral principles rest today, and which swerves as an almost unique link between its members, is violated and it would be upset if this violation could be committed quite freely. How could it maintain the slightest authority if, when it is offended, the moral conscience did not protest? As soon as the human being is and must be considered as a sacred thing which neither the individual nor the group can dispose of freely, any attack on it must be forbidden. It is irrelevant that the guilty party and the victim are one and the same: the social ill that results from the act does not go away just because the author of it also suffers. If in ourselves and in general we are repelled by the fact of the violent destruction of a man's life and see it as a sacrilege, then we cannot tolerate it in any circumstances. A collective sentiment that relaxed to that extent would soon be powerless. (149)

From these statements it is clear that Durkheim believed in legal and other kinds of regulation of suicide because of harm to 'the individual', because of the need to protect the sacredness of the individual as it permeates the collective conscience, rather than because of particular harm to particular, actual empirical individuals. When discussing the legal prohibition of suicide, Durkheim wrote that the harm consists in suicide's subversion of human individuality. Durkheim's evolutionary perspective on why suicide is regulated is that 'Suicide is thought immoral in and for itself, whoever they may be who participate in it. Thus, with the progress of history, the prohibition, instead of being relaxed, only becomes more strict'

(Durkheim 1951: 333). Earlier a person who commits suicide was viewed as an 'unscrupulous debtor to society'. Now the act of suicide is treated as a graver offence because today he has acquired a kind of dignity which places him above himself as well as above society. So long as his conduct has not caused him to forfeit the title of man, he seems to us to share in some degree in that quality *sui generis* ascribed by every religion to its gods which renders them inviolable by everything moral. He has become tinged with religious value; man has become a god for men. Therefore any attempt against his life suggests sacrilege. Suicide is such an attempt. No matter who strikes the blow, it causes scandal by violation of the sacrosanct quality within us which we must respect in ourselves as well as in others. Hence, suicide is rebuked for derogating from 'this cult of human personality on which all our morality rests' (Durkheim 1951: 334).

It is this cult of the individual which is a feature of modern morality and which Durkheim considered needs protection. In the case of suicide, such protection is afforded not just by laws, but also by religious traditions and popular sentiment. But Durkheim saw such protection taking multiple forms in various contexts. In the economic and industrial sphere, he so regarded policies favouring social justice and reducing exploitation. His conception of socialism was that it would alleviate 'the functioning of the social machine, still so harsh to individuals, to place within their reach all possible means of developing their abilities without hindrance, to work finally to make a reality of the famous precept: "to each according to his labour"' (Durkheim 1974: 56). And in the sphere of education he saw, and sought through his teaching to encourage, the development of what he called individualism, through moral education and enlightened pedagogy in the schools (see Durkheim 1961).

This, then, was the later Durkheim's account of the moral foundations of modern law. Unfortunately for the sociologist of law, he did not, however, inquire further into its implications for modern law and legal practice. Nor did he confront the tough questions of how to resolve conflicts, including legal conflicts, over what 'the sacredness of the individual' means and what its practical, substantive implications are, socially and politically. Is the language of 'individualism' just empty rhetoric available to all factions and parties? Clearly, one might argue, such language is rhetorical, but is it *merely* so? Does its ever-wider use have practical bearing on what can be seen as legitimate? These are questions all the more pertinent at a time when the discourse of human rights is ever more pervasive and harnessed to widely diverse and opposed agendas (Moyn 2010).

Roger Cotterrell makes an interesting attempt to confront these questions, noting, in sympathy with Durkheim's (distinctly functionalist) approach, that moral individualism becomes more important (because functionally necessary) the more complex and differentiated societies become. On the one hand, there will be a societal need for laws that enable 'individuals to play a role; appropriate to their talents and abilities, in the economic division of labour of modern complex society'. This, he suggests, implies that one must 'feel in control of one's life conditions, which means free from the tyranny of instincts that dominate one's choices, from external controls and arbitrary prohibitions, and from exploitations that undermine one's sense of identity'. On the other, ideas of common humanity become 'sociologically necessary' as

> social interactions become less localized, more varied and wider-reaching in their effects; as they become elements in ever more extensive networks of economic and social intereraction. (Cotterrell 2010:8)

So far as Durkheim himself was concerned, the secular, civic 'religion of individualism' – the moral framework alone capable of ensuring the cohesion of diverse, fractured modern societies – furnished grounds for regulating in distinctive ways contracts, the inheritance of property and divorce. As Cotterrell (1999: 132) has remarked, contract 'is the framework of commerce and industrial relations—the very fields where Durkheim sees the most serious problems of anomie and disruption in modern society'. Thus he favoured regulating contracts through socialist planning to 'moralize' the economy and the development of 'secondary', pluralistic cross-class 'occupational' and industry-based secondary associations or groupings (as explained in the preface to the second edition of *The Division of Labour,* and in *Professional Ethics and Civic Morals* (Durkheim 1957)), generating locally appropriate norms (see Didry 2000). As for property rights, while tracing their origin in the sacred setting apart of property under the control of certain persons, he focused on the egalitarian thrust of modern individualism, arguing against rights of inheritance or succession. And he rejected divorce by mutual consent as endangering the stability of marriage and thus the future of the nuclear family, which he saw as a bulwark of individualist values. In all three cases, plainly, Durkheim was advancing a distinctive interpretation of the morality of individualism that contrasts sharply with how 'individualism' has typically been understood by economic liberals and libertarians, just as his sociology of law contrasts with the economic analyses of law.

Durkheim on Law: Sociology's Debt

The central place occupied by the study of law in the Durkheimian corpus makes a consideration of his work on the subject mandatory for those seeking to understand the nature of his contribution to sociology. Beyond its obvious importance for any attempt to assess Durkheim's own distinctive vision of the field, one must, however, ask what, if anything, his work on law has lastingly contributed to the field, in the light of more recent sociological research and approaches to the subject. In this concluding section, we shall focus on what later sociologists have made of his view of crime and of the nature and function of punishment. Necessarily the assessment of Durkheim's contribution, here as elsewhere, must be qualified, for Durkheim's treatment of a subject so close to the core of his sociological concerns shares all the defects and limitations implicit in his whole theoretical approach (see Pearce 1989). Conversely, it also embodies the very features that have rescued his work from the dustbin of history and made it a continuing source of inspiration and theoretical stimulation (Deflem 2008; Vogt 1993).

During the last third of the twentieth century, some of Durkheim's more uncritical admirers sought to find in his work on law anticipations and adumbrations of emerging work in the sociology of deviance and social control (Jones 1981; and, to a more limited extent, Traugott 1978: Introduction). His insistence on viewing crime as a social phenomenon has been praised as the foundation for a 'fully social theory' of deviance (Taylor *et al.* 1973: Ch. 3). His ironic view of crime as 'a factor in public health, an integrative element in any healthy society' (114), his insistence upon the symbiotic relationship of crime and punishment, and his assertion that 'what confers upon [deviations] this character is not the intrinsic importance of the acts but the importance which the common consciousness ascribes to them' (116), were together seen as foreshadowing the central insights of labelling or societal reaction theory (Jones 1981). Finally, given the revival of concern from the mid-1970s onwards with developing a historically informed sociology of social control, and more especially with the inter-relationships of punishment and social structure, there were a number of efforts to draw attention to Durkheim's pioneering work on the subject, for his status as one of the classical sociology theorists, and the detailed and extended nature of his treatment of penal law tended to constitute these texts as a respectable repository of conceptual tools with which to organize and make sense of the mass of empirical data produced by penological research (see Garland 1983).

Labelling or societal reaction theory (the two terms may for most purposes be taken as equivalent) is a perspective primarily associated with such mid- to late-twentieth century sociologists as Edwin Lemert, Howard Becker and Thomas Scheff. It emphasizes the centrality of more or less organized societal reaction to otherwise mundane examples of rule-breaking in creating stable deviant identities. Irony is central to this perspective. Social control is no longer viewed as simply a benign and defensive response to individual pathology. Labelling theorists emphasize that society helps to create or aggravate deviance in the very process of attempting to control it, whether through stigmatization and punishment, or through the actual or symbolic segregation of the offender. These reactions, in Lemert's words, 'become central facts of experience for those experiencing them, altering psychic structure, producing specialized organization of social roles and self-regarding attitudes. ...In effect, the original causes of the deviation recede and give way to the central importance of the disapproving, degradational, and labeling reactions of society' (Lemert 1967: 63, 17; see also Lemert 1951; Becker 1963, 1974; Scheff 1966). Though penologists in these years drew upon a somewhat different set of theoretical inspirations – the work of Marxist historians like E.P. Thompson and his students (Thompson 1975; Hay *et al.* 1975), and the treatises of the French philosopher and social theorist, Michel Foucault (Foucault 1965; 1977) – they too saw deviance and social control as intimately intertwined.

Since Durkheim too had viewed crime and society's reactions to it as inseparably linked together, and not in any simple or straightforward fashion, it is perhaps not surprising that some have been tempted to draw a direct connection between his work and more recent scholarship in this arena. In important respects, however, such genealogies distort and exaggerate the value of Durkheim's contributions. Consider, for example, the alleged affinity of his ideas with those of societal reaction theory. Early on in his career, Durkheim (2013a: 291, footnote) saw crime in essentially negative, conventional terms. He sought to distinguish 'the differentiation ... which disintegrates (cancerous, microbic, criminal) ... from that which concentrates vital forces (division of labour)', and saw the criminal as someone who seeks 'to live at the expense of' society and crime itself as 'the very negation of solidarity' (Durkheim 2013a: 277). His subsequent abandonment of this stance and inversion of 'common sense' (crime, he now claimed, was 'linked to the basic conditions of social life', and was 'indispensable to the normal evolution of morality and law' (Durkheim 2013b: 63) does mark a welcome move away from the purely 'correctional' viewpoint that continued to dominate criminology till past the midpoint of the twentieth century. Yet he remains remote from the 'appreciative naturalism' which David Matza (1969) sees as one of labelling theory's major contributions to the study of deviance.

Some of Durkheim's ideas *can* be shown to have had a quite direct influence on labelling theory. Kai Erikson's (1966) *Wayward Puritans* borrows, in a wholly uncritical way, a number of Durkheimian notions – the conception of punishment as a symbolic reaffirmation of the community's moral values and beliefs, the idea that a certain level of crime is 'normal' for a given society, and the realization that deviance is a social creation: 'we should not say that an act offends the common consciousness because it is criminal, but that it is criminal because it offends that consciousness. We do not condemn it because it is a crime, but it is a crime because we condemn it' (this vol.: 70). Erikson's work, while embedded in a functionalism generally foreign to the societal reaction literature, nevertheless became a central point of reference for those working within that tradition, not least because it appeared to demonstrate the socially contingent nature of deviant labels, and the crucial role of audience reactions in the manufacture of deviance and the constitution of deviant identity.[5]

It would be a mistake, however, to see any very close affinity between Durkheim's views and those of the societal reaction theorists. The primary inspiration for the latter was the distinctively American tradition of the Chicago School (Matza 1969). While Durkheim does, indeed, argue that criminality is not an inherent quality of a particular class of actions, but rather the outcome of a process of social definition, he also insists on the existence and importance of a set of universally accepted rules, which are absolute, clear and obvious to all members of a society in all situations – a proposition which, if accepted, renders the central concerns of the societal reaction theorists moot. In Durkheim's case, then, the claim that the nature of crime (and, by extension, the nature of other forms of deviance) does not lie in 'the intrinsic importance of the acts' did not and could not lead to an exploration of the practical uses of social rules or of the processes by which some rule violators and not others come to be defined as deviant. His most basic theoretical premises led him 'to assume that the major social norms generally express the sentiments of the total society. He never seriously entertained the idea that they might only express the sentiments of a specific stratum within it' (Coser 1960: 218). The idea that moral meanings are to a high degree uncertain and variable, that they are not uniformly distributed through the social structure, indeed that it may not be possible to specify major social norms about which there is general agreement (all central assumptions of this body of work on deviance) were notions radically incompatible with the Durkheimian vision of the ways in which societies are held together.

On the contrary, Durkheim (this vol.: 65) was disposed to argue that 'the only feature common to all crimes is that ... they comprise acts universally condemned by the members of each society'. So far from prompting concern with the existence of conflicting or ambiguous moral evaluations, and hence with the crucial roles played by power and 'respectability' in the application of deviant labels, it was Durkheim's view that 'crime disturbs those feelings which, in any single type of society, are to be found in every healthy conscience' (65). Evidence that moral rules do not generally command such universal acceptance was rendered innocuous by claiming that such situations were pathological and atypical (the product, for example of 'the forced division of labour'), or by the assertion that 'ignorance or insubordination [to the fundamental rules of society] are irrefutably symptoms of a pathological perversion' (66). Hence, Durkheim's work has proved of only limited value to those modern theorists concerned to emphasize the basically problematic nature of deviance, especially in modern, highly differentiated societies.

One may go further: Durkheim's central methodological presuppositions are such that, as long as one adheres to them, sustained attention to subjective meanings and actors' conceptions of reality as constitutive of the social order is simply impossible. Notwithstanding his increasing concern with 'collective representation' and the cultural or ideational dimension of social reality, Durkheim remains committed to a vision of sociology within which knowledge is built up on the basis of hard data – 'social facts' that in principle are supposedly identifiable wholly without reference to subjective or inter-subjective meanings, and whose inter-relationships are then subjected to causal analysis. From within such a rigid, absolute conception of social reality, the essentially *meaningful* character of social interaction is systematically obscured.

It was, of course, precisely this methodological viewpoint that led Durkheim to study law in the first place. Vital to his project of treating social facts as things, to be discovered through empirical investigation, was the use of indicators to allow 'external' observation of aspects of the social world otherwise inaccessible to scientific observation and measurement. Such indices were for him the key to understanding characteristics of social life which though less apparent are doubtless more essential (Durkheim 2013b: 41). Thus, 'social solidarity is a wholly moral phenomenon which by itself, does not lend itself to exact observation and especially not to measurement'. Fortunately, however, a solution is at hand: 'We must therefore substitute for this internal datum, which escapes us, an external one which symbolizes it, and then study the former through the latter. That visible symbol is the law' (57). Law 'is nothing more than the most stable and precise element in this very organization ... Thus we may be sure to find reflected in the law all the essential varieties of social solidarity' (58).

For law to fulfil the role Durkheim had assigned it, it was essential that it 'exist permanently...and constitute a fixed object, a constant standard which is always at hand for the observer, and which leaves no room for subjective impressions or personal observations' (Durkheim 2013b: 47). Inescapably, therefore, he was driven to treat law as a given set of standards by which behaviour is judged, and to assert that this judgment is inherently non-problematic. Only by adopting this viewpoint could he plausibly claim to by-pass actors' conceptions of social reality, and to rest his analysis upon externally defined brute facts, grasped purely objectively. Within a few years of Durkheim's death, Bayet (1925, quoted in Douglas 1966: 63) subjected the assumption that law could be analysed in this way to withering criticism:

> I know well that law has the advantage of being an easily gotten social fact. Morality seems to be rolled up in it for the greatest convenience of sociologists and it is the real morality of actions, since it provides for sanctions. But from

the first, it remains to be known if these sanctions are to be applied: the existence of the law is a fact, but the application of the law is also a fact ...Moreover ... the law registers morality only in simplifying it. All that is nuance or diversity falls out.

Subsequent studies of the day-to-day administration of the legal system and of the ways in which the personnel mediating this process modify and distort the formal provisions of the law, have lent empirical substance to these objections (see, for example, Skolnick 1966; Sudnow 1965; Cicourel 1967), and one must conclude that only the radical rejection of Durkheim's views on the subject opened up this domain of sociological inquiry.

Perhaps even more strikingly, those engaged in developing a historical sociology of punishment long tended to ignore Durkheim's pioneering work on the subject. That neglect has begun to abate in the past two decades, as we shall examine at more length below. But the reason for the earlier persistent tendency to ignore his work was almost certainly Durkheim's own extraordinary neglect of the phenomenon of power, and the generally under-developed nature of his political sociology. The revival of interest in the sociology of penality occurred initially in two somewhat distinct intellectual traditions: the neo-Marxist work of E.P. Thompson and his students, most notably in the essays collected as *Albion's Fatal Tree* (Hay *et al.*, 1975; see also Thompson 1975; Spitzer and Scull 1977; Ignatieff 1978; Cohen and Scull 1983); and in the body of work inspired by the late Michel Foucault's book, *Discipline and Punish* (Foucault 1977). Despite the considerable intellectual gulf that separated these two bodies of theory, both regarded systems of punishment as inextricably linked with the asymmetrical relationships of control and dependency characteristic of the larger society, and both stressed their connections with the changing forms and extent of state power and economic organization. Law, for Thompson and his students, is one of the focal points of conflict and struggle and their resolution in modern societies, a major means by which power is legitimized, and the form in which coercion is most routinely exercised. Foucault, influenced by the Weberian emphasis on rationalization and the growth of instrumental reason as defining features of modernity, saw punishment, and the more general process of 'disciplining' modern societies, as involving a transition from, in David Garland's (1991: 97) elegant summary, 'a morally-charged and emotive set of ritual practices into an increasingly passionless and professionalized instrumental process'. With their focus on conflict and power, and on how punitive institutions serve as mechanisms of positive disciplinary power, both traditions gave little space or credence to the Durkheimian insistence that modern punishment at its core remains 'irrational' and emotional, that it is, as the word itself implies, punitive, concerned to inflict pain.

Durkheim's one overt gesture at incorporating political variables into his analysis, the claim in 'Two Laws of Penal Evolution' that absolutist forms of government operate to intensify the severity of punishment independently of a society's level of social development, certainly provided no basis for a more extended Durkheimian treatment of state forms and their relation to law. In his eagerness to claim that absolutism exercises a wholly independent influence upon the intensity of punishment, Durkheim made the extraordinary claim that this (and by implication any other) form of political organization is not 'a consequence of the fundamental nature of society, but rather depends on unique, transitory and contingent factors' (this vol.: 83). Almost uniquely among social phenomena, therefore, much of the political realm is portrayed as lying outside what Durkheim otherwise insists is the all-pervasive influence of *la société*. He is at least consistent on this point: the analysis of political phenomena was excluded from discussion in the *Année sociologique* on the grounds of their contingency and unpredictability. Consistency in this instance, however, is scarcely a virtue.

One can only conclude that in appealing to what for him was the residual category of the organization of state power (which he contends in any event is of only secondary importance), Durkheim is inventing an illegitimate *deus ex machina* designed to explain away facts which otherwise all too visibly contradict his first 'law' of penal evolution. Such special pleading is, as we have noted, his characteristic way of dealing with awkward evidence. Here, however, it involves him in a further confusion. In general, Durkheim insists that positive law is no more than an index or expression of 'social life', and that the state and the law-makers function as neutral transmitters of general social values: the authorized 'interpreters of...collective sentiments' (68). But in the case of absolutism, at least, he allows that the constitution and structure of state power decisively affects the content of the law, and thus that 'the state is more than a cipher without effects' (Garland 1983: 53). Quite reasonably, recent researchers have declined to put on this Durkheimian straitjacket, and have instead sought to explore the impact of a variety of political structures and processes on the constitution and administration of the penal law.

Sociological and socio-historical analyses of systems of punishment undertaken in the 1970s and 1980s also rejected Durkheim's insistence on viewing penality as essentially reducible to retribution. Rather than concentrating the study of punitive mechanisms on their repressive effects alone, most such work, and even the more elaborated discussions that were developed in the subsequent decades, have continued to endorse Foucault's injunction to 'regard punishment as a complex social function' (Foucault 1977: 23. Foucault is explicitly critical of Durkheim on these grounds). The consequence has been to make available for analysis a whole spectrum of phenomena that Durkheim's essentialist definition would have artificially insulated from scrutiny: attempts to reform and to rehabilitate; to prevent and to deter; and their associated 'discourses, rhetorics, and techniques'. As Garland (1983: 57) insists, 'the purpose of theory must be to open up such complexities to analysis and significance – not to banish them by decree of an imperial Essence'.

Yet if Durkheim's insistence on reducing punishment to its retributive elements met with general scepticism in the 1970s and 1980s, his associated analysis of the symbolic aspects of punishment had an often barely acknowledged, yet pervasive, impact on this whole body of scholarship. Foucault (1977), who is loftily dismissive of the value of Durkheim's work, develops a semiology of punishment which unquestionably owes much to Durkheim's earlier exploration of related themes – the drawn-out ritual destruction of the body of the would-be regicide Damiens, contrasted with the minutely proportioned, rule-governed confinement of the anonymous individual offender in the nineteenth-century penitentiary: punishment as spectacle, or as the most hidden part of the penal process. Linebaugh's (1975) discussion of the rituals attending public executions at Tyburn Tree has obvious Durkheimian overtones. Douglas Hay's (1975) analysis of the majesty, the ritualistic pomp and circumstance of the administration of eighteenth-century English criminal law, with its emphasis on the contributions such symbolism and ritual made to the ideological integration of English society, likewise owes much to Durkheim, as well as to the more obvious inspiration of Marx.

What was borrowed from Durkheim in these discussions, it must be said, were particular insights and suggestive hypotheses extracted from a theoretical matrix which, as a totality, these scholars rejected. In discussing the ideological functions of the criminal law, Hay is explicit about its role as a weapon in the struggle of a patrician ruling class to maintain its hegemony, a means of *producing* political sentiments and loyalties rather than an occasion for expressing them and thereby reinforcing them. In delimiting the shift from penalties visited upon the body to those involving confinement and the temporary suspension of rights, Foucault is explicitly *not* endorsing a Durkheimian vision of the progressive humanization of punishment: for Foucault, the goal of the system is 'not to punish less, but to punish better; to punish with an attenuated severity, perhaps, but in order to punish with more universality and necessity; to inset the power to punish more deeply into the social body' (Foucault 1977: 82).

A later generation of scholars has been much more open about their debt to Durkheim, and quite vocal about the continuing importance of his central concerns in any systematic sociology of punishment. If a revived interest in the phenomenon of punishment first assumed a historical garb, it soon began to focus its attention on more contemporary phenomena. David Garland, at once one of the most astute commentators on the penological scene, and one of the seminal voices in advancing our understanding of punishment in modern societies, has suggested that the move from penology being a narrowly technical, administrative literature, of little interest to those outside the ranks of those running the punitive apparatus, to a vibrant intellectual enterprise concerned to provide a much broader social and political analysis of the institutions, practices, techniques and personnel through which the power to punish is exercised, has its roots in an ideological crisis: a loss of faith in the prison and other forms of punishment encapsulated in the slogan 'nothing works' – the conclusion many drew in the light of an influential essay by the American criminologist Robert Martinson (1974; see also Rothman 1974, Stone 1987). As long as the key questions at hand seemed to be how to fine-tune the existing system, and make sure it worked as efficiently as possible, more fundamental questions about punishment as a social phenomenon were ignored or obfuscated. 'Now, however, when penologists have lost faith in the institutional project [and the value of the prison] and have become critical and self-reflective, they are once again beginning to assess the axioms upon which punishment is based' (Garland 1990: 9).

There is a measure of truth in such contentions. Equally salient, however, is the fact that, at the very historical moment when notions of prisons as engines of rehabilitation were being greeted with apparently terminal scepticism, and the penal apparatus thrown into apparent ideological crisis, the fraction of the citizenry subjected to incarceration was increasing by leaps and bounds. From the mid-1970s to the present, we appear to have entered a period of what Loïc Wacquant has called 'hyper-incarceration'. The massive expansion in the proportion of the population confined in prisons has manifested itself most dramatically in the United States, which has witnessed an explosive growth in its prison census. Though crime rates were stagnant and then declining over the relevant period, from 1975 to 2000, the number of inmates in state and federal prisons grew from 240,593 to 1,310,710, while the population in local jails increased from 138,800 to 621,149, taken together an increase of some 509 per cent. (As Wacquant (2009:114) dryly remarks, 'If it were a city, the carceral system of the United States would be the country's fourth largest metropolis, behind Chicago'.) Nor does the trend show signs of slackening: by 2008, the numbers incarcerated had grown to 2,310,984. While no other advanced society even approaches this level of incarceration, other Western democracies like Britain and France have also experienced explosive growth in their prison populations. Prisons and borstals in England and Wales, for instance, held 39,820 inmates in 1975, but more than twice that number, 85,115, were incarcerated as of 2010. The punitive turn in state policy, as evident at the level of rhetoric as in the numbers imprisoned, and encompassing substantial increases in the length of prison sentences and the emergence of preventive detention measures like California's three strikes law, has been so remarkable that it could not escape notice, particularly as the associated fiscal costs of these policy shifts greatly exacerbated the fiscal crisis of the state.

So it is that the problem of the sociological significance of punishment, its social role, and its place in modern culture has once more come to the fore. One sign of its growing salience has been the appearance of a specialized journal, *Punishment and Society* in 1997, alongside a burgeoning scholarly literature. A broad array of theoretical ideas has been brought to bear on the question of how to account for, or even adequately grasp the contours of, this remarkable reversal of long-term trends towards lower rates of imprisonment. By no means has this led to a wholesale re-embrace of Durkheimian ideas about punishment. The racial and class-based inequalities that mark America's criminal justice system and go some way towards explaining its starkly great rates of imprisonment have weaker echoes elsewhere. Few modern analysts doubt that questions of power and control have to remain central to any accounting we provide of juridical punishment, and Foucauldian, Weberian, and neo-Marxist theoretical perspectives continue to be ransacked for ideas that can make sense of contemporary realities. But the more astute scholars among them have grown discontented with the notion that this complex social institution can be wholly or even mainly explained in such terms. Amidst what Garland (1990: 5) has commented is a 'growing conviction among social scientists that the modern methods of punishment are neither obvious nor self-evidently rational; that on the contrary they stand in serious need of explication', it is to Durkheim that a number of them have turned.

For more than two decades, Roger Cotterrell (for an early statement, see Cotterrell 1977; and for a later, more comprehensive analysis, Cotterrell 1999) had staunchly maintained an at first rather lonely insistence on the continuing relevance of Durkheim's theoretical ideas, with their stress on the moral foundations of secular societies, despite the apparent growth of instrumental reason as their central organizing principle. Law and its sanctions addressed the pressing issue of how to symbolize social unity, while simultaneously allowing those thus regulated to play an active role in a social order that was not just, as he put it, 'an economic free-for-all'. So far from complexity and differentiation making moral bonds unimportant, the reverse is true, but the morality in question itself is necessarily more complex, nuanced, and sophisticated. Cotterrell's (1991: 935) insistence on the value and importance of considering how law, and by extension punishment, help to frame and maintain 'the balance of moral interdependence which constitutes social solidarity in modern conditions' was now taken up and elaborated by others.

Early in his career, for example, David Garland had published a quite critical review of Durkheim's œuvre (Garland 1983), but within less than a decade, he had become far more sympathetic to elements of Durkheim's approach, particularly those found in his later work. Garland insisted that more instrumental accounts of punishment, and attempts to explain its major features as the product of a drive for control, had been found severely wanting. Punishment also, and quite crucially, communicates meaning. It teaches, constructs, supports and regenerates sensibilities and social meanings, allowing members of a complex society to evaluate the conduct of others, while simultaneously displaying 'a positive capacity to produce meaning and create "normality"' (Garland 1990: 253). All these were insights he derived directly and centrally from Durkheim's work, most especially the latter's discussion in the central chapters of *Moral Education* (Durkheim 1961). Garland then devotes considerable space to illustrating how valuable these notions can be in making sense of aspects of modern penality alternative theoretical traditions pass over in silence, or lack the ability to grapple with in any serious or sustained fashion. And when he subsequently attempted to make sense of 'the dramatic developments that have occurred in our social response to crime in the last thirty years and ... the social, cultural, and political forces that gave rise to them', his proffered explanation drew heavily on these Durkheimian ideas (Garland 2001: vii).

Perhaps the chief rival account of these developments has been offered by the Berkeley sociologist, Loïc Wacquant, who trained under Pierre Bourdieu in Paris and William Julius Wilson in Chicago. Wacquant's work is marked by a far more critical stance towards contemporary capitalist societies (one which extends Bourdieu's concept of the 'bureacratic field', linking it with a concern for the mutual implication of penalty and ethno-racial divisions) and he sharply distances his approach to understanding what has been happening from Garland's (see Wacquant 2009a: 298–303). (Wacquant's massive promised trilogy of monographs, of which only the first two volumes have appeared to date (Wacquant 2009a; 2009b; forthcoming), designed to lay bare the dynamics of the neo-liberal state, places the penal apparatus – and related developments in the administration of 'welfare' – at the centre of his analysis; and he argues that 'punitive containment has proved to be a remarkably successful political strategy', whereas for Garland it 'both marks and masks a political failing'.) Nonetheless, though their explanations of the contemporary culture of control do indeed differ in major respects, Wacquant emphatically concurs with Garland on a central interpretative issue, the importance of assimilating Durkheim's ideas, and about their value for exploring the contemporary realities of punishment if one is to understand contemporary developments. In Wacquant's (2009a: xv–xvi) words, 'To understand why and how the law-and-order upsurge that has swept most postindustrial countries around the close the century ... it is both necessary and sufficient to break with the ritual opposition of intellectual schools and to wed the virtues of a *materialist* analysis, inspired by Karl Marx and Friedrich Engels, and the strengths of a *symbolic* approach, initiated by Emile Durkheim and amplified by Pierre Bourdieu.' The convergence between the two disparate contemporary theorists extends further, as they both point to how Durkheim anticipated and accounted for one of the paradoxes of punishment: while stigmatizing and incarcerating the criminal may serve important positive functions for society at large, for those subjected to it, the consequences are far otherwise:

> All punishment, once applied, loses a part of its influence by the very fact of its application. What lends it authority, what makes it formidable, is not so much the misery that it causes as the moral discredit implied by the blame that it expresses. This feeling of moral sensitivity that stands guard against misdeeds is one of the most delicate of sentiments. It is not strong, it is not completely itself, it lacks its full power of influence except among those for whom it has lost nothing of its original purity. We often say that the first offense leads to others. This is because, once we have felt it, we are less sensitive to this shame. Punishment has this very great limitation of clashing with one of the chief resources of the moral life, and thus of reducing its own efficacy in the future. It retains all its force only when it constitutes a threat ... the influence of punishment declines with frequency of repetition. (Durkheim 1961: 198–9)

Thus, in Wacquant's (2009a: 280) words, the sorts of 'high frequency imprisonment' that has become characteristic of American and, to a lesser degree, European responses to crime 'induces a process of *penal inoculation* among the populations it strikes with regularity, making them less and less susceptible to the preventive or retributive effects sought by the authorities'. Or, in Garland's (1990: 74–5) gloss, 'Precisely because punishment involves moral condemnation, but cannot by itself produce moral attachment, it serves to alienate further offenders rather than to improve their conduct. Moral reproach produces guilt, remorse, and reform only where the offender is already a member of the moral community represented by the law, and, in such cases, self-reproach makes formal punishment more or less redundant. But in other cases, where attachment is weak and self-reproach is minimal, punishment is prone to have the opposite effect.' Hence the problem of massive recidivism among the criminal classes.

As the preceding discussion makes clear, some of Durkheim's central ideas about law and its sanctioning process have been enjoying something of a revival in recent years, particularly the previously overlooked arguments that he advanced in his later work. His stress on the symbolic properties of law, and his more subtle arguments about its role, and the role of legal sanctions, in underpinning social solidarity in complex societies have deservedly attracted considerable attention, and are among the many reasons why his work on the sociology of law enjoys a continuing contemporary relevance, and can fairly be said to be worthy of our close attention. To be sure, what is valuable are particular insights and suggestive hypotheses, not his theoretical system as a whole, but this should scarcely occasion surprise, for the same could be said of the work of any of the major classical sociological theorists.

Notes

1. In the Preface to the second volume of the *Année sociologique*, Durkheim wrote: 'Religion contains in itself from the very beginning, even in an indistinct state, all the elements which in dissociating themselves from it, articulating themselves, and combining with one another in a thousand ways, have given rise to the various manifestations of collective life. From myths and legends have issued forth science and poetry; from religious ornamentations and cult ceremonials have come the plastic arts; from ritual practice were born law and morals' (Durkheim 1899: iv).
2. Mauss here expanded on Durkheim's basic thought that 'it is certain that penal law was essentially religious in its origin' (Durkheim 2013a: 72).
3. Vogt notes that a number of the Durkheimians pursued their studies in faculties of law, nearly a quarter of them had formal training in a law faculty and that, with the passing of the *Année*, six contributed to a new journal, founded in 1931, the *Archives de philosophie de droit et de sociologie juridique*.
4. Dubow (1974: 8) likewise concludes that 'when the law of simple local communities is compared with the law of the more complex state systems of which they become a part, the direction of legal change is from an emphasis on restitution to a greater reliance on repressive criminal law'.
5. Erikson, incidentally, failed to resolve (indeed appeared oblivious to) the problems inherent in the Durkheimian ideas he embraced. Perhaps significantly, there have been few attempts to emulate his work.

CHAPTER 1

The Durkheimian View of Morality and the Law

Introduction

Durkheim saw sociology, like other sciences, as fundamentally a collective enterprise.[1] He had, however, very strong – some might say dogmatic – views about the nature of the social, and the ways in which society might form an object of study in its own right, and a determination to see the new discipline of sociology established on a firm and lasting foundation. From the very beginning of his academic career, his intense personal commitment and the polemical power of his early academic publications attracted a legion of students and younger colleagues to his cause. He saw in the advancement of their careers a means to further the intellectual project to which he devoted his life, and he sought to create an environment where what had begun as a personal crusade to advance the study of society could be transformed into a collective enterprise – albeit one animated by a common sense of purpose and a shared (Durkheimian) vision of how to bring a new science of society into existence. And to a remarkable extent he succeeded. Until the horrors of the 'war to end all wars' intervened, decimating its ranks (including his only son André), the Durkheimian school of sociology went from strength to strength. All across France, Durkheim succeeded in placing his students and collaborators in provincial lycées and eventually in university posts. A handful of early scholarly studies inaugurated a burgeoning new discipline. Adopting a common intellectual framework and methodology, a talented generation of scholars with a shared vision constituted themselves the shock troops of the novel intellectual enterprise.

More than Durkheim's intellectual charisma and his remarkable skills as an academic politician were at work here. Central to the sense of collective purpose, the élan, *and the collective discipline that distinguished the emerging Durkheimian school of sociology was an organizational innovation that provided a forum for the exchange of views, an outlet and a testing ground for their scholarly work, and a very public demonstration of the scope, the reach, and the reality of an emerging science of society. It was an intellectual weapon that gave focus and visibility to an increasingly self-confident scholarly enterprise.*

That weapon, that innovation, was the publication of a new journal, the Année sociologique.[2] *Durkheim had first conceived the idea of such an enterprise in 1896, and its first issue appeared two years later. The journal had a sizeable group of collaborators who contributed regularly to its pages, but there was no question about who stood as* primus inter pares. *Durkheim supervised everything, going so far as to scrutinize and comment upon even the shortest book review that appeared in the journal. Not content with being a hands-on editor and the inspiration behind its intellectual orientation, Durkheim also contributed extensively to the new journal's scholarly content. When he decided to revisit the question of the evolution of punishment that had formed such a central element in his examination of the division of labour and the nature of social solidarity in modern societies, it was in the pages of the* Année *that he chose to publish his further thoughts on the subject. 'Two Laws of Penal Evolution' appeared in the* Année's *fourth volume (see Chapter 4). Though its early volumes displayed some degree of intellectual eclecticism (it published monographs by the German sociologist Georg Simmel and his fellow-countryman and geographer Friedrich Ratzel in its first three volumes), it increasingly articulated the Durkheimian orthodoxy. That was at once its weakness and its strength. It attracted criticism from those outside Durkheim's charmed circle, but it made it easier to develop a formidable sense of shared intellectual endeavours, and to create and defend what had begun as a marginal and suspect intellectual enterprise.*

In addition to monographs, it consisted primarily in reviews of books and even articles from many disciplines, selected for their relevance to the ongoing task of constructing the synthetic discipline of sociology. In this first chapter we include four extracts – two prefaces and two reviews – that reveal this process at work, showing the Durkheimians' developing approach to law. The goal was in part to define what distinguishes the sociological perspective. Thus Durkheim writes that 'one of the principal tasks of L'Année *is precisely to work progressively to determine the natural boundaries of sociology'. And in part it was a classificatory task: to construct sub-fields on the basis of what the best research and current literature suggested, as in Durkheim's discussion here of crime and punishment, and to develop historically based typologies, as he sought to do here in respect of juridical systems.*

The two reviews we include, both by Durkheim, succinctly summarize, through commentary on others' writings, how Durkheim viewed law and morality and the relations between them. Law and morality are not, he thought, distinct domains. Legal rules are not distinguished from moral rules by their character: for example, by their content or form or by the nature of the behaviour they regulate, but rather by the way that sanctions are administered. Moral sanctions are diffuse, *administered by anyone, whereas legal sanctions are* organized, *applied only by specially authorized representatives charged with the task of such enforcement. Thus law involves an institutionalized means for publicly declaring and enforcing norms. The organization and institutionalization of law renders it publicly visible. Law, he wrote in* The Division of Labour, *'is nothing more than the most stable and precise element of this very organization … Thus we may be sure to find reflected in the law all the essential varieties of social solidarity.' In this way Durkheim sought to 'operationalize' social solidarity. He wrote '…we must substitute for this internal datum, which escapes us, an external one which symbolizes it and then study the former through the latter. That visible symbol is the law' (this vol.: 57–8).*

The review of Lévy-Bruhl's book offers a very revealing brief account of Durkheim's way of viewing morality and of how his way differed from the philosopher's way. Lucien Lévy-Bruhl was, indeed, a philosopher. Durkheim's friend, colleague and intellectual ally, his intellectual career largely consisted in a tireless pursuit of the philosophical implications of (mainly Durkheimian) sociological ideas and ethnographic findings. (They did not, however, always agree. Durkheim was to take sharp issue with Lévy-Bruhl's theory of 'pre-logical' thinking in a later volume of the Année *(Durkheim 1913). But Lévy-Bruhl was persuaded that morality is 'the subject-matter of science': that there can and should be a science of morality and that, far from having 'power to explain', morality is 'a matter to be explained'.)*

There are in this review some very striking formulations of Durkheim's distinctive views about morality. Philosophers suppose, he wrote, that they can find a basis to prescribe and legislate, dictating 'duties to mankind' and pronouncing upon the priority of the ends people ought to pursue, and they suppose this because they assume that human nature is always and everywhere the same and that the 'moral conscience possesses an inner unity'. But in proceeding in this fashion, they are typically just echoing the ideas and sentiments of their time, reproducing and presenting in systematic form the ethical practices of their contemporaries. For human nature varies across time and space, varying with 'the diversity of the societies in which the human type functions' – hence the need for 'comparative history'. There is no such entity as 'man in general'. And, as for the 'moral conscience,' it is 'made up of very heterogeneous elements, since all the social forms from the past have reverberations in the present'. The task of the sociology of morality must be to study 'the diverse moral standards that have been effectively in use in different societies'. The science of morality must devote itself to studying 'maxims, customs and beliefs' viewed as natural because 'grounded in the nature of the societies which practise them'. This 'science des mœurs' is, he argued, a latecomer in the history of social science precisely because morality has always been 'stamped with a religious character' and masked with a 'veneer of beliefs' which 'make of it a holy thing which it is not permitted to handle in accordance with the usual procedures of the positive sciences'. And as for the practical implications of such a science, they can only be limited, for morality cannot be 'constructed all in one piece'. Revealingly, Durkheim compared the sociologist of morality with the physiologist offering his scientific findings to the 'clinician' who faces the task of intervention in the world. The clinicians, deciding on whether 'we should or should not want, socialism, divorce, etcetera' are, presumably, bureaucrats and politicians in a democratic state, but about these matters Durkheim has little to tell us.

Durkheim's Review of Ernst Neukamp, *The Historical Development of Legal Constraint* in *L'Année sociologique*

Law is often distinguished from morality and religion by saying that actions that break the law can be dealt with by material sanctions, whereas the merely moral never relies upon more than moral suasion. Our author easily shows that this method of distinguishing the two domains is fallacious. There are a multitude of legal rules to which physical sanctions are not attached, such as the purely moral stigma certain juridical precepts impose. Laws which permit the indefinite suspension of the sentence imposed, like our Bérenger Law,[3] are of the same character. Debtors cannot be physically forced to pay their debts; all that can be done is, indirectly, to seize their goods with court approval. Contrariwise, religion has often imposed itself on the faithful by physical means. From this point of view, it is thus impossible to draw up a line of demarcation between these two different orders of facts. What does serve to distinguish them is that, in the case of law, the coercion directed towards the offenders, whether it takes a physical or a moral form, is always organized. That organized form is manifested in two ways. The rules that the coercion is mobilized to enforce are created by clearly defined entities and in a clearly defined form, and, furthermore, the whole system that the law relies upon to enforce its precepts is regulated and organized, the author asserts, down to the last detail.

In the second part of his work, he shows how this organization of legal coercion has grown more and more significant over time: he takes as the point of departure for the pattern he traces Greece, Rome and the German tribes. He shows how the violent, confused, disorganized elements that made up the primitive vendetta steadily became more fixed, rule-governed and organized as they were made subject to the moderating and organizing influence of the state. This first claim leads Neukamp to offer another finding. To the extent that legal constraint becomes more organized, it becomes more spiritualized. While, at the outset, it consists of an exercise of physical force, designed simply to externally restrain offenders, it attempts more and more to break into the inner life of the guilty party, changing his mental and moral make-up. It seeks to correct his beliefs, to transform those who offend, etc. It thus becomes a sort of pedagogy, an instrument of re-education, which is to say that as coercion it disappears.

We have no problem with accepting the way in which the author defines law, having proposed the same definition ourselves. 'The difference that distinguishes these two kinds of punishments,' as we put it (speaking of moral punishment and legal punishment), 'doesn't inhere in their intrinsic characters, but in the manner in which they are administered. The former is applied by each and everyone, the other by a distinct, defined entity; the former is diffuse, the latter is organized.' We are very pleased to acknowledge a concordance that serves as a guarantee of objectivity. Yet this definition is equally applicable to a multitude of religious as well as legal prescriptions. From this perspective, one cannot distinguish law and religion. The author recognizes this himself (p. 42) in a brief parenthetical remark. But he ought not to have posed the problem in these terms and to have announced that he was going to distinguish these two domains, for they are not distinguishable with repect to their form.

As for the law of the progressive spiritualization of legal coercion, it is true of penal sanctions, but we do not see any way in which it applies to civil sanctions. However, the characteristic coercion of the law cannot be peculiar to a particular type of law; it must apply to all its forms. It's thus not correct to say that, as a general principle, law is more and more losing its previous salient feature.

Durkheim's Review of Lucien Lévy-Bruhl's *Morality and the Science of Morals* in *L'Année sociologique*

One finds in this monograph, analyzed and laid out with rare dialectical vigour, the same idea that is the foundation of everything we undertake in these pages [the *Année sociologique*], knowing that there is a science of morals, and that the practical speculations of the moral philosophers must depend upon this science.

To establish this claim, the author begins by undertaking a critique of the traditional conception of morality, bringing to light the confusion and incoherence that it rests upon. Ordinarily, in looking at morality, we distinguish two parts and two distinct disciplines: on the one hand, theoretical morality, on the other, practical morality. It is the former that is regarded as being the scientific part. But Lévy-Bruhl has no trouble at all demonstrating that it is in no respect whatsoever a science. It does not aim, indeed, to grasp a given reality, but to determine the general principles of what <u>ought to be done</u>. It seeks to discover what ends man <u>ought</u> to pursue, and in what order these ends <u>ought</u> to be subordinated to one another. But the sciences, whatever they may be, are only concerned with knowing what is, not with prescribing or with legislating. Some attempt to get around this objection by calling theoretical morals a normative science, but the linking of these two words, logically incompatible as they are, only succeeds in making clear, without diminishing it, the inherent contradiction of the concept. Science may arrive at some conclusions that permit the establishing of norms; it is not itself normative. The notion of a theoretical morality is thus misbegotten; properly scientific and theoretical considerations are mixed up with practical considerations; and lastly, it is the latter which are, by a large margin, the preponderant ones.

This confusion of theory and practice – with the subordination of the former to the latter – is not, moreover, limited to morality; it can be found in the early stages of all the human sciences. As it is the necessities of action that stimulate reflection, the latter finds itself directly orientated towards practical ends. It is only very slowly that patterns of thought were set free and learned to pursue purely speculative ends, to study things with the sole goal of getting to know them, without being preoccupied with the possible applications of the theoretical results it sought to attain. But it is above all in the study of moral facts that this progress must be slow and difficult. For morality is marked by a religious character, which screens it from properly scientific thought, that is to say free thought. Morality as actually practised by people is camouflaged over time with an overlay of beliefs, of symbols which make of it a holy thing which is not allowed to be treated according to the ordinary procedures of the positive sciences.

But then, if theoretical morality is not a science of moral facts, what is it? It is, simply enough, a means of coordinating as rationally as possible the ideas and sentiments which make up the moral conscience at a given point in time. In reality, the moralist legislates less than he thinks; he merely echoes his time; he can only reproduce the moral practices of his contemporaries, putting into an order that is easier to lay out, the moral practices of his contemporaries. This is why the moral speculations of the philosophers have worried the public conscience much less often than the discoveries of science. There are no 'moral theories' that have ever produced mental revolutions comparable to those which resulted from the teaching of Galileo, for example. That is because moral theory, far from dictating laws to practice, only reflects it and translates it into a more abstract language. It is only another aspect of moral reality. It is thus, in part, the thing that needs explaining and far from what provides the explanation: an object of science, not the science itself.

This coordination that it supplies, moreover, rests upon postulates that are presented as evidence when in reality they lack warrant. In order to construct a deductive morality, moral theorists begin by admitting the abstract idea of a human nature, always and everywhere with the self-same identity, and sufficiently known that they can prescribe to the person the kind of conduct that best suits him in the principal circumstances of his life. Further, when they attempt to construct a system, they presume that normally the moral conscience possesses an internal unity, that the precepts which it enacts are propped up one upon another by irreproachable logical links. But both of these contentions are belied by the facts. Human nature varies over time; it was not yesterday what it is today. It varies in space; the Australian's [aborigine's] is not ours. The notion of what it consists of cannot be constructed by a piece of sleight of hand. We must, preliminarily, recognize the different types that have appeared in the past or that coexist in the present. As to what accounts for this diversity, it is the diversity of the societies in which the human type functions; consequently, since man is a product of his history, it is only by comparative history that he can be understood. For that to happen, all sorts of researches need to be under-taken that are barely under way; it won't do therefore to borrow from contemporary psychology the notion that it deals with general human nature. Furthermore, precisely because the moral conscience is a historical product, it is often made up of extremely heterogeneous elements; because all the social forms of the past echo into the present.

We must thus renounce this contradictory conception of a normative science and resolve definitively to break apart science and practice. Instead of only treating of morality to dictate what man's duties are, we must begin by studying morality, or rather the diverse moralities which have been effectively in use in different societies, and this with the sole goal of under-standing them, knowing what they consist of and on what factors they depend. Each social type has a moral discipline appropriate to it; it is made up of maxims, customs, beliefs that are as real as other natural phenom-ena. There, then, are the facts that are an object of scientific study, which can be described and which one may seek to explain. The morality of a people, taken at a given moment in its history, can't be made up; it exists, it has an independent reality. The old conception according to which there is a natural morality and only one, knowledge of which is founded upon general human nature, is no longer tenable. All the moral institutions that we encounter in history are equally natural, in the sense that they are grounded in the nature of the societies that practise them. Given that a society is constituted in a particular way, it is impossible for it not to have the corresponding morality. It thus doesn't obtain its morality at the hands of a thinker of genius; it gets it from its organization, in other words from its way of living. The science of moral reality, thus considered, is <u>the science of customs and morals</u> [*mœurs*] that the author sharply contrasts to the theoretical morality which he began by critiquing. Since, manifestly, the causes and conditions on which each moral standard depends at each moment in time are social in character, the science of customs and morality is a branch of sociology.

It is this science that alone can provide a rational basis for practical applications. To the degree to which we understand the laws of moral reality, we shall be in a better position to modify it rationally, to say what it ought to be. These methodical interventions will, however, be limited; for morality is not there to be constructed in its entirety. We can't make the whole thing up; it exists and it functions and we can only watch over its functioning. Doubtless there will always be numerous cases where science will not be in a position to provide us with the necessary information to usefully guide our action; for science only moves slowly towards its results which are always provisional. But there is nothing there which is unique to morality. Isn't it constantly the case that the clinician faces problems for which physiology provides no solution? What to do then? He decides on the path that, given the current state of our knowledge, seems the most reasonable. Rational moral art will act likewise.

This circumspect response will doubtless not satisfy those enamoured of absolutes, for whom provisional assurances, grounded in science, would not suffice. It seems to them that the art of morality is only truly itself when it issues its rulings with a sense of infallibility. Alas! Every time we pass from general and theoretical propositions, in whatever manner these have been established, to reaching practical decisions, we court, whatever we do, risks that no method can mechanically do away with; we can only arrive at very uncertain approximations and isn't the best course of action to be resolutely aware of this? The abstract theories of the Kantians or of the utilitarians have no advantage over the method Lévy-Bruhl recommends: they do not point more surely towards the end we ought to favour, the path we ought to follow in the concrete circumstances of life. Between the categorical imperative, if admitted for a moment, and the question of knowing if, today, we should or should not want socialism, divorce, etc., there is an enormous logical chasm which further thought can only traverse gingerly, having recourse to procedures, to ways of deciding that are not in the least conducive to absolute certainty. In this respect, all possible ways forward are equally imperfect and, it follows from this common and unavoidable imperfection, that we cannot take issue with any of them.

Durkheim, 'Moral and Juridical Systems' in *L'Année sociologique*

Until now, in this section we have brought together in a higgledy-piggledy fashion all the juridical systems which the books published in the past year have allowed us to study in their entirety. The time has come to introduce into this confused mass of facts a little order and some distinctions.

A juridical system is defined by the social order which it expresses: it is that social order which best marks the direction towards which it is oriented. Now, with this understanding, the following distinctions are presently possible.

In the first place, there is the sort of societies commonly called primitive [*inférieures*]. But as we have already shown, with respect to religious systems, this category is much too indeterminate. One can, in fact, discern within it three discrete types.

The crudest juridical system is the one to be found in societies of the Australian type: these are made up of totemic clans, perfectly equal among themselves, each juxtaposed one against another without any hierarchy; it is an aggregate of homogeneous groups between which there is no functional differentiation.

Following this come societies like those of the North American Indians. The totemic clan survives there, but it tends to fade into the background; on this earlier base there develops a more or less complex system of classes, of military orders, of religious brotherhoods, of colleges of priests, of diverse social elements. We shall call these differentiated societies based on totemic clans.

Finally, all trace of organization along totemic lines disappears; the tribe, while it may include clans, above all clans linked in the masculine line, is more conscious of itself and its unity. Often enough, it may even have a permanent central government. These we call tribal societies.

Beyond tribal societies, there are nations. We don't hide the fact that this term is uncertain and vague. It can be applied to very different societies and there must ultimately be a way of distinguishing, for example, between the great monarchies of Asia and the city-states of Greece and of Italy. We must thus ask the reader to accept this terminology as purely provisional. The classifications we make use of in the *Année* are not dictated by *a priori* considerations; they are themselves constructed from contact with the things that reveal themselves to us. They can thus only be built up progressively, and it is natural that, on more than one point, the first terms on which one may settle may be still very crude and can only be gradually made more precise. In parallel fashion, one must above all shy away from a premature perfection which can only be obtained artificially.

One may readily acknowledge that this classification corresponds closely to the one we have previously proposed for religious systems; and this ought not to occasion surprise if, as we believe, religion, like law, is a social thing, bound up with the general organization of society. Nevertheless, one must not expect from this that this correspondence will extend to a perfect parallelism. There is indeed an important difference between juridical systems and religious systems which prevents them always and in every case being classified in the same manner. The former are narrowly national: they are intimately tied to the structure of society; they are an essential element of its social distinctiveness and cannot be detached from it. Our legal code may resemble those of the other states of Europe, but each European state has its own. Religions, by contrast, are much more likely to jump frontiers; all the peoples of Europe share the same religion. One might even say, in a larger sense, that perhaps there is no religion that is not to some degree international. Therefore, it can happen that a society practises a religion that is not exactly in harmony with the structure of that society, or, consequently, with its judicial system. Thus, Islam figures among the national religions, but Arab juridical systems among tribal systems. That is because there is a religion common to all the Arabs, but no politically constituted Arab nation.

Durkheim, 'Sociology of Crime and of Moral Statistics' in *L'Année sociologique*

(The study of juridical rules and morality from the point of view of their functioning.)

When we founded the *Année*, we thought it best not to adopt immediately too systematic a classification, one that an ill-prepared audience would have had a difficult time accepting. Besides, the material we were covering was too vast to be organized at a stroke and *a priori*; it was essential to wait upon the lessons that could not fail to emerge from our common endeavours. But if we forbade ourselves to resolve the problem prematurely, we insisted on never losing sight of it; for we believe that one of the principal tasks of the *Année* is precisely to seek progressively to determine the natural framework of sociology. This is, it turns out, the best means of defining definite objects to research, and at the same time, of liberating our science from the vague generalities that hold it back. It also allows us, simultaneously, to gain a better sense of the whole, whereas the actual classifications in use too often obscure it, precisely because they are formed in a completely empirical manner, each independently of the others. That is why not a year has gone by in which we haven't sought to perfect our original classification. On this occasion, it is in our fourth section that we are going to introduce an improvement of this sort.

Until now, the section was exclusively devoted to criminal sociology, and, if moral statistics appeared there, it was solely insofar as it was an auxiliary discipline to criminology; it was criminal statistics that were relevant. In proceeding in this fashion, we were conforming to a tradition that makes the study of crime a scientific enterprise, with its own subject-matter and special methods. But however distinctive in certain respects this branch of sociology may be, it is tightly related to other areas of research which it is important to bring together, if one wants the classification of the sciences to correspond to the natural order of things.

If crime or, more generally, immoral action is a sociological phenomenon, it is because it consists in the violation of moral or juridical rules. It is the social character of these rules which imparts itself to the actions that violate them. But actions taken in conformity with these same precepts are evidently social phenomena in the same fashion and for the same reason as those just mentioned. They are thus both of the same sort, or at the very least they constitute two varieties of the same type, which includes all the diverse and even contradictory ways in which law and morality are put into practice by societies; for to violate a rule is one way of practising it. They are only, in the end, different expressions of one and the same reality, which is the moral state of the collectivity being examined. This state can equally well be assessed from the number and nature of the conforming actions that are performed daily as from the number and nature of the felonious ones. Positive morality, as one may call it, and negative morality, or criminality, are only two aspects of collective morality. All these facts thus belong in the same area of research, because they mutually complete and clarify each other. To assess the conjugal morality of a given country, it is not sufficient to calculate the rate of adultery; one must also take account of the state of marriage, the conditions under which marriages are contracted, their average length, the respective ages of the spouses, the nature of the matrimonial regimes adopted, etc. There are even forms of action about which it is difficult to say whether they are forms of positive of negative morality: for example, divorce.

One can easily see what links there are between this category of facts and those that were previously treated under the heading of Moral and Juridical Sociology. Both are connected to rules of law and morality, but these rules are considered, in the two instances, from two different points of view. What we were seeking in the third section [of the *Année*] was the manner in which they are progressively constituted; it is their origins that one tries to uncover. The inquiry was genetic. Here, one takes them as given, and observes the manner in which, once formed, people apply them. These are the conditions, not of their formation, but of their functioning, that we seek to determine. Assuredly, there is a close linkage between these two kinds of inquiry. In fact, to understand a rule, we must know its true import and that import resides in part in the manner in which it is understood and practised. We would misconstrue, for example, what the *patria potestas* [power of the father] was in certain periods of Roman history, if we knew only what we learn from juridical texts. From another point of view, the mental states from which a moral precept is derived are to be found among the factors that determine the manner in which it is applied.

It goes without saying that these two sorts of studies are very different and oriented, one may say, in two almost opposite directions. In the one, we turn towards the past and consider the moral rule in the course of its evolution; because this is the only way of discovering the elements from which it was composed. In the other, we fix upon a precise moment in time to measure the degree of authority it exercises, at that moment, over people's consciences, and the factors that account for variations in the limits of its authority. Moreover, the research process differs in the two cases: in the former, we make use of history and comparative ethnography; in the latter, we rely above all on statistics.

We thus plan from now on to bring together, in the fourth section [of the *Année*], under the same heading, everything having to do with the functioning of moral and juridical rules, whether this functioning is studied through a focus on honest and proper behaviour, or looks at immoral and criminal actions. For these different phenomena are inseparably linked with each other. In principle, each sub-heading of the preceding section ought to have its counterpart here. With respect to domestic organization there are the statistics of domestic life (celibacy and marriage, divorces, those widowed, the number of children per family, the number of children raised outside a family, the number of adoptions, and so forth); with respect to political organization, everything bearing upon the intensity of public life (the numbers of voters in elections, measures of legislative and administrative activity, etc.); with respect to criminal law, all studies bearing upon the manner in which the injunctions of this law are violated (criminology in the strict sense), for which the penalties dictated by the code are imposed by judges or applied in the prisons (penology). Because all these areas of research necessarily draw their data from the actions of individuals – because social institutions only exist and function in and through the actions of citizens, functionaries, etc. – we might have thought of calling the science that treats of this material 'pragmatology', to give a greater sense of their unity. But since, from another point of view, every neologism that is not established and more or less called for by customary usage has scarcely any chance of establishing itself, we shall limit ourselves provisionally to calling this branch of sociology after the two principal disciplines that make it up: criminal sociology and moral statistics, without deceiving ourselves about the drawbacks of this terminology that we would be happy to see vanish.

Notes

1.   'Science,' he wrote in his preface to the first volume of the *Année*, 'because it is objective, is an essentially impersonal affair and cannot progress except through collective labour' (Durkheim 1898: vii).

2. Perhaps not so coincidentally, one of the few other 'schools' of sociology to establish itself as a distinctive strand of the discipline, the Chicago School, also consolidated itself around an academic journal, the *American Journal of Sociology*, still edited by faculty (and graduate students) at the University of Chicago.

3. The Bérengers, father and son, were nineteenth-century French penal reformers. René, the son (1830–1915) was the author of laws creating a system of parole (1885) and suspended sentences (1891). The latter became known as the Bérenger Law. [Translator.]

CHAPTER 2

Law as an Index of Social Solidarity

Introduction

French academics in Durkheim's day were required to write two doctoral theses.[1] *Durkheim's major thesis subsequently became his first important monograph,* The Division of Labour in Society, *which was published six years after he had taken up his initial academic post at the University of Bordeaux in 1887. His appointment there was as a lecturer (*Chargé d'un Cours de Science Sociale et de Pédagogie*) in pedagogy and social science – not, be it noted, sociology. As much as two-thirds of his lecturing was given over to courses for schoolteachers, an obligation that served as a constant interruption, in the words of his nephew Marcel Mauss, to 'his preferred studies' (Mauss 1925: 15). The mere reference to social science in Durkheim's official title was controversial, and had been granted as a special favour to him. One measure of how fraught the atmosphere was at the time is the fact that, a year after he had taken up his post, there were continuing quarrels among the faculty about whether sociology was a legitimate field of inquiry, and who should house this unwanted intruder, the Faculty of Letters or the Faculty of Law.*

Scepticism about the value of the infant discipline was widespread at the time. Only a decade before, Alfred Espinas had been forced to remove all references to Auguste Comte (the man who had coined the term 'sociology') from his doctoral thesis, and when the dissertation was published, in a further indication of the disrepute in which sociology was held in many academic circles, it was given the subtitle 'Essay in Comparative Psychology' (Delprat 1900). But Durkheim's inaugural lecture at Bordeaux for a course to which he gave the title 'La solidarité sociale' ['Social Solidarity'] made it clear that developing the young science of sociology would be his central aim, a goal he would seek to advance in his teaching, but even more centrally in his research and publications. Throughout his career, his work would be marked, overtly or subtly, by this overarching desire to make manifest the value of a scientific perspective on the social, and by the polemical aim of persuading a sceptical audience that sociology could tackle questions hitherto the province of philosophers, historians and legal scholars, and in so doing, provide novel and compelling new answers to old puzzles. It would be a task he pursued, as one of his listeners remarked, not through 'literary displays and rhetorical periods, appeals to sentiment and metaphysical flights, to which sociological subjects seem at first sight to be so well suited. It is obvious that M. Durkheim denies himself "phrases", generalities and vast syntheses, and that he wishes neither to generate "problems" nor construct systems. He observes facts, he analyses them and explains them by laws' (Delprat 1900: 357).

Georges Davy once commented that morality was the centre and end of [Durkheim's] work' (Davy 1920: 71) and it was a crucial theme of Durkheim's inaugural address. Ethics, he informed the philosophers present, should be examined scientifically, seen, that is 'as a system of natural phenomena which we will subject to analysis and whose causes we will seek' (Durkheim 1888a: 45). 'Morality,' he had already concluded, 'is nothing if it is not a social discipline' (Durkheim 1886: 75) and, together with law and religion, it formed 'the three great regulating functions of society' (Durkheim: 1886: 69). It was here that one would find the ties that bound individuals to a larger whole, the 'solid and durable links' (Durkheim 1886: 75) that the maintenance of social order ultimately depended upon.

These, then, would be the central themes his new social science would examine, and he announced that he planned a major attempt to work out 'how law is formed under the pressure of social needs, how it gradually becomes established, through what degrees of crystallization it successively passes and how it is transformed' (Durkheim 1888a: 47). For if social solidarity, morality, and law were to form the analytical core of his sociology, and explicitly were the organizing themes of his first major publication on the division of labour, it was law that could be most easily and directly brought under the sociological microscope. Through law and legal codes, he would soon come to argue, one could indirectly measure and make sense of other and more elusive realms, those that were not amenable to direct observation and measurement.

Early on his academic career, Durkheim was forced to spend most of his time and energy instructing future teachers. Only on Saturdays, in a course open to the public, was he permitted to lecture on sociology. His central aim in these lectures, and later in a stream of publications, was to establish that the social was a distinctive realm of nature, with its own laws and its own sui generis *features. Week after week, he sought to inculcate this lesson, and to persuade his audience of the validity of the sociological enterprise.*

The appearance of his first major monograph in 1893 (Durkheim 1893), followed in rapid succession by a second monograph directly addressing the methodological question of how once might go about studying the realm of the social (Durkheim 1895), and a further substantial book advancing a sociological explanation of suicide (Durkheim 1897), ostensibly the most individual of actions, constituted a carefully thought-out plan to introduce his claims for sociology to a far larger virtual audience than those who could experience his powers of persuasion at first hand in his Saturday performances in Bordeaux. The fundamental question he had put forth in the lecture with which he began a course on the sociology of the family in 1888, 'What are the bonds which unite men one with another?' (Durkheim 1888b: 257), had broadened by the time he wrote The Division of Labour *into a larger concern with 'the relations between the individual personality and social solidarity'. 'How,' as Durkheim now posed the question, 'does it come about that the individual, whilst becoming more autonomous, depends ever more closely upon society? How can he become at the same time more of an individual and yet more linked to society? For it is indisputable that these two movements, however contradictory they appear to be, are carried on in tandem' (Durkheim 2013a: 7).*

The passage reprinted in the present chapter is drawn from some of the earliest pages of the monograph devoted to providing a systematic answer to this conundrum. How, then, is society held together? What is the basis of social solidarity, regardless of the differing forms that solidarity may assume over the course of history, and how can one simultaneously take account of and explain the burgeoning of the individual? Durkheim's response begins with the assertion that solidarity is 'a wholly moral phenomenon'. But that poses an immediate problem for the social scientist because, as such, it is not amenable to direct observation, measurement and analysis. How then is one to proceed? One needs to find an entity one can observe and measure.

For Durkheim, that external indicator is, quite simply, the law. Whenever societies exist, he contends, social life assumes a regular, organized form. And wherever it does so, there we find law. Law, in this way, is necessarily central to Durkheim's sociological project, and he argues in the pages that follow this passage that the sociologist approaches the legal realm with aims and methods that are quite distinct from those of traditional legal scholarship. Law, for him, is an inescapable part of organized social life. If morality is about regulation and constraint (as for Durkheim it indubitably was), then law is its necessary concomitant, the social phenomenon that embodies the consolidation and the stabilization of organized social relationships and traces out the major forms that social solidarity has taken over the course of human history. Most crucially, towards the end of the discussion that follows, Durkheim argues for a broad distinction between two types of law, distinguished by the differing sanctions to which they are attached. One type of law meets violations by imposing suffering on the perpetrator. It seeks to hurt the deviant to repress his or her behaviour. Its counterpart operates according to a very different logic, replacing the deliberate infliction of pain with an attempt to restore the previous state of affairs, thereby repairing the breach of morality.

Extract from Durkheim, *The Division of Labour in Society*

We have not merely to investigate whether, in these kinds of societies, there exists a social solidarity arising from the division of labour. This is a self-evident truth, since in them the division of labour is highly developed and it engenders solidarity. But above all we must determine the degree to which the solidarity it produces contributes generally to the integration of society. Only then shall we learn to what extent it is necessary, whether it is an essential factor in social cohesion, or whether, on the contrary, it is only an ancillary and secondary condition for it. To answer this question we must therefore compare this social bond to others, in order to measure what share in the total effect must be attributed to it. To do this it is indispensable to begin by classifying the different species of social solidarity.

However, social solidarity is a wholly moral phenomenon which by itself is not amenable to exact observation and especially not to measurement. To arrive at this classification, as well as this comparison, we must therefore substitute for this internal datum, which escapes us, an external one which symbolizes it, and then study the former through the latter.

That visible symbol is the law. Indeed where social solidarity exists, in spite of its non-material nature, it does not remain in a state of pure potentiality, but shows its presence through perceptible effects. Where it is strong it attracts men strongly to one another, ensures frequent contacts between them, and multiplies the opportunities available to them to enter into mutual relationships. To state the position precisely, at the point we have now reached it is not easy to say whether it is social solidarity that produces these phenomena or, on the contrary, whether it is the result of them. Likewise it is a moot point whether men draw closer to one another because of the strong effects of social solidarity, or whether it is strong because men *have* come closer together. However, for the moment we need not concern ourselves with clarifying this question. It is enough to state that these two orders of facts are linked, varying with each other simultaneously and directly. The more closely knit the members of a society, the more they maintain various relationships either with one another or with the group collectively. For if they met together rarely, they would not be mutually dependent, except sporadically and somewhat weakly. Moreover, the number of these relationships is necessarily proportional to that of the legal rules that determine them. This is because social life, wherever it becomes lasting, inevitably tends to assume a definite form and become organized. Law is nothing more than this very organization in its most stable and precise form. The overall life of society cannot enlarge in scope without legal activity simultaneously increasing in proportion. Thus we may be sure to find reflected in the law all the essential varieties of social solidarity.

It may certainly be objected that social relationships can be forged without necessarily taking on a legal form. Some do exist where the process of regulation does not attain such a level of consolidation and precision. This does not mean that they remain indeterminate; instead of being regulated by law they are merely regulated by custom. Thus law mirrors only a part of social life and consequently provides us with only incomplete data with which to resolve the problem. What is more, it is often the case that custom is out of step with the law. It is repeatedly stated that custom tempers the harshness of the law, corrects the excesses that arise from its formal nature, and is even occasionally inspired with a very different spirit. Might then custom display other kinds of social solidarity than those expressed in positive law?

But such an antithesis only occurs in wholly exceptional circumstances. For it to occur law must have ceased to correspond to the present state of society and yet, although lacking any reason to exist, is sustained through force of habit. In that event, the new relationships that are established in spite of it will become organized, for they cannot subsist without seeking to consolidate themselves. Yet, being at odds with the old law, which persists, and not succeeding in penetrating the legal domain proper, they do not rise beyond the level of custom. Thus opposition breaks out. But this can only happen in rare, pathological cases, and cannot even continue without becoming dangerous. Normally custom is not opposed to law; on the contrary, it forms the basis for it. It is true that sometimes nothing further is built upon this basis. There may exist social relationships governed only by that diffuse form of regulation arising from custom. But this is because they lack importance and continuity, excepting naturally those abnormal cases just mentioned. Thus if types of social solidarity chance to exist which custom alone renders apparent, these are assuredly of a very secondary order. On the other hand the law reproduces all those types that are essential, and it is about these alone that we need to know.

Should we go further and assert that social solidarity does not consist entirely in its tangible manifestations; that these express it only partially and imperfectly; that beyond law and custom there exists an inner state from which solidarity derives; and that to know it in reality we must penetrate to its heart, without any intermediary? But in science we can know causes only through the effects that they produce. In order to determine the nature of these causes more precisely science selects only those results that are the most objective and that best lend themselves to quantification.

Science studies heat through the variations in volume that changes in temperature cause in bodies, electricity through its physical and chemical effects, and force through movement. Why should social solidarity prove an exception?

Moreover, what remains of social solidarity once it is divested of its social forms? What imparts to it its specific characteristics is the nature of the group whose unity it ensures, and this is why it varies according to the types of society. It is not the same within the family as within political societies. We are not attached to our native land in the same way as the Roman was to his city or the German to his tribe. But since such differences spring from social causes, we can only grasp them through the differences that the social effects of solidarity present to us. Thus if we neglect the differences, all varieties become indistinguishable, and we can perceive no more than that which is common to all varieties, that is, the general tendency to sociability, a tendency that is always and everywhere the same and is not linked to any particular social type. But this residual element is only an abstraction, for sociability *per se* is met with nowhere. What exists and what is really alive are the special forms of solidarity – domestic, professional, national, that of the past and that of today, etc. Each has its own special nature. Hence generalities can in any case only furnish a very incomplete explanation of the phenomenon, since they necessarily allow to escape what is concrete and living about it.

Thus the study of solidarity lies within the domain of sociology. It is a social fact that can only be thoroughly known through its social effects. If so many moralists and psychologists have been able to deal with this question without following this method, it is because they have avoided the difficulty. They have divested the phenomenon of everything that is more specifically social about it, retaining only the psychological seed from which it develops. It is certain that solidarity, whilst being pre-eminently a social fact, is dependent upon our individual organism. In order to be capable of existing it must fit our physical and psychological constitution. Thus, at the very least, we can content ourselves with studying it from this viewpoint. But in that case we shall perceive only that aspect of it which is the most indistinct and the least special. Strictly speaking, this is not even solidarity itself, but only what makes it possible.

Even so, such an abstract study cannot yield very fruitful results. For, so long as it remains in the state of a mere predisposition of our psychological nature, solidarity is something too indefinite to be easily understood. It remains an intangible virtuality too elusive to observe. To take on a form that we can grasp, social outcomes must provide an external manifestation of it. Moreover, even in such an indeterminate state, it depends on social conditions that explain it, and cannot consequently be detached from them. This is why some sociological perspectives are not infrequently to be found mixed up with these purely psychological analyses. For example, some mention is made of the influence of the *gregarious state* on the formation of social feeling in general; or the main social relationships on which sociability most obviously depends are rapidly sketched out. Undoubtedly such additional considerations, introduced unsystematically as examples and at random as they suggest themselves, cannot suffice to cast much light on the social nature of solidarity. Yet at least they demonstrate that the sociological viewpoint must weigh even with the psychologists.

Thus our method is clearly traced out for us. Since law reproduces the main forms of social solidarity, we have only to classify the different types of law in order to be able to investigate which types of social solidarity correspond to them. It is already likely that one species of law exists which symbolizes the special solidarity engendered by the division of labour. Once we have made this investigation, in order to judge what part the division of labour plays it will be enough to compare the number of legal rules which give it expression with the total volume of law.

To undertake this study we cannot use the habitual distinctions made by jurisprudents. Conceived for the practice of law, from this viewpoint they can be very convenient, but science cannot be satisfied with such empirical classifications and approximations. The most widespread classification is that which divides law into public and private law. Public law is held to regulate the relationships of the individual with the state, private law those of individuals with one another. Yet when we attempt to define these terms closely, the dividing line, which appeared at first sight to be so clear-cut, disappears. All law is private, in the sense that always and everywhere individuals are concerned and are its actors. Above all, however, all law is public, in the sense that it is a social function, and all individuals are, although in different respects, functionaries of society. The functions of marriage and parenthood, etc. are not spelt out or organized any differently from those of ministers or legislators. Not without reason did Roman law term guardianship a *munus publicum*. Moreover, what is the state? Where does it begin, where does it end? The controversial nature of this question is well known. It is unscientific to base such a fundamental classification on such an obscure and inadequately analysed idea.

In order to proceed methodically, we have to discover some characteristic which, whilst essential to juridical phenomena, is capable of varying as they vary. Now, every legal precept may be defined as a rule of behaviour to which sanctions apply. Moreover, it is clear that the sanctions change according to the degree of seriousness attached to the precepts, the place they occupy in the public consciousness, and the role they play in society. Thus it is appropriate to classify legal rules according to the different sanctions that are attached to them.

These are of two kinds. The first consist essentially in some injury, or at least some disadvantage imposed upon the perpetrator of a crime. Their purpose is to do harm to him through his fortune, his honour, his life, his liberty, or to deprive him of some object whose possession he enjoys. These are said to be repressive sanctions, such as those laid down in the penal code. It is true that those that appertain to purely moral rules are of the same character. Yet such sanctions are administered in a diffuse way by everybody without distinction, whilst those of the penal code are applied only through the mediation of a definite body – they are organized. As for the other kind of sanctions, they do not necessarily imply any suffering on the part of the perpetrator, but merely consist in *restoring the previous state of affairs,* re-establishing relationships that have been disturbed from their normal form. This is done either by forcibly redressing the action impugned, restoring it to the type from which it has deviated, or by annulling it, that is depriving it of all social value. Thus legal rules must be divided into two main species, according to whether they relate to repressive, organized sanctions, or to ones that are purely restitutive. The first group covers all penal law; the second, civil law, commercial law, procedural law, administrative and constitutional law, when any penal rules which may be attached to them have been removed.

Note

1. Durkheim's second thesis, in Latin, was *Quid Secundatus Politicae Scientae Instituendae Contulerit,* 1892, translated into English as *Montesquieu and Rousseau: Forerunners of Sociology*, Ann Arbor, MI: University of Michigan Press, 1960.

CHAPTER 3

From Repressive to
Restitutive Law

Introduction

Having established in the opening pages of The Division of Labour, *to his own satisfaction at least, that law could serve as an adequate index of morality and thus provide an empirical means of grasping the underpinnings of social solidarity, Durkheim proceeded to make an examination of law the centrepiece of his analysis of the changing forms of social organization as one transitioned from less to more advanced and differentiated societies. The broad distinction he had made between repressive and restitutive forms of law is further elaborated, and then deployed in an attempt to delineate two ideal types of social solidarity, mechanical and organic. Taking matters a step further, Durkheim claims to identify an essentially unilinear progression from one to the other, corresponding fundamentally to the growth of the division of labour.*

As he discussed these issues, Durkheim was led to confront the question of the relationships between crime and punishment, and how to delimit and define the criminal, – in other words, 'what crime consists of in essence'. Crime was, he proclaimed, those actions which offend 'strong and definite states of the conscience collective'. *Hence its symbiotic relationship to punishment, as the passionate condemnation of actions that arouse universal disapproval. In a sort of feedback mechanism, in punishing crime, society not only makes manifest the abhorrence upright consciences feel towards the offender, but it simultaneously reaffirms and reinforces those sentiments.*

But in advanced societies, at least, law is not reducible to criminal or penal law, and Durkheim is at pains to try to elaborate the different foundations upon which criminal and civil law rest, and the fundamental divergences that exist between them. These, as the following passages make clear, extend much beyond their differing relationship to shared moral beliefs. But if the relationship of civil or restitutive law to the social is of a very different character, if the characteristic reactions to violations of civil

62

law are of a contrasting sort, if civil law is much more specialized and more dependent upon specialized officials for its enforcement, it remains the case, Durkheim insists, that society is present in this sphere of activity. Contra Spencer, what is at stake is not merely the self-interested actions of the parties to a contract. On the contrary, as Durkheim phrases it, 'if a contract has binding force, it is society which confers that force...Every contract ... presumes that, behind the parties binding each other, society is there, quite ready to intervene and enforce respect for undertakings entered into.' These passages broach one of Durkheim's seminal arguments that retains all its force and relevance today. Chapter 9, and our introduction to those texts, will provide a more extended and developed discussion of the issues at stake here.

Extract from Durkheim, *The Division of Labour in Society*

The bond of social solidarity to which repressive law corresponds is one the breaking of which constitutes the crime. We use the term 'crime' to designate any act which, regardless of degree, provokes against the perpetrator the characteristic reaction known as punishment. To investigate the nature of this bond is therefore to ask what is the cause of the punishment or, more precisely, what in essence the crime consists of.

Assuredly crimes of different species exist. But it is no less certain that all these species of crime have something in common. This is proved by the reaction that they provoke from society: the fact that punishment, except for differences in degree, is always and everywhere the same. The oneness of the effect reveals the oneness of the cause. Undoubtedly essential resemblances exist not only among all crimes provided for in the legislation of a single society, but among all crimes recognized as such and punished in different types of society. No matter how different these acts termed crimes may appear to be at first sight, they cannot fail to have some common basis. Universally they strike the moral consciousness of nations in the same way and universally produce the same consequence. All are crimes, that is, acts repressed by prescribed punishments. Now the essential properties of a thing lie in those observed wherever it exists and which are peculiar to it. Thus if we wish to learn in what crime essentially consists, we must distinguish those traits identical in all the varieties of crime in different types of society. Not a single one of these types may be omitted. Legal conceptions in the lowest forms of society are as worthy of consideration as those in the highest forms. They are facts that prove no less instructive. To rule them out of court would be to run the risk of perceiving the essence of crime where it is not. It would be like the biologist whose definition of living phenomena would be very inexact if he had scorned to observe single-cell entities. If he had looked at organisms alone – and particularly the higher organisms – he would have wrongly concluded that life consists essentially in the organization of cells.

The way to discover this permanent, general element is clearly not to go through all those acts which have been designated as crimes at all times and in all places, in order to note the characteristics they present. For, despite what has been stated, if there are acts that have been universally regarded as criminal, these constitute a tiny minority. Thus such a method would provide us with only a singularly distorted notion of the phenomenon, because it would apply only to exceptions. The variations in repressive law at the same time prove that this unchanging character is not to be found in the intrinsic properties of acts imposed or prohibited by penal rules, because these display so great a diversity, but in the relationship they entertain with some condition outside themselves.

This relationship was believed to lie in the kind of antagonism existing between these acts and the larger interests of society. It has been claimed that penal rules have expressed for each type of society the basic conditions for collective life. Their authority thus sprang from necessity. Moreover, since these needs vary according to societies, one could in this way explain the variations in repressive law. We have already given our views on this point. Such a theory ascribes much too large a part to deliberate calculation and reflection in directing social evolution. There are a whole host of acts which have been, and still are, regarded as criminal, without in themselves being harmful to society. The act of touching an object that is taboo, or an animal or man who is impure or consecrated, of letting the sacred fire die out, of eating certain kinds of meat, of not offering the traditional sacrifice on one's parents' grave, of not pronouncing the precise ritual formula, or of not celebrating certain feasts, etc. – how have any of these ever constituted a danger to society? Yet we know the prominent position occupied in the repressive law of a large number of peoples by such a regulation of ritual, etiquette, ceremonial and religious practices. We need only open the Pentateuch to be convinced of it. Moreover, as these facts are found normally in certain social species, we cannot regard them as mere anomalies or pathological cases which we may legitimately dismiss.

Even where the criminal act is certainly harmful to society, the degree of damage it causes is far from being regularly in proportion to the intensity of repression it incurs. In the penal law of most civilized peoples murder is universally regarded as the greatest of crimes. Yet an economic crisis, a crash on the stock market, even a bankruptcy, can disorganize the body social much more seriously than the isolated case of homicide. Assuredly murder is always an evil, but nothing proves that it is the greatest evil. What does one human being the less matter to society? Or one cell fewer in the organism? It is said that public safety would be endangered in the future if the act remained unpunished. But if we compare the degree of danger, however real it may be, to the penalty, there is a striking disproportion. All in all, the instances just cited show that an act can be disastrous for society without suffering the slightest repression. On any score, therefore, this definition of crime is inadequate.

Modifying the definition, can it be asserted that criminal acts are those that *seem* harmful to the society that represses them? Can we also say that penal rules express, not the conditions essential to social life, but those that *appear* to be so to the group observing the rules? Yet such an explanation explains nothing: it does not allow us to understand why, in so many cases, societies have mistakenly enforced practices which in themselves were not even useful. In the end this alleged solution to the problem really amounts to a truism. If societies therefore force every individual to obey these rules it is plainly because, rightly or wrongly, they esteem this systematic and exact obedience to be indispensable, insisting strongly upon it. This therefore comes down to our saying that societies deem the rules necessary because they deem them necessary! What we should be saying is why they judge them necessary. If the view held by societies was based upon the objective necessity for prescriptive punishments, or at least upon their utility, this would be an explanation. But this goes against the facts, so the entire problem remains unsolved.

However, this latter theory is not without some foundation. It is correct in seeking the conditions that constitute criminality in certain states of the individual. Indeed, the only feature common to all crimes is that, saving some apparent exceptions to be examined later, they comprise acts universally condemned by the members of each society. Nowadays the question is raised as to whether such condemnation is rational and whether it would not be wiser to look upon crime as a mere sickness or error. But we need not launch into such discussions, for we are seeking to determine what is or has been, not what should be. The real nature of the fact we have just established cannot be disputed, viz., that crime disturbs those feelings that in any one type of society are to be found in every healthy consciousness.

We can determine in no other way the nature of these sentiments nor define them in relation to their special purposes, for these purposes have varied infinitely, and can vary again. Nowadays it is altruistic sentiments that manifest this characteristic most markedly. But at one time, not at all distant, religious or domestic sentiments, and a host of other traditional sentiments, had precisely the same effect. Even now, despite what Garofalo says, a mere negative sympathy for others is by no means the only condition for bringing about such an effect. Even in peacetime do we not feel as much aversion for the man who betrays his country as for the robber and swindler? In countries where feeling for the monarchy is still alive, do not crimes of *lèse-majesté* arouse the general indignation? In democratic countries do not insults levelled at the people unleash the same anger? Thus we cannot draw up a catalogue of those sentiments the violation of which constitutes the criminal act. Such feelings are indistinguishable from others, save for one characteristic: they are shared by most average individuals in the same society. Thus the rules forbidding those acts for which the penal law provides sanctions are the sole ones to which the celebrated legal axiom, 'No man is presumed ignorant of the law', can be applied without exaggeration. Since the rules are inscribed upon everyone's consciousness, all are aware of them and feel they are founded upon right. At least this is true for the normal condition. If adults are encountered who are ignorant of these basic rules or refuse to recognize their authority, such ignorance or refusal to submit are irrefutably symptoms of a pathological perversion. Or if by chance a penal rule persists for some time although disputed by everyone, it is because of a conjunction of exceptional circumstances, which are consequently abnormal – and such a state of affairs can never endure.

This explains the special manner in which penal law becomes codified. All written law serves a dual purpose: to prescribe certain obligations, and to define the sanctions attached to them. In civil law, and more generally in every kind of law where sanctions are restitutive, the legislator approaches and resolves these two problems separately. Firstly, he determines the nature of the obligation as exactly as possible; only then does he state the manner in which a sanction should be applied. For example, in the chapter of the French civil code devoted to the respective duties of husband and wife, these rights and duties are spelt out in a positive way, but nothing is said as to what happens when these duties are not fulfilled by one or the other party. The sanction must be sought elsewhere in the Code. Occasionally the sanction is even taken totally for granted. Thus Article 214 of the civil code prescribes that the wife must live with her husband; one may deduce that the husband can oblige her to return to the marital home, but this sanction is nowhere formally laid down. By contrast, penal law prescribes only sanctions and says nothing about the obligations to which they relate. It does not ordain that the life of another person must be respected, but ordains the death of the murderer. It does not first state, as does civil law: This is the duty; but states immediately: This is the punishment. Undoubtedly if an act is punished, it is because it is contrary to a mandatory rule, but this rule is not expressly spelt out. There can be only one reason for this: it is because the rule is known and accepted by everybody. When a customary law acquires the status of a written law and is codified, it is because litigious questions require a solution more closely defined. If the custom continued quietly to function, provoking no argument or difficulty, there would be no reason for it to undergo this transformation. Since penal law is only codified so as to establish a sliding scale of penalties, it is therefore because a custom by itself can give rise to doubt. Conversely, if rules whose violation entails punishment need no juridical expression it is because they are not at all a subject of dispute, and because everyone feels their authority.

It is true that sometimes the Pentateuch does not lay down sanctions, although, as we shall see, it contains little else than penal rules. This is the case for the Ten Commandments, as they are formulated in Exodus 20 and Deuteronomy 5. But this is because the Pentateuch, although it fulfilled the function of a code, is not properly one. Its purpose is not to gather together into a single system, and to detail with a view to their application, the penal rules followed by the Jewish people. So far short does it fall of forming a codification that the various sections comprising it do not even seem to have been drawn up at the same time. It is above all a summary of the traditions of all kinds through which the Jews explained to themselves, and in their own way, the origins of the world, of their society and of their main social practices. Thus if the Pentateuch enunciates certain duties to which punishments were certainly attached, this is not because they were unknown or failed to be acknowledged by the Jews, or because it was necessary to reveal them to them. On the contrary, since the book is merely a compilation of national legends, we may be sure that all it contained was graven on everyone's consciousness. Nevertheless it was essential to recapitulate in a set form the popular beliefs about the origins of these precepts, the historical circumstances in which it was assumed that they had been promulgated, and the sources of their authority. From this viewpoint, therefore, the determination of punishments becomes something incidental.

For the same reason the operation of repressive justice always tends to some extent to remain diffuse. In very different types of society it is not exercised through a special magistrate, but society as a whole shares in it to a greater or lesser degree. In primitive societies where, as we shall see, law is wholly penal in character, it is the people assembled together who mete out justice. This was the case for the primitive Germans. In Rome, whereas civil matters fell to the praetor, criminal ones were judged by the people, at first by the *cornices curiates,* and then, from the law of the Twelve Tables onwards, by the *cornices centuriates.* Until the end of the Republic, although in fact the people had delegated its powers to standing commissions, they remained the supreme judges in these kinds of cases. In Athens, under the legislation of Solon, criminal jurisdiction fell in part to the Ηλίαια, a huge collegial body which nominally included all citizens over the age of thirty. Lastly, in Germano-Roman nations society intervened in the exercise of these same functions in the form of the jury. Thus the diffuse state that pervades this sphere of judicial power would be inexplicable if the rules whose observance it ensures, and in consequence the sentiments these rules reflect, were not immanent in everyone's consciousness. It is true that in other cases the power was held by a privileged class or by special magistrates. Yet these facts do not detract from the value as proof of the other ones mentioned. Although the feelings of the collectivity are no longer expressed save through certain intermediaries, it does not follow that these feelings are no longer of a collective nature just because they are restricted to the consciousnesses of a limited number of people. Their delegation to these people may be due either to an ever-increasing growth in cases necessitating the appointment of special officials, or to the extreme importance assumed by certain personages or classes in society, which authorizes them to be the interpreters of its collective sentiments.

Yet crime has not been defined when we have stated that it consists of an injury done to the collective sentiments, since some of these may be wounded without any crime having been committed. Thus incest is fairly generally an object of aversion, and yet it is a purely immoral act. The same holds good for breaches of sexual honour committed by a woman outside marriage, either by yielding her liberty utterly to another or by receiving the surrender of his liberty. Thus the collective sentiments to which a crime corresponds must be distinguished from other sentiments by some striking characteristic: they must be of a certain average intensity. Not only are they written upon the consciousness of everyone, but they are deeply written. They are in no way mere halting, superficial caprices of the will, but emotions and dispositions strongly rooted within us. The extreme slowness with which the penal law evolves demonstrates this. It is not only less easily modified than custom, but is the one sector of positive law least amenable to change. For instance, if we observe what the law-givers have accomplished since the beginning of the century in the different spheres of the law, innovations in penal law have been extremely rare and limited in scope. By contrast, new rules have proliferated in other branches of the law – civil, commercial, administrative or constitutional. If we compare penal law as laid down in Rome by the Law of the Twelve Tables with its condition in the classical era, the changes we note are minimal beside those that civil law underwent over the same period. Mainz states that from the Twelve Tables onwards the main crimes and offences were fixed: 'For ten generations the calendar of public crimes was not added to save by a few laws which punished embezzlement of public funds, conspiracy and perhaps *plagium*.' As for private offences, only two new ones were recognised: plundering (*actio bonorurn vi raptorum*) and malicious damage (*damnum injuria datum*). Such is the position everywhere. In the lower forms of society, as will be seen, law is almost exclusively of a penal kind, and consequently remains unchanged. Generally religious law is always repressive: it is essentially conservative. This unchangeable character of penal law demonstrates the strength of resistance exerted by the collective sentiments to which it corresponds. Conversely, the greater malleability of purely moral laws and the relative swiftness with which they evolve demonstrates the lesser strength of the sentiments underlying them. They have either developed more recently and have not yet had time to penetrate deeply the individual consciousness, or their roots are in a state of decay and are floating to the surface.

A last addition is needed for our definition to be accurate. If, in general, the sentiments that purely moral sanctions protect, that is, ones that are diffuse, are less intense and less solidly organized than those protected by punishments proper, exceptions still remain. Thus there is no reason to concede that normal filial piety or even the elementary forms of compassion for the most blatant forms of misery are nowadays more superficial sentiments than is the respect for property or public authority. Yet the wayward son and even the most arrant egoist are not treated as criminals. Consequently it is not enough for these sentiments to be strongly held; they must be precise. Indeed, every single one relates to a very clearly defined practice. Such a practice may be simple or complex, positive or negative, that is, consisting in an action undertaken or avoided; but it is always determinate. It is a question of doing or not doing this or that, of not killing or wounding, or uttering a particular formula, or accomplishing a particular rite, etc. By contrast, sentiments such as filial love or charity are vague aspirations to very general objects. Thus penal rules are notable for their clarity and precision, whilst purely moral rules are generally somewhat blurred in character. Their indeterminate nature not infrequently makes it hard to formulate any clear definition of them. We may state very generally that people should work, or have compassion for others, etc., but we cannot determine precisely the manner or extent to which they should do so. Consequently there is room here for variations and shades of meaning. By contrast, because the sentiments embodied in penal rules are determinate, they possess a much greater uniformity. As they cannot be interpreted in different ways, they are everywhere the same.

Extract from Durkheim, *The Division of Labour in Society*

Thus, summing up the above analysis, we may state that an act is criminal when it offends the strong, well-defined states of the collective consciousness.

This proposition, taken literally, is scarcely disputed, although usually we give it a meaning very different from the one it should have. It is taken as if it expressed, not the essential characteristics of the crime, but one of its repercussions. We well know that crime offends very general sentiments, but ones that are strongly held. But it is believed that their generality and strength spring from the criminal nature of the act, which consequently still remains wholly to be defined. It is not disputed that any criminal act excites universal disapproval, but it is taken for granted that this results from its criminal nature. Yet one is then hard put to it to state what is the nature of this criminality. Is it in a particularly serious form of immorality? I would concur, but this is to answer a question by posing another, by substituting one term for another. For what *is* immorality is precisely what we want to know – and particularly that special form of immorality which society represses by an organized system of punishments, and which constitutes criminality. Clearly it can only derive from one or several characteristics common to all varieties of crime. Now the only characteristic to satisfy that condition refers to the opposition that exists between crime of any kind and certain collective sentiments. It is thus this opposition which, far from deriving from the crime, constitutes the crime. In other words, we should not say that an act offends the common consciousness because it is criminal, but that it is criminal because it offends that consciousness. We do not condemn it because it is a crime, but it is a crime because we condemn it. As regards the intrinsic nature of these feelings, we cannot specify what that is. They have very diverse objects, so that they cannot be encompassed within a single formula. They cannot be said to relate to the vital interests of society or to a minimum of justice. All such definitions are inadequate. But by the mere fact that a sentiment, whatever may be its origin and purpose, is found in every consciousness and endowed with a certain degree of strength and precision, every act that disturbs it is a crime. Present-day psychology is increasingly turning back to Spinoza's idea that things are good because we like them, rather than that we like them because they are good. What is primary is the tendency and disposition: pleasure and pain are only facts derived from this. The same holds good for social life. An act is socially evil because it is rejected by society. But, it will be contended, are there no collective sentiments that arise from the pleasure or pain that society feels when it comes into contact with their objects? This is doubtless so, but all such sentiments do not originate in this way. Many, if not the majority, derive from utterly different causes. Anything that obliges our activity to take on a definite form can give rise to habits that result in dispositions which then have to be satisfied. Moreover, these dispositions alone are truly fundamental. The others are only special forms of them and are more determinate. Thus to find charm in a particular object, collective sensibility must already have been constituted in such a way as to be able to appreciate it. If the corresponding sentiments are abolished, an act most disastrous for society will not only be capable of being tolerated, but honoured and held up as an example. Pleasure cannot create a disposition out of nothing; it can only link to a particular end those dispositions that already exist, provided that end is in accordance with their original nature.

Extract from Durkheim, *The Division of Labour in Society*

The very nature of the restitutive sanction is sufficient to show that the social solidarity to which that law corresponds is of a completely different kind.

The distinguishing mark of this sanction is that it is not expiatory, but comes down to a mere restoration of the *'status quo ante'*. Suffering in proportion to the offence is not inflicted upon the one who has broken the law or failed to acknowledge it; he is merely condemned to submit to it. If certain acts have already been performed, the judge restores them to what they should be. He pronounces what the law is, but does not talk of punishment. Damages awarded have no penal character: they are simply a means of putting back the clock so as to restore the past, so far as possible, to its normal state. It is true that Tarde believed that he had discovered a kind of civil penal law in the awarding of costs, which are always borne by the losing party. Yet taken in this sense the term has no more than a metaphorical value. For there to be punishment there should at least be some proportionality between the punishment and the wrong, and for this one would have to establish exactly the degree of seriousness of the wrong. In fact the loser of the case pays its costs even when his intentions were innocent and he is guilty of nothing more than ignorance. The reasons for this rule therefore seem to be entirely differ-ent. Since justice is not administered free, it seems equitable that the costs should be borne by the one who has occasioned them. Moreover, although it is possible that the prospect of such costs may stop the over-hasty litigant, this is not enough for them to be considered a punish-ment. The fear of ruin that is normally consequent upon idleness and neglect may cause the businessman to be energetic and diligent. Yet ruin, in the exact connotation of the term, is not the penal sanction for his shortcomings.

Failure to observe these rules is not even sanctioned by a diffused form of punishment. The plaintiff who has lost his case is not disgraced, nor is his honour impugned. We can even envisage these rules being different from what they are without any feeling of repugnance. The idea that murder can be tolerated sets us up in arms, but we very readily accept that the law of inheritance might be modified, and many even conceive that it could be abolished. At least it is a question that we are not unwill-ing to discuss. Likewise, we agree without difficulty that the laws regard-ing easements or usufruct might be framed differently, or that the mutual obligations of buyer and vendor might be determined in another way, and that administrative functions might be allocated according to different principles. Since these prescriptions do not correspond to any feeling within us, and as generally we do not know their scientific justification, since this science does not yet exist, they have no deep roots in most of us. Doubtless there are exceptions. We do not tolerate the idea that an undertaking entered into that is contrary to morals or obtained either by violence or fraud can bind the contracting parties. Thus when public opinion is faced with cases of this kind it shows itself less indifferent than we have just asserted, and it adds its disapprobation to the legal sanction, causing it to weigh more heavily. This is because there are no clear-cut partitions between the various domains of moral life. On the contrary, they form a continuum, and consequently adjacent areas exist where different characteristics may be found at one and the same time. Nevertheless the proposition we have enunciated remains true in the overwhelming majority of cases. It demonstrates that rules where sanctions are restitutive either constitute no part at all of the collective consciousness, or subsist in it in only a weak state. Repressive law corresponds to what is the heart and centre of the common consciousness. Purely moral rules are already a less central part of it. Lastly, restitutive law springs from the farthest zones of consciousness and extends well beyond them. The more it becomes truly itself, the more it takes its distance.

This characteristic is moreover evinced in the way that it functions. Whereas repressive law tends to stay diffused throughout society, restitutive law sets up for itself ever more specialized bodies: consular courts, and industrial and administrative tribunals of every kind. Even in its most general sector, that of civil law, it is brought into use only by special officials – magistrates, lawyers, etc., who have been equipped for their role by a very special kind of training.

But although these rules are more or less outside the collective consciousness, they do not merely concern private individuals. If this were the case, restitutive law would have nothing in common with social solidarity, for the relationships it regulates would join individuals to one another without their being linked to society. They would be mere events of private life, as are, for instance, relationships of friendship. Yet it is far from the case that society is absent from this sphere of legal activity. Generally it is true that it does not intervene by itself and of its own volition: it must be solicited to do so by the parties concerned. Yet although it has to be invoked, its intervention is none the less the essential cog in the mechanism, since it alone causes that mechanism to function. It is society that declares what the law is, through its body of representatives.

However, it has been maintained that this role is in no way an especially

social one, but comes down to being that of a conciliator of private interests. Consequently it has been held that any private individual could fulfil
it, and that if society adopted it, this was solely for reasons of convenience.
Yet it is wholly inaccurate to make society a kind of third-party arbitrator
between the other parties. When it is induced to intervene it is not to
reconcile the interests of individuals. It does not investigate what may be
the most advantageous solution for the protagonists, nor does it suggest a
compromise. But it does apply to the particular case submitted to it the
general and traditional rules of the law. Yet the law is pre-eminently a
social matter, whose object is absolutely different from the interests of the
litigants. The judge who examines a divorce petition is not concerned to
know whether this form of separation is really desirable for the husband
and wife, but whether the causes invoked for it fall into one of the categories stipulated by law.

Yet to assess accurately the importance of the intervention by society it
must be observed not only at the moment when the sanction is applied, or
when the relationship that has been upset is restored, but also when it is
instituted.

Social action is in fact necessary either to lay a foundation for, or to
modify, a number of legal relationships regulated by this form of law, and
which the assent of the interested parties is not adequate enough either to
institute or alter. Of this nature are those relationships in particular that
concern personal status. Although marriage is a contract, the partners can
neither draw it up nor rescind it at will. The same holds good for all other
domestic relationships, and *a fortiori* for all those regulated by administrative law. It is true that obligations that are properly contractual can be
entered into or abrogated by the mere will to agreement of the parties. Yet
we must bear in mind that, if a contract has binding force, it is society
which confers that force. Let us assume that it does not give its blessing to
the obligations that have been contracted; these then become pure promises possessing only moral authority. Every contract therefore assumes
that behind the parties who bind each other, society is there, quite
prepared to intervene and to enforce respect for any undertakings entered
into. Thus it only bestows this obligatory force upon contracts that have
a social value in themselves, that is, those that are in conformity with the
rules of law. We shall even occasionally see that its intervention is still
more positive. It is therefore present in every relationship determined by
restitutive law, even in ones that appear the most completely private, and
its presence, although not felt, at least under normal conditions, is no less
essential.

Since the rules where sanctions are restitutive do not involve the
common consciousness, the relationships that they determine are not of
the sort that affect everyone indiscriminately. This means that they are
instituted directly, not between the individual and society, but between

limited and particular elements in society, which they link to one another. Yet on the other hand, since society is not absent it must necessarily indeed be concerned to some extent, and feel some repercussions. Then, depending upon the intensity with which it feels them, it intervenes at a greater or lesser distance, and more or less actively, through the mediation of special bodies whose task it is to represent it. These relationships are therefore very different from those regulated by repressive law, for the latter join directly, without any intermediary, the individual consciousness to that of society, that is, the individual himself to society.

But these relationships can assume two very different forms. Sometimes they are negative and come down to a mere abstention; at other times they are positive, or ones affording co-operation. To the two categories of rules that determine either kind of relationship correspond two kinds of social solidarity between which a distinction must be drawn.

Extract from Durkheim, *The Division of Labour in Society*

In a small society, since everybody is roughly placed in the same conditions of existence, the collective environment is essentially concrete. It is made up of human beings of every kind who people the social horizon. The states of consciousness that represent it are therefore of the same character. At first they relate to precise objects, such as a particular animal, tree, plant, or natural force, etc. Then, since everyone is similarly placed in relation to these things, they affect every individual consciousness in the same way. The whole tribe, provided it is not too extensive, enjoys or suffers equally the advantages and inconveniences of sun and rain, heat and cold, or of a particular river or spring, etc. The collective impressions resulting from the fusion of all these individual impressions are thus determinate in their form as in their objects. Consequently the common consciousness has a definite character. But this consciousness alters in nature as societies grow more immense. Because they are spread over a much vaster area, the common consciousness is itself forced to rise above all local diversities, to dominate more the space available, and consequently to become more abstract. For few save general things can be common to all these various environments. There is no longer question of such and such an animal, but of such and such a species; not this spring, but these springs; not this forest, but forest *in abstracto*.

Moreover, because living conditions are not the same everywhere, these common objects, whatever they may be, can no longer determine everywhere feelings so completely identical. The results for the collectivity thus lack the same distinctness, and this is even more the case because the component elements are more dissimilar. The more differences between the individual portraits that have served to make a composite portrait, the more imprecise the latter is. It is true that local collective consciousnesses can retain their individuality within the general collective consciousness and that, since they encompass narrower horizons, they can more easily remain concrete. But we know that gradually they vanish into the general consciousness as the different social segments to which they correspond fade away.

Perhaps the fact that best demonstrates this increasing tendency of the common consciousness is the parallel transcendence of the most vital of all its elements – I refer to the notion of divinity. Originally the gods were not apart from the universe, or rather there were no gods, but only sacred beings, without the sacred character with which they were invested being related to some external entity as its source. The animals or plants of the species that serve as the clan totem are the object of worship. But this is not because a principle *sui generis* coming from outside communicates to them their divine nature. This nature is intrinsic within them. They are divine in themselves. But gradually the religious forces become detached from the things of which they were at first only the attributes, and are reified. In this way is formed the notion of spirits or gods who, whilst preferring this or that location, nevertheless exist outside the particular objects to which they are more especially attached. This fact alone renders them less concrete. However, whether they are many or have been reduced to a certain unity, they are still immanent in the world. Partly separated from things, they still exist in space. Thus they remain very close to us, continually intermingling with our life. Greco-Roman polytheism, which is a higher and better organized form of animism, marks a new step towards transcendence. The dwelling-place of the gods becomes more clearly distinct from that of man. Having withdrawn to the mysterious heights of Olympus or to the depths of the earth, they no longer intervene personally in human affairs, except intermittently. But it is only with Christianity that God finally goes beyond space; His Kingdom is no longer of this world. The dissociation of nature and the divine becomes so complete that it even degenerates into hostility. At the same time the notion of divinity becomes more general and abstract, for it is formed not from sensations, as it was in the beginning, but from ideas. The God of humanity has necessarily a less defined meaning.

Moreover, at the same time as religion, legal rules become universalized, as do those of morality. First bound to local circumstances, to racial or climatic peculiarities, etc., they gradually free themselves from these and simultaneously become more general. What makes this increase in generality more apparent is the unbroken decline in formalism. In lower societies the form of behaviour – even its external form – is predetermined even down to the detail. The way in which men must take food or dress in every situation, the gestures they must perform, the formulas they must pronounce, are precisely laid down. On the other hand, the more distant the point of departure, the more moral and legal prescriptions lose clarity and preciseness. They no longer regulate any save the most general forms of behaviour, and these only in a very general way, stating what should be done, but not how it should be done. Now everything definite is expressed in a definite form. If collective sentiments were as determinate as once they were, they would be expressed in no less determinate a fashion. If the concrete details of action and thought were as uniform, they would be obligatory as well.

The fact has often been remarked upon that civilization has tended to become more rational and logical. We can now see the cause of this. That alone is rational that is universal. What defies the understanding is the particular and the concrete. We can only ponder effectively upon the general. Consequently, the closer the common consciousness is to particular things, the more exactly it bears their imprint, and thus the more unintelligible it is. This is whence derives the effect that primitive civilizations have upon us. Not being able to reduce them to logical principles, we are inclined to view them only as bizarre, strange and fortuitous combinations of heterogeneous elements. In reality, there is nothing artificial about them. But we must look for their determining causes in sensations and impulsions of the sensibility, and not in concepts. If this is so, it is because the social environment for which they have been made is not sufficiently extensive. On the other hand, when civilization is developed over a vaster field of action, when it relates to more people and things, general ideas necessarily appear and there become paramount. The notion of mankind, for example, replaces in law, morality and religion that of the Romans which, being more concrete, is more difficult to understand. Thus it is the growth in the size of societies and their greater density that explains this great transformation.

The more general the common consciousness becomes, the more scope it leaves for individual variations. When God is remote from things and men, His action does not extend to every moment of time and to every thing. Only abstract rules are fixed, and these can be freely applied in very different ways. Even then they have neither the same ascendancy nor the same strength of resistance. Indeed, if usages and formulas, when they are precise, determine thought and action with a compulsion analogous to that of the reflexes, by contrast these general principles can only be translated into facts with the assistance of the intelligence. Yet once reflective thinking has been stimulated, it is not easy to set bounds to it. When it has gathered strength, it spontaneously develops beyond the limits assigned to it. At the beginning certain articles of faith are stipulated to be beyond discussion, but later the discussion extends to them. There is a desire to account for them and justify them, and however they fare in this examination, they relinquish some part of their strength. For ideas arising from reflection never have the same constraining power as instincts. Thus actions that have been deliberated upon have not the instant immediacy of involuntary acts. Because the collective consciousness becomes more rational, it therefore becomes less categorical and, for this reason again, impedes less the free development of individual variations.

CHAPTER 4

The Evolution of Punishment

Introduction

In our introduction to Chapter 1, we have pointed out the central part the Année sociologique *played in the consolidation of the Durkheimian school of sociology. Not content with being a hands-on editor and the inspiration behind its intellectual orientation, Durkheim also contributed extensively to the new journal's scholarly content. When he decided to revisit the question of the evolution of punishment that had formed such a central element in his examination of the division of labour and the nature of social solidarity in modern societies, it was in the pages of the* Année *that he chose to publish his further thoughts on the subject. 'Two Laws of Penal Evolution' appeared in the* Année's *fourth volume, to which Durkheim also contributed a shorter note on 'The Sociology of Crime and Moral Statistics', as well as a host of book reviews.*

Durkheim's further thoughts about punishment had been stimulated by a new lecture course he had begun at Bordeaux in 1896. 'Physique générale du droit et des mœurs' ['General Structure of Law and Normative Behaviour'], as its title suggests, ranged far more widely across the territory of legal and moral obligations in relation to the state, the family and society in general, seeking to examine the traditional subject matter of moral philosophy from an empirical perspective. It was a lengthy course extending over two years, and the discussion of the evolution of punishment occupied the final portion of the first year's lectures.

As compared with the largely unilinear account of the changing forms and content of penal law offered in The Division of Labour, *reproduced in Chapters 2 and 3, Durkheim's later discussion is more nuanced and complex, incorporating in particular the ideas that political power can by itself influence the intensity of punishment; that the degree of centralization of government power and authority was historically contingent and thus could vary to some degree independently of changes in social structure; and therefore that the structure of government could act to neutralize, even reverse, the influence of social organization on the nature and intensity of punishment. Under absolute forms of government, crime inevitably came to acquire a political dimension, to be seen as an attack on the sovereign, and thus, as a form of* lèse-majesté, *to be repressed with almost religious fury.*

In that sense, crime and its necessary concomitant, punishment, came under such regimes to resemble the forms they took in less advanced societies, where offences were characteristically seen as directed against 'collective things', including customs and traditions and public authorities, and ultimately were 'offences against religion'. Being seen as sacrilegious, crimes against God or the gods, they were 'exceptionally odious' and aroused collective fears, prompting fierce and exemplary punishment. But such types of 'religious criminality' (absent the countervailing effect of absolutist forms of rule) became, Durkheim contended, steadily less salient as societies evolved, with crime increasingly involving offences against the person rather than the collectivity. Punishment, in turn, became less harsh, less extreme, more humane.

Durkheim's theory of punishment fundamentally, therefore, continued to emphasize its gradual humanization, and its increasing mildness. He emphasized the ways in which punishment visited on the body of the offender came more and more to be replaced by fines and imprisonment, and while he insisted that punishment could never entirely disappear, he expected its pains to alleviate over time. In his account of the torturous execution of the would-be regicide Damiens in 1757, Foucault (1977: 3–6) clearly borrows from Durkheim's insights about the political dimensions of punishment in absolutist states. But though Foucault likewise emphasizes a transition from corporal punishment to an ever greater reliance on the impersonal prison, in most respects the two theorists could not be further apart. For Foucault, the prison serves, not to punish less, but to punish better, to substitute the manipulation and transformation of offenders into docile bodies via an ever more intrusive technology of power for the brutal demonstration of the awfulness of absolute power. Durkheim, meanwhile, sees in the evolution of punishment the struggles of society to reconcile the need to recognize the suffering and the dignity of the victims of crime with an analogous respect for the common humanity of the criminal. There is, as he puts it below, 'a real and irremediable contradiction in avenging the human dignity offended in the person of the victim by violating it in the person of the criminal'. Hence his expectation that punishment would become steadily milder and less draconian.

Theoretically, Durkheim's account of the evolution of punishment in the pages that follow depends heavily on his developing sense that collective sentiments and beliefs are crucially relevant to the explanation of social practices. More specifically, he argues that modern differentiated societies give rise to individualism and must embrace it – that the individual, paradoxical as it may seem, is the product of society, not its fons et origo. *One must look to the growing emphasis on the dignity to be accorded to the individual, and modern society's encouragement of individual initiative, spontaneity, and freedom of thought, for the explanation of the long-term amelioration of punishment.*

Durkheim had provided a more extended analysis of the social foundations of individualism and its ramifying implications for the social order in a polemical essay written at the height of the Dreyfus affair in 1898. 'Individualism and the Intellectuals' is reprinted below as Chapter 7. In our introduction to that section, we shall provide some further reflections on Durkheim's emerging views on this vital issue.

Durkheim, 'Two Laws of Penal Evolution'

In the present state of the social sciences, one can, in most cases, only render the most general aspects of social life intelligible. Undoubtedly this leads one now and then to what are merely gross approximations, but these are not without their usefulness; for they are a preliminary means of coming to grips with reality and, however schematic they may be, they form the essential precondition of subsequent more precise formulation.

Keeping this proviso in mind, we shall seek to establish and to explain two laws which seem to us to prevail in the evolution of the apparatus of punishment. It is quite clear that we shall direct our attention only to the most general tendencies; but if we succeed in introducing a little order into this confused mass of facts, however imperfect it may be, our labours will not have been in vain.

The variations through which punishment has passed in the course of history are of two sorts, quantitative and qualitative. The laws governing each of these are, of course different.

I. THE LAW OF QUANTITATIVE CHANGE

This may be formulated as follows:

> *The intensity of punishment is the greater the more closely societies approximate to a less developed type- and the more the central power assumes an absolute character.*

Let us first explain the meaning of these propositions. The first of them does not really need much further definition. It is relatively easy to determine whether one social type is more or less advanced than another: one has only to see whether they are more or less complex and, as to the extent of similar composition, whether they are more or less organized. This hierarchy of social types, moreover, does not imply that the succession of societies takes a unilinear form; to the contrary, it is certain that the sequence must rather be thought of as a tree with many branches all diverging in greater or lesser degree. But, on this tree societies are found at differing heights, and are found at differing distances from the common trunk. It is on condition that one looks at in this way that one can talk in terms of a general evolution of societies.

The second factor which we have distinguished must concern us at more length. We say that governmental power is absolute when it encounters among the other social functions nothing which serves to counterbalance it and to limit it effectively. In reality, the complete absence of all such limitations is nowhere to be found: one might even say that it is inconceivable. Traditions and religious beliefs act as brakes on even the strongest governments. Beyond this, there are always certain lesser social institutions which now and then are capable of making themselves felt and resisting governmental power. The subordinate elements which are subjected to a supreme regulatory function are never deprived of all their individual energy. But this factual limitation may be in no sense legally required of the government which submits to it; although it exercises a certain amount of care in the exercise of its prerogatives, it is not held back by written or by customary law. In such a case, it exercises a power which we may term absolute. Undoubtedly, if it goes too far, the social forces which it is harming may unite to react to this and to contain it; it may even be that the government, foreseeing that such a reaction may arise, and in order to forestall it, may impose restrictions on itself. But this development, whether it is the result of the government's own actions or is imposed on it, is essentially contingent; it does not arise out of the normal functioning of institutions. When it arises out of the government's initiative, it is presented as gracious concession, as a voluntary relinquishment of legitimate rights; when it is produced by a collective resistance, it has a frankly revolutionary character.

One can characterize an absolute government in yet another way. The legal sphere is entirely centred around two poles; either the relations which are central to it are unilateral, or they are, on the contrary, bilateral and reciprocal. These are, at least, two ideal types [*types idéaux*] around which they oscillate. The first consists exclusively of rights given to one of the parties to the agreement over the other without the latter enjoying any rights corresponding to his duties. In those of the second type, on the other hand, the legal bond provides for complete reciprocity in the rights conferred on both parties to the agreement. Real rights and more particularly the right of property, represent the purest form of the first type: the owner has rights over his property, which has none over him. The contract, and above all the just contract, i.e., one where there is an exact equivalence in the social value of the objects or benefits exchanged, exemplifies the case of reciprocal connections. Now, the more the relations of the supreme power with the rest of the society have a unilateral character, in other words the more these relationships resemble those which unite the possessor and the thing possessed, the more absolute is the government. Conversely, the more completely bilateral are its relations with other social groups, the less absolute it is. Thus, the purest example of absolute supremacy is the Roman *patria potestas,* as the old civil code defines it, since the son was likened to an object.

Therefore, what makes the central authority more or less absolute in character, is the degree to which all counterweights organized with a view to restraining it are missing. One can therefore foresee that this kind of power structure comes into being when all the directive functions of society are more or less completely brought together into one and the same hand. In fact, because of their vital significance, they cannot be concentrated in one and the same person, without giving him an extraordinary hold over the rest of society, and this dominance is what is meant by the term absolutism. The person who wields such an authority finds himself possessed of a power which frees him from any collective restraint, and which to some extent means that he only takes into account himself and his own whims and can impose all his wishes. This hypercentralization releases a social force *sui generis* which is of such intensity that it dominates all the others and holds them in thrall. And this does not simply amount to a *de facto* dominance, but is seen as being as of right, for the person who has such a privilege is possessed of such an aura of prestige that he seems to be in a sense superhuman; as a consequence we do not even conceive that he could be subject to ordinary restraints, as is the common run of humanity.

However brief and imperfect this analysis may be, it will at least suffice to caution us against committing certain errors which are still common. One sees, for instance, that, contrary to the mistaken notion perpetrated by Spencer, whether or not a government assumes an absolutist character does not depend on the number and importance of governmental functions. However numerous these may be, if they are not concentrated in the hands of one person, the government is not an absolute one. This is the situation found today in our great European societies, particularly in France. The sphere of State action is very much more extensive than it was under Louis XIV; but with the rights which it exercises over society go reciprocal duties; in no sense does it resemble a property-right. In practice, it is not only that the supreme regulatory functions are split up among distinct and relatively autonomous organs, however interdependent, but also that they do not exercise their powers without a degree of participation by other elements of society. Thus, from the fact that the State makes itself felt in a greater number of directions, it does not follow that it becomes more absolute. True, this may happen, but if this is to be the case there must be circumstances quite other than the greater complexity of functions which devolve upon it. On the other hand, the modest scope of its functions does not prevent a government taking on this character. Actually, if these functions are few in number and not very actively pursued, this is because social life itself on the more general level is impoverished and languishing; for the greater or lesser extent to which the central directive organ is developed only reflects the development of social life in general, just as the extent of the individual's nervous system varies with the importance of the organic exchanges. The society's directive functions accordingly are only rudimentary when the social functions are of the same type; and thus the relationship between them remains constant. Consequently, the former retain their primacy, and these functions need only be concentrated in the hands of a single person to put him beyond criticism and to raise him infinitely far above the rest of society. Nothing is more simple than the rule of some barbarian chieftains; nothing is more absolute.

This observation leads us to another more closely related to the issue at hand: namely the fact that the degree to which a government possesses an absolutist character is not linked to any particular social type. Indeed, if one may find such a government as often in an extremely complex society as in a very simple one, it is no more tied exclusively to primitive societies than to other types. True, one might surmise that this concentration of governmental power always accompanies the concentration of the social mass, regardless of whether it be caused by this factor, or whether it helps bring it about. But it is not so. The Roman City, especially following the overthrow of the monarchy, was, until the last phase of the Republic, quite free of absolutism; yet, it was precisely under the Republic that the various segments or sub-groupings *(gentes)* which made up the city attained a very high degree of concentration and unity. Besides, we in fact observe examples of governments which deserve to be called absolute in the most diverse of social types, in seventeenth-century France as much as in the latter period of the Roman State or in a multitude of primitive kingdoms. Conversely, the same people, depending on the circumstances, can move from an absolute form of government to a completely different type; yet the same society can no more change its type in the course of its evolution than can an animal change its species during its own lifetime. France in the seventeenth and France in the nineteenth centuries belonged to the same social type and yet its major regulatory institutions were quite different. One cannot maintain that between Napoleon I and Louis-Philippe, French society moved from one kind of society to another, only to undergo a shift in the opposite direction from Louis-Philippe to Napoleon III. Such changes contradict the very notion of species.

This special kind of political organization is not, therefore, a consequence of the fundamental nature of the society, but rather depends on unique, transitory, and contingent factors. This is why these two causes of the evolution of punishment – the nature of the social type and of the governmental organ – must be carefully distinguished. For being independent, they act independently of one another, on occasion even in opposite directions. For example, it happens that, in passing from a primitive type of society to other more advanced types, we do not see punishment decreasing as we might have expected, because the organization of government acts at the same time to neutralize the effects of social organization. Thus, the process is a very complex one.

Having explained the nature of the law, we must now show that it conforms to the facts. Since there can be no question of examining every society, we shall choose the ones we are going to compare from among those where penal institutions have reached a certain degree of development and are known fairly precisely. For the rest, as we have tried to show elsewhere, the essence of a sociological explanation does not lie in piling up facts, but rather in organizing series of regular variations whose terms are bound together as closely as possible, and which are also sufficiently wide-ranging.

In a very large number of ancient societies death pure and simple is not the supreme punishment; it is augmented, in the case of those offences deemed most frightful, by further torments which are aimed at making it still more dreadful. Thus, among the Egyptians, above and beyond hanging and beheading, we find burning at the stake, 'death by ashes', and crucifixion. In the case of punishment by fire, the executioner used to begin by inflicting numerous wounds in the hands of the criminal using sharpened stakes, and only after this was the latter placed on a fire and burned alive.· 'Death by ashes' consisted of suffocating the condemned man to death under a pile of ashes. 'It is even probable,' says Thonissen, 'that the judges were accustomed to inflicting on the criminals whatever additional suffering they felt was required by the nature of the crime or the exigencies of public opinion.' The Asian peoples would seem to have taken cruelty to even further lengths.

Among the Assyrians, criminals were thrown to ferocious animals or into a fiery furnace; they were cooked to death in a brass pot placed over a slow fire; they had their eyes put out. Strangulation and beheading were spurned as being too mild! Among the various tribes of Syria, criminals were stoned to death, they were shot full of arrows, they were hanged, they were crucified, their ribs and entrails were burned with torches, they were drawn and quartered, they were hurled from cliffs ... or they were crushed beneath the feet of animals, etc.

The code of Manu itself distinguishes between an ordinary death sentence, consisting of beheading, and a severe or aggravated death sentence. The latter was divided into seven categories: impalement on a pointed stake, being burned to death, being crushed to death under elephant's feet, judicial drowning, having boiling oil poured into one's ears and mouth, being torn apart by dogs in public, being cut into pieces with razors.

Among these same peoples, the ordinary death sentence was widely used. It is impossible to list all the offences punished in this way. A single fact illustrates how numerous they were: according to Diodorus' account, one Egyptian king, by banishing those condemned to death into the desert, managed to establish a new city there, and another, by employing them in a programme of public works, succeeded in building numerous dikes and digging canals.

Punishments symbolic of the crime committed were used as less drastic penalties than the death sentence. Thus in Egypt, forgers, those who altered public documents, used to have their hands cut off; rape of a free-born woman was punished by castration; spies had their tongues torn out, etc. Likewise, after the laws of Manu, the tongue of a man in the lowest caste who had gravely insulted the twice-born[1] was to be cut out; a Sudra who had the audacity to sit down next to a Brahmin was to be branded on the buttocks, etc. Over and above these characteristic mutilations, all sorts of corporal punishment were customary in one tribe or another. This type of punishment was usually inflicted at the discretion of the judge.

The Hebrews certainly did not possess a higher type of society than these other peoples; indeed, the concentration of the society only occurred at a relatively late period, under the monarchy. Before this, there was no Israeli nation, but merely a more or less autonomous grouping of tribes or clans, which only united briefly if faced by a common threat. And yet Mosaic law is much less harsh than the law of Manu or the sacred books of Egypt. Capital punishment is no longer accompanied by the same refined cruelties. It even seems that, for a considerable period of time, stoning was the only way it was done; it is only in the rabbinical texts that there is mention of burning, beheading and strangulation. Mutilation, so widely practised by the other Oriental peoples, is only mentioned once in the Pentateuch. True, the principle of retaliation, when the crime involved wounding someone, might involve mutilation; but the guilty party could always escape this by means of a financial settlement; this practice was only forbidden in case of murder. As for other physical punishments, which are reduced to whipping, they were certainly used for a great number of offences, but the maximum penalty was fixed at 40 lashes, and in practice this number was really 39. Where does this relative mildness come from? From the fact that among the Hebrews absolutist government was never able to establish itself on a lasting basis. We have seen that for much of the time they lacked any sort of political organization. Later on, of course, a monarchy was formed; but the king's power remained very limited: 'There always existed a very lively belief in Israel that the king was there for the sake of the people and not the people for the sake of the king; he ought to seek to help Israel, and not to further his own self-interest.'

Even though certain individuals occasionally succeeded, by dint of their personal prestige in winning an exceptional degree of authority, the temper of the people remained profoundly democratic.

Yet we have been able to see that the penal law still remained a very harsh one there. If we move from the preceding sorts of society to the City-State, which is without doubt a more advanced type of society, we observe a more marked decline in the severity of punishment. Although capital punishment at Athens was, in certain instances, accompanied by other penalties, *this* was, nevertheless, highly exceptional. Such punishment consisted, in principle, of death by drinking hemlock, by the sword, by strangulation. Symbolic mutilation disappeared. It even seems that the same thing happened with corporal punishment, except for the slaves and, perhaps, the lower classes. Yet Athens, even viewed at its apogee, represents a relatively archaic form of the City. Indeed, organization based on the clan system (*gene, phratres*) was never as completely obliterated there as it was at Rome, where, from a very early period, *curias* and *gentes* became mere historical survivals, of whose meaning even the Romans themselves were uncertain. Consequently the system of punishments was much harsher at Athens than at Rome. First, Athenian law, as we noted above, did not completely avoid adding other punishments to the death sentence. Demosthenes alludes to culprits being nailed to the gallows; Lyseas cites the names of assassins, highwaymen, and spies beaten to death; Antiphon speaks of a poisoner dying on the rack. Sometimes death was preceded by torture. Besides this, the number of offences for which the death penalty was invoked was considerable: 'Treason, harming the Athenian people, assaults on the political institutions, debasing the national law, lying to the tribune of the people's assembly, abuse of diplomatic office ... extortion, impiety, sacrilege, etc., etc., immediately brought forth the intervention of "The Eleven".'[2] At Rome, on the other hand, capital crimes were much less numerous and the *Leges Porciae*[3] limited the employment of capital punishment throughout the Republic. Beyond this, except for totally exceptional circumstances, execution was never accompanied by lesser tortures, or by any further mistreatment. Crucifixion was only permitted for slaves. Moreover, the Romans were apt to boast of the relative leniency of their system of punishment: '*Nulli gentium mitiores placuisse pocuas,*' said Titus Livy, and Cicero commented: '*Vestram libertatem, rum acerbitate suppliciorum infestam, sed lenitate legum munitam esse voluerunt.*'

But when, with the advent of the Empire, governmental power tended to become absolute, the penal law became more severe. First, the number of capital crimes grew. Adultery, incest, all sorts of offences against public morals, and above all the constantly growing number of crimes of lese-majesty were punished by death. At the same time, harsher forms of punishment were instituted. Burning at the stake, formerly reserved for political crimes of an exceptional nature, was used against arsonists, the sacrilegious, sorcerers, parricides, and certain other crimes of lese-majesty; the sentence '*ad opus publicum*' was established, and mutilations visited upon some classes of criminals (for example, castration in the case of certain offences against public morals, severing the hands of forgers, etc.). Finally, torture made its appearance; it was the Imperial period that the Middle Ages was later to borrow from.

If we move on from the City to the case of Christian societies, we observe punishment evolving according to the same law. It would be a mistake to estimate the kind of punishment employed in feudal times according to the reputation for atrocity which the Middle Ages have been given. When we examine the facts we cannot but see that punishment was much milder than in earlier types of society, at least if one looks at them at the corresponding phase in their evolution, which is to say in their formative period and, so to speak, their first flush of youth; and it is only in these circumstances that the comparison has any illustrative value. Capital crimes were not very numerous. According to Beaumanoir, the only things which could not by some means be atoned for were man-slaughter, treason, homicide, and rape. The laws of Saint Louis added to these abduction and arson. These were the major concerns of the higher courts. However, although robbery was not so termed, it too was a capi-tal crime. The same thing happened with respect to two offences which were considered particularly threatening to the rights of the lord; these were the breaking of contracts and crimes of the highway (robbery of toll-houses with violence). As for religious crimes, the only ones which were then controlled by means of the death penalty were heresy and athe-ism. Those who committed sacrilege had only to do penance, as did blas-phemers; indeed, Saint Louis having decided, in the first flush of the religious enthusiasm of his youth, that they ought to be branded on the forehead and to have their tongues pierced, found himself censured by Pope Clement IV. It was only somewhat later that the Church displayed an implacable severity against its enemies. As for the punishments them-selves, there was nothing outrageous about them. The only additions to the death penalty consisted in being dragged to execution on a hurdle and in being burned alive. Mutilations were uncommon. In other respects we know how humane the Church's system of control was. Its preferred modes of punishment were penances and abstinence. It spurned public humiliations, the pillory and its iron collar [the means of attaching a criminal to the pillory] although such punishments did not seem to it beyond its province. It is true that, when the Church judged a bloody repression to be necessary, it delivered up the guilty to secular justice. Nevertheless, the fact that the most influential moral force of the time bore witness in this manner to its horror of such punishments was of the greatest significance.

This was roughly the situation up until about the fourteenth century. From then on the king's power became more and more firmly established. One sees that punishment increased in proportion to its consolidation. First, crimes of lese-majesty which were non-existent in feudal times, make their appearance, and the list of such crimes is a long one. Religious crimes take on this quality. Consequently sacrilege becomes a capital crime. The same applies to any trafficking with unbelievers, to all attempts 'to persuade others of or argue for any and all beliefs which are, or might be, contrary to the sacred teachings of Our Lord'. Simultaneously, a greater rigour is manifested in the application of punishments. Those convicted of capital crimes may be stretched on the rack (it is at this stage that torture on the rack makes its appearance), buried alive, drawn and quartered, flayed alive, or boiled to death. Sometimes the condemned man's children were punished with him.

The apogee of the absolute monarchy coincides with the period of the greatest repression. In the seventeenth century the forms of capital punishment in use were still those we have just enumerated. Beyond this, a new punishment was introduced, the galleys, and this form of punishment was so terrible that the wretches condemned to it would sometimes sever their own arm or hand in order to escape it. The practice was even so common that a decree of 1677 made it punishable by death. As for corporal punishments, these were countless: there was the ripping out or the piercing of tongues, cutting off of lips, cutting or tearing off ears, branding with a hot iron, beating with cudgels, the cat-o'-nine tails, the pillory, etc. Finally, we must not forget that torture was used not only as a means of getting information, but also as a means of punishment. At the same time, the number of capital crimes increased because the crimes of lese-majesty were growing ever more numerous.

Such was the state of the criminal law until the middle of the eighteenth century. There then occurred, throughout Europe, the protest to which Beccaria has given his name. Doubtless it would be a distortion to claim that the Italian criminologist was the initial cause of the reaction which was to subsequently proceed without interruption. The movement had begun before him. A whole series of works, now forgotten, had already appeared demanding the reform of the penal system. Yet it is incontestably the case that it was the 'Treatise on Crimes and Punishments' which delivered the mortal blow to the old and hateful routines of the criminal law.

An ordinance of 1788 had already introduced certain reforms which were not unimportant; but it was above all with the Penal Code of 1810 that the new aspirations were at last really satisfied. Accordingly, the appearance of the new code was received with great admiration, not only in France, but in all the major European countries. It represented, indeed, considerable progress in the direction of mitigating earlier severity. However, in point of fact, it still remained much too closely tied to the past. Thus it was not long before new reforms were being sought. There were complaints that the death penalty was still very widely employed, even if it could not be augmented as it was under the *ancien régime*. The retention of branding, the pillory, and mutilation of the parricide's hands was seen as inhuman. It was in response to these criticisms that the revision of 1832 took place. This introduced a much greater leniency into the penal system, suppressing all mutilations, decreasing the number of capital crimes, and at last giving the judges the power of lessening all penalties if there were extenuating circumstances. It is unnecessary to show that things have continued in the same direction since then, so that today there are beginning to be complaints that things are being made too comfortable for criminals.

II. THE LAW OF QUALITATIVE CHANGES

The law which we have just established refers exclusively to the severity or the quantity of punishments. The one which will now concern us is concerned with their qualitative aspects. It may be formulated thus:

Deprivations of liberty, and of liberty alone, varying in time according to the seriousness of the crime, tend to become more and more the normal means of social control.

Primitive societies almost completely lack prisons. Even in the laws of Manu, there is at most one passage which seems to concern itself with prisons. 'Let the king place all the prisons on the public highway, so that the criminals, hideous and humiliated, may be exposed in full view of everyone.' Yet such a prison has a completely different character than ours; it is more nearly analogous to the pillory. The guilty party was held prisoner so that he could be put on display and also because imprisonment was a necessary condition of the punishments being imposed on him; but not because this itself was the punishment. That consisted rather of the harsh existence imposed on all the detainees. The silence of the Mosaic law on this point is even more complete. There is not even a single mention of prison in the Pentateuch. Later on, in the Chronicles, in the book of Jeremiah, one does come across passages which speak of prisons, of fetters, of damp dungeons; but, in all these cases, what is in question is preventive custody, places of detention where people accused of crimes, are held while awaiting trial, and where they had to submit to a regime of greater or lesser severity, depending on their particular circumstances. It is only in the book of Ezra that imprisonment appears, for the first time, as a punishment properly so-called. In the ancient law of the Slavs and the Germans, punishments simply involving deprivation of liberty would seem to have been similarly missing. The same was true of the old Swiss cantons until the nineteenth century.

In the City-States such punishments had begun to make their appearance. Contrary to what Schoemann says, it seems certain that at Athens imprisonment was inflicted as a special punishment in some situations. Demosthenes expressly states that the tribunals were empowered to punish by imprisonment or by any other punishment. Socrates speaks of life imprisonment as a penalty which could be invoked against him. Plato, outlining in *The Laws* the plans of the ideal city, proposes to repress quite a large number of offences by imprisonment, and we know that his utopia is nearer to historical reality than it was at one time thought to be. However, everyone recognizes that at Athens this type of punishment remained little developed. In the orators' speeches, prison is most often put forward as a way of preventing the flight of those accused of a crime or as a convenient way of forcing some debtors to pay their debts, or indeed as a supplementary form of punishment, a *prostimema*. When the judges restricted themselves to imposing a fine they had the right to supplement this with a term of five days in the public prison with one's feet shackled. At Rome, the situation was not very different. 'Prison,' states Rein, 'was originally no more than a place for preventive detention. Later it became a means of punishment. However, it was rarely used, except for slaves, soldiers and actors.'

It is only in the Christian societies that it has completely developed. The Church, indeed, from very early on was accustomed to prescribe temporary detention or life in a monastery for some criminals. At first this was thought of as no more than a means of surveillance, but later on incarceration, or imprisonment properly so-called, came into existence, being regarded as a genuine punishment. The maximum sentence was permanent solitary confinement in a cell which had been bricked up, as a sign of the irrevocability of the sentence. It is from here that the practice passed over into the secular legal system. However, as imprisonment was simultaneously used as an administrative measure, the sense in which it was a punishment remained for a long time rather ambiguous. It is only in the eighteenth century that criminologists ended up agreeing to recognize imprisonment as a kind of punishment in certain definite situations, when it was for life, when it was substituted by a commutation for the death penalty, etc.; in a word, every time it had been preceded by a legal investigation. With the penal law of 1791, it became the basis of the system of control, which, other than the death penalty and the pillory, consisted of no more than various kinds of imprisonment. Nevertheless, imprisonment by itself was not considered a sufficient punishment; but deprivations of another kind were added to it (belts or chains which the inmates had to wear, and a miserable diet). The Penal Code of 1810 left aside these additional penalties, except for hard labour. The two alternative punishments involving deprivations of liberty scarcely differed from one another except in respect of the amount of time during which the prisoner was shut up. Since that time, hard labour has lost a great part of its distinctive character and is tending to become simply another kind of imprisonment. At the same time, the death penalty has been utilized less and less frequently; it has even disappeared completely from some legal codes, to such an extent that virtually the whole field of punishment is now found to consist in the suppression of liberty for limited period of time or for life.

III. EXPLANATION OF THE SECOND LAW

Having shown how punishment has varied through time, we will now seek the causes of the established variations; in other words, we shall try to explain the two laws previously established. We will begin with the second.

As we have just seen, incarceration first appears only as a simple preventive measure; it later takes on a repressive character, and finally becomes equated with the very notion of punishment. To account for this evolution, we must in turn search for what gives birth to imprisonment in its original form – and then see what has determined its subsequent transformations.

It is easy to understand why imprisonment is not present in relatively under-developed societies: it does not serve any need. In these societies responsibility is collective; when a crime is committed, it is not only the guilty party who pays penalty or reparation. The clan also takes part, either together with or in place of the transgressor. At a later time, when the clan has lost its familial character, it is replaced by a still fairly extensive circle of kinsmen. Under these conditions, there is no reason to arrest and hold under guard the presumed author of an act. For if, for one reason or another, he is missing, others remain. Furthermore, the moral and legal independence, which characterizes each familial group at this time, serves to restrain the demand that one of its members be handed over in this way on mere suspicion. But to the extent that society is centralized, these elementary groups lose their autonomy and become merged with the total mass, and responsibility becomes individual. Consequently, some measures are necessary to prevent punishment being evaded by the flight of those who have earned it and at the same time these measures are less offensive to established morality. We find it in Athens, Rome, and among the Hebrews after the time of the Exile. But it is so contrary to the principles of ancient social organization that it runs up against obstacles which narrowly restrict its use, at least wherever the power of the State is subject to some limitation. It is for this reason that in Athens preventive detention was authorized only in particularly serious cases. Even the murderer was able to remain at liberty right up until the day of sentence. In Rome, the accused 'was at first only made a prisoner in the case of a flagrant and manifest misdemeanour, or when there was a confession; ordinarily, a bail-bond sufficed'.

One must beware of explaining these apparent restrictions on the right of pre-trial detention by a sentiment of personal dignity and a sort of precocious individualism, which were scarcely part of the morality of the ancient City-State. What limits the legal power of the State is not the just claim of the individual, but that of the clan or the family, or at least what remains of it. This is not an anticipation of our modern morality, but an archaic survival.

However, this explanation is incomplete. To explain an institution, it is not enough to establish that when it appeared it served some useful end; for just because it was desirable it does not follow that it was possible. In addition, one must discover how the necessary conditions for the realization of that goal came into existence. However strong a need may be, it cannot create *ex nihilo* the means for its own satisfaction; we must therefore search out where these came from. No doubt at first sight it would seem just common sense that from the day that the prison would have served a useful function for societies, men would have had the idea of building it. In reality, however, this development presupposes the realization of certain conditions without which it could not come about. In practice, it implies the existence of sufficiently spacious public establishments, run on military lines, managed in such a manner as to prevent communications with the outside, etc. Such arrangements are not improvised on the spur of the moment. Indeed, there exist no traces of them in primitive societies. The very meagre, very intermittent public life which then exists requires nothing more for its development than a place for popular assemblies. Houses are constructed with exclusively private ends in mind; in places where there are permanent chiefs, their houses are scarcely distinguished from the others; temples themselves are of relatively late origin; finally, ramparts do not exist, for they appeared only with the rise of the City State. In these conditions, the concept of a prison cannot arise.

But as the social horizon extends, as collective life, instead of being dispersed in a multitude of small centres where it can only be weak, is concentrated in a more limited number of places, it becomes at the same time more intense and more continuous. Because this sphere assumes greater importance, so the dwelling places of those who direct it are transformed. They are enlarged, they are organized in terms of the wider and more permanent functions which are laid upon them. The more the authority of those who live there grows, the more their homes are marked off and distinguished from the rest of the dwellings. They take on a lofty air, they are protected behind higher walls, deeper ditches, in such a way as to visibly mark the line of demarcation which henceforth separates the holders of power from the mass of their subordinates. The conditions for the creation of the prison are now present. What makes one suppose that the prison must have arisen in that way is that in the beginning it often appears in the shadow of a royal palace, in the outbuildings of temples and similar buildings. Thus, in Jerusalem we know of three prisons during the period of the invasion of the Chaldeans: one was 'at the high gate of Benjamin', and we know that the gates were fortified places; another was in the court of the royal palace; and the third was in the house of a royal functionary. In Rome, it is in the royal fortress that the most ancient prisons are found. In the Middle Ages, it is in the manorial castle, in the towers of the ramparts which surround the towns.

Thus, at the very time when the establishment of a place of detention was becoming useful in consequence of the progressive disappearance of collective responsibility, buildings were arising which could be utilized for this purpose. The prison, it is true, was still only a place of pre-trial detention. But once that it had been set up on this basis, it quickly assumed a repressive character, at least partially. In fact, all those who were thus kept prisoner were suspects; they were also most frequently those suspected of serious crimes. Furthermore, they were subjected to a severe regimen which was already virtually a punishment. Everything that we know about these primitive prisons, which, let it be remembered, are still not penitentiaries in the strict sense, paints them in the blackest of colours. In Dahomey, the prison is a hole, in the form of a pit where the condemned wallow in refuse and vermin. In Judaea, we saw that they used dungeons. In ancient Mexico, it consisted of wooden cages where the prisoners were kept; they were scarcely fed. In Athens, the prisoners were subjected to the dishonourable punishment of shackles. In Switzerland, to make escape more difficult, they put iron collars on the prisoners. In Japan, the prisons are called hells. It is natural that a sojourn in such places should have been very early considered as a form of punishment. Petty crimes, especially those which have been committed by the people of slender means, the *personae humiles,* as the Romans called them, were dealt with in this way. It was a penalty which the judges could impose more or less arbitrarily.

As to the juridical development of this new punishment from the time of its formation onward, it can be accounted for by combining the preceding considerations with the law relating to the progressive weakening of punishment. In practice, this weakening takes place from top to bottom of the penal code. In general, it is the most serious punishments which are the first to be affected by this regression, that is to say, which are the first to grow milder, then to disappear. The process begins with the diminution of the aggravated forms of capital punishment, which continues until the day is reached when they are completely done away with. The crimes to which capital punishment is applied are gradually curtailed; mutilations are subject to the same law. It follows from this that lesser punishments must be developed to fill the gaps which this regression produces. In proportion as the penal law abandons the archaic forms of repression, new forms of punishment invade the free spaces which they then find before them. Now the various modes of imprisonment are the last punishments to develop. At first, they are lowest in the scale of penalties, since they begin by not being punishments at all, properly so called, but only the condition of true repression; and for a long time, they retain a mixed and indecisive character. For this reason, the future was reserved for them. They were the necessary and natural substitutes for the other punishments which were fading away. But from another perspective, they were themselves influenced by the trend towards moderation. This is why, whereas originally they were mingled with other hardships to which they were occasionally only ancillary, they are gradually disentangled from them. They are reduced to their simplest forms, which is to say, to deprivation of liberty alone, varying only with respect to the length of that deprivation.

Thus, the qualitative changes in punishment are in part dependent on the simultaneous quantitative changes it undergoes. In other words, of the two laws which we have established, the first contributes to an explanation of the second. Thus, the time has now arrived to explain it in its turn.

IV. EXPLANATION OF THE FIRST LAW

In order to facilitate this explanation, we will consider the two factors which we have distinguished separately; as the second is the one which plays the least important role we will leave it on one side for the moment. Let us look, therefore, at how it is that punishments become less severe as one moves from the most primitive to the most advanced societies, without bothering ourselves temporarily with those perturbations which may be due to the more or less absolute character of governmental power.

One might be tempted to explain this decline in severity in terms of a corresponding softening of mores. We have more and more horror of violence; violent, that is to say cruel, punishments must therefore inspire in us a growing repugnance. Unfortunately, this explanation may be reversed. For while, on the one hand, our greater humanity makes us recoil from inflicting painful punishments, it must simultaneously make the inhuman acts which these punishments repress seem more odious to us. If our more developed altruism finds the idea of making others suffer repugnant, for the very same reason the crimes which offend these sentiments must seem to us more abominable; and consequently we will inevitably tend to repress them more severely. Not only is this so, but this tendency can be only partially and weakly neutralized by the opposing tendency, which leads us to make the guilty suffer as little as possible, even though they both have the same origin. For it is undeniable that our sympathy must be less for the offender than for his victim. Consequently, greater moral sensitivity would rather have led to a harsher punishment, at least for all the crimes which inflict harm on other human beings. In fact, when it begins to appear to a marked degree in the course of history, this is just the way it manifests itself. In primitive societies, murder and simple theft are only feebly repressed, since the mores there are coarse. In Rome, for a long time, violence was not regarded as invalidating contracts, let alone as something penal. But from the time that man's sympathetic feelings for man were affirmed and developed these crimes have been punished more severely. The movement must necessarily have continued if some other cause had not intervened.

Since punishment results from crime and expresses the manner in which it affects the public conscience, it is in the evolution of crime that one must seek the cause determining the evolution of punishment. Without it being necessary to go in detail into the proofs which justify the distinction, we think it will be readily conceded that all acts deemed criminal in every known society may be divided into two basic categories: those which are directed against collective things (whether ideal or material, it matters not) of which the principal kinds are offences against public authority and its representatives, the mores, traditions and religion; and those which only injure the individual (murders, thefts, violence and fraud of all types). These two forms of criminality are sufficiently distinct that there is every reason to designate them by different words. The first may be called religious criminality because outrages against religion are the most essential part of it, and because crimes against tradition or chiefs of state have always had a more or less religious character; the second, one might term human criminality. Granting this distinction, we know that the penal law of primitive societies consists almost exclusively of crimes of the first type; but, as evolution advances, so they decline, while outrages against the person take up more and more space. For primitive peoples, crime consists almost uniquely in not performing cult practices, in violating ritual prohibitions, in straying from ancestral morality, in disobeying authority where it is quite firmly established. By contrast for the European of today, crime consists essentially in the injury of some human interest.

Now, these two kinds of criminality differ profoundly because the collective sentiments which they offend are not of the same type. As a result, repression cannot be the same for one as for the other.

The collective sentiments which are contradicted and offended by the criminality characteristic of primitive societies are collective, as it were, in a double sense. Not only have they the collectivity as their subject, so that they are found in the majority of individual consciences, but more than that *they have collective things as their object*. By definition, these things are outside the circle of our private interests. The ends to which we are thus attached infinitely surpass the narrow horizon we each have as individuals. It is not us personally with which they are concerned, but with the collective existence. Consequently, the acts which we must perform in order to satisfy them do not correspond to our own individual inclinations; but rather they do violence to them since they consist in all kinds of sacrifices and privations which a man has to impose upon himself whether it be for the purpose of humouring his god, to conform to custom, or to obey authority. We do not have an inclination to fast, to mortify ourselves, to forbid ourselves one or another kind of meat, to sacrifice our favourite animals on the altar, to inconvenience ourselves out of respect for custom, etc. Consequently, just as with the sensations which come to us from the external world, such sentiments are in us but not of us; even exist, in a sense, in spite of us; and they appear to us in this way in consequence of the constraint which they exercise over us. We are thus obliged to alienate them, to assign as their cause some external force, just as we do for our sensations. Moreover, we are obliged to conceive of this force as a power which is not only extraneous, but even superior to us, since it gives the orders and we obey them. This voice which speaks within us in such an imperious tone, which enjoins us to do violence to our nature, can come only from a being other than ourselves, and one, moreover, which dominates us. In whatever special form men have portrayed it (god, ancestors, august personages of all kinds), it always has in its relation to them something transcendent, superhuman about it. That is why this part of morality is wholly imbued with religiosity. The duties which it prescribes for us bind us to a personality which infinitely surpasses our own; the collective personality, which we may think of as a pure abstraction, or with the help of what are properly religious symbols, the guise in which it most frequently appears.

In the case of crimes which violate these sentiments and which consist of the neglect of special obligations, these cannot fail to appear to us as directed against these transcendent beings, since they do indeed strike at them. It is because of this that they appear exceptionally odious; for an offence is the more revolting when the person offended is higher in nature and dignity than the offender. The more one is held in respect, the more abominable is lack of respect. An act which is simply reprehensible when directed at an equal becomes sacrilegious when it concerns someone who is superior to us; the horror which it produces can therefore only be calmed by a violent repression. Normally, when simply trying to please his gods, the faithful man must submit to a thousand privations if he is to maintain regular relations with them. To what privations must he not be subjected when he has outraged them? Even were the pity which the guilty party inspires quite strong, it could not serve to effectively counterbalance the indignation aroused by the act of sacrilege, nor, consequently, to modify appreciably the punishment; for the two sentiments are too unequal. The sympathy which men experience for one of their kind, especially one disgraced by an offence, cannot restrain the effects of the reverential fear which they feel for the divinity. In the face of a power which is so much greater than him, the individual appears so insignificant that his sufferings lose their relative importance and become a negligible quantity. For what is an individual's suffering when it is a question of appeasing a God?

It is otherwise with collective sentiments which have the individual for their object; for each of us is an individual. What concerns humankind concerns us all; for we are all men. Consequently we take sentiments protecting human dignity personally to heart. Of course, I do not mean to say that we respect the life and property of our fellows out of a utilitarian calculation and to obtain from them a just reciprocity. If we reprove acts which lack humanity, it is because they offend the sentiments of sympathy which we have for man in general, and these sentiments are disinterested precisely because they have a general object. This is the great difference which separates the moral individualism of Kant from that of the utilitarians. Both, in a sense, make the development of the individual the object of moral conduct. But for the latter the individual in question is the tangible, empirical individual, as realized in each particular conscience; for Kant, on the other hand, it is the human personality, it is humanity in general, in abstraction from the concrete and diverse forms under which it presents itself to the observer. Nevertheless, however universal it may be, such a conception is closely related to that towards which our egoistic tendencies incline us.

Between man in general and the man whom we are there is not the same difference as that between a man and a god. The nature of this ideal being differs only in degree from our own; it is only the model of which we are various examples. The sentiments which attach us to it are thus, in part, the extension of those which attach us to ourselves. It is this which is expressed in the popular saying: 'Do not do unto others that which you would not wish done to you.'

Consequently, for us to explain these sentiments and the acts towards which they impel us, it is not necessary, to the same degree, to seek some transcendent origin of them. To account for the respect we feel for humanity, there is no need to suppose that it is imposed on us by some power exterior to and superior to humanity; it already appears intelligible to us just because we feel we are men ourselves. We are aware that it conforms more to the natural inclination of our sensibility. Unlike the previous type, the crimes which offend this will not, therefore, seem to us to be directed against some super-human being. We shall not see in them acts of 'lèse-divinity', but simply of 'lèse-humanity'. Unquestionably, this ideal is far from being deprived of all transcendence; it is in the nature of every ideal to surpass reality and to dominate it. But this transcendence is much less marked. If this abstract man is not to be confused with any one of us, each of us realizes him in part. Since it is essentially human, no matter how elevated this end may be, it is also immanent in us to some degree.

Consequently, the conditions of repression are no longer the same as in the first case. There is no longer the same distance between the offender and the offended; they are more nearly on the same level. This is the more so as, in each particular case, the victim of the crime offers himself in the guise of a particular individuality, in all respects identical to that of the transgressor. The moral scandal which the criminal act constitutes is, therefore, less severe, and consequently does not call for such violent repression. The offence of man against man cannot arouse the same indignation as an offence of man against God. At the same time, the sentiments of pity which he who suffers punishment evokes in us can no longer be so easily nor so completely extinguished by the sentiments he has offended and which react against him; for both are of the same nature. The first sentiments are only a variety of the second. What tempers the collective anger, which is the essence of punishment, is the sympathy which we feel for every man who suffers, the horror which all destructive violence causes us; it is the same sympathy and the same horror which inflames this anger. And so the same cause which sets in motion the repressive apparatus tends also to halt it. The same mental state drives us to punish and to moderate the punishment. Hence an extenuating influence cannot fail to make itself felt. It might appear quite natural to freely sacrifice the human dignity of the transgressor to the outraged divine majesty. But there is a real and irremediable contradiction in avenging the offended human dignity of the victim by violating that of the criminal. The only way, not of eliminating the difficulty (for strictly speaking it is insoluble), but of alleviating it, is to lessen the punishment as much as possible.

Seeing as, in the course of time, crime is reduced more and more to offences against persons alone, while religious forms of criminality decline, it is inevitable that punishment on the average should become weaker. This weakening does not come from the fact that morals become less harsh, but from the fact that religiosity, which was earlier imprinted in both the penal law and the collective sentiments which underlay it, steadily declines. Doubtless, the sentiments of human sympathy simultaneously become livelier; but this greater liveliness is not sufficient to explain this progressive moderation in punishments; since, by itself, it would tend to make us more severe towards all those crimes of which man is the victim, and to increase the repression of such crimes. The true reason is that the compassion of which the condemned man is the object is no longer overwhelmed by the contrary sentiments which would not let it make itself felt.

But, you may say, if this is the case, how is it that punishments attached to crimes against persons participate in the general decline? For, if they have declined less than the others, it is still certain that they too are, in general, less harsh than they were two or three centuries ago. If, however, it is in the nature of this type of crime to call forth less severe punishments, the effect should have shown itself from the first, as soon as the criminal character of these acts was formally recognized; punishments directed against them ought to have immediately and at a single stroke attained the degree of mildness which they allow of, rather than becoming progressively milder. But what determines this progressive softening, is that at the time when these crimes, having remained for a long time on the threshold of the criminal law, were brought within it and finally classed as part of it, religious criminality held almost complete sway in this area. As a result of this preponderant situation, it began by pulling into its orbit those new offences which had just been created and marked them with its imprint. So much so, that just as crime is essentially conceived as an offence directed against the divinity, so crimes committed by man against man are also conceived on this same model. We believe that they also repel us because they are defended by the gods and, by the same token, outrage them. The habits of mind are such that it does not even seem possible that a moral precept can have a sufficiently well-founded authority if it does not derive from what is at the time considered as the unique source of all morality. Such is the origin of these theories, still so widespread today, according to which morality lacks all basis if it does not rest upon religion, or, at the very least, on a rational theology; that is to say, if the categorical imperative does not emanate from some transcendent being. But to the extent that human criminality develops and religious criminality recedes, the former shows more and more clearly its own physiognomy and distinctive traits, such as we have described. It frees itself from the influences to which it used to be subjected and which prevented it from being itself. If, even today, there are a good many people for whom the penal law, and more generally all morality, are inseparable from the idea of God, yet their number is diminishing; and even those who lag behind in this archaic conception are no longer as narrowly tied to these ideas as a Christian of earlier times used to be. Human morality progressively sheds its primitively confessional character. It is in the course of this development that that regressive evolution of punishments which makes the most grave breaches in the prescriptions of this morality occurs.

But a reciprocal influence must be noted, for as human criminality gains ground, it reacts in its turn on religious criminality and, so to speak, assimilates it. If it is offences against persons which constitute the principal crimes today, offences against collective things (crimes against the family, against morals, against the State) nevertheless still exist. However, these collective things themselves tend to lose more and more that religiosity which formerly marked them. From the divinities which they were, they are becoming human realities. We no longer hypostasize the family or society in the form of transcendent and mystical entities; we see scarcely more than human groups who coordinate their efforts with a view to achieving human goals. As a result, crimes directed against these collectivities partake of the characteristics of those which directly injure individuals; and punishments which are aimed at the former themselves become milder.

Such is the cause which had determined the progressive weakening of punishments. One can see that this result is produced mechanically. The manner in which collective sentiments reacted against crime changed because these sentiments changed. New forces came into play; the result could not remain the same. This great transformation has not taken place with a view to a preconceived end nor under the direction of utilitarian considerations. But, once accomplished, it finds itself quite naturally adjusted to useful ends. For the very reason that it had necessarily resulted from the new conditions in which societies found themselves placed, it could not be other than in relationship and harmony with those conditions. In fact, the intensity of punishments serves only to make individual consciences aware of the force of collective constraint; so it is useful only if it varies with the same intensity as this constraint. It is fitting that it becomes milder as collective coercion becomes lighter, more flexible, becomes less inaccessible to free examination. Now this is the great change produced in the course of moral evolution. Although social discipline, of which morality properly so-called is only the highest expression, progressively extends its field of action, it loses more and more of its authoritarian rigour. Because it becomes more human, it leaves more room for the spontaneity of individuals; it even solicits it. It has therefore less need to be violently imposed. And for this to occur, the sanctions which assure it respect must also become less constricting on all initiative and thought.

We may now return to the second factor of penal evolution, which we have up until now left out of account; namely the nature of the means of government. The preceding considerations will readily allow us to explain the manner in which they act. In truth, the constitution of an absolute power necessarily has the effect of raising the one who wields it above the rest of humanity, making of him something superhuman; the more so as the power with which he is armed is more unlimited. In fact, wherever the government takes this form, the one who controls it appears to people as a divinity. When they do not make an actual god of him, they at the very least see in the power which is invested in him an emanation of divine power. From that moment, this religiosity cannot fail to have its usual effects on punishment. On the one hand, offences directed against a being so palpably superior to all its offenders will not be considered as ordinary crimes, but as sacrilegious acts and, by virtue of this, will be violently repressed. From this stems the exceptional position that the penal law assigns to crimes of lese-majesty among all peoples subjected to an absolutist government. From another point of view, as in these same societies almost all the laws are supposed to emanate from the sovereign and express his will, so the principal violations of the law appear to be directed against him. The reprobation which these acts arouse is thus much stronger than if the authority to which they cause injury was more dispersed, and consequently more moderate. The fact that it is concentrated at this point, rendering it more intense, also makes it more sensitive to all who offend it, and more violent in its reactions. Thus the gravity of most crimes is heightened by degrees; consequently, the average intensity of punishment is extraordinarily increased.

V. CONCLUSIONS

Understood in this way, the law which we have just described takes on a quite different significance.

In fact, if one goes to the root of things, one can now see that it explains not merely, as it might seem at first sight, the quantitative variations through which punishment has passed, but also qualitative variations. If the punishment is milder today than formerly it is not because former penal institutions, while remaining intact, have little by little lost their rigour; but rather that they have been replaced by different institutions. The motive forces which have determined each of these are not of the same type. It is no longer that sudden explosion, that indignant bewilderment aroused by an outrage directed against a being whose value immeasurably surpasses that of the aggressor; it *is* more that calmer and more reflective emotion provoked by offences which take place between equals. Blame is no longer the same and does not exclude pity; by itself, *it* calls for moderation. Hence, the necessity for new punishments which are in accord with this new mentality.

This allows us to avoid an error to which the immediate observation of the facts might have led. Seeing with what regularity repression seems weaker the further one goes in evolution, one might believe that the movement is destined to continue without end; in other words, that punishment is tending toward zero. Now, such a consequence would be in contradiction *with* the true sense of our law.

In fact, the cause which has determined this regression would not produce its attenuating effects indefinitely. For it does not result from a kind of sluggishness of the moral conscience which, gradually losing its strength and its original sensitivity, would become more and more incapable of all energetic penal reaction. We are not more complacent today than formerly toward all crimes indiscriminately, but only toward some of them; there are some, on the contrary, towards which we are more severe. However, those to which we show increasing indulgence, turn out to be also those which provoke the most violent repression, inversely, those for which we reserve our severity call forth only moderate punishments. Consequently, as the former, ceasing to be treated as crimes, are removed from the penal law and give place to others, *it* must necessarily produce a weakening of the average punishment. But this weakening can last only as long as this substitution goes on. The moment must come – and it has almost arrived – when this will be accomplished, when offences against the person will fill the whole of criminal law, or even when what remains of the other offences will be considered no more than an appendage of the previous sort. Then the movement of retreat will cease. For there is no reason to believe that human criminality must in its turn regress as have the penalties which punish it. Rather, everything points to its gradual development; that the list of acts which are defined as crimes of this type will grow, and that their criminal character will be accentuated. Frauds and injustices, which yesterday left the public conscience almost indifferent, arouse it today, and this sensitivity will only become more acute with time. There is not in reality, therefore, a general weakening of the whole apparatus of repression; rather, one particular system weakens, but it is replaced by another which, while being less violent and less harsh, does not cease to have its own severities, and is certainly not destined to an uninterrupted decline.

This explains the state of crisis in which the penal law of all the civilized peoples is found. We have arrived at the time when penal institutions of the past have either disappeared or are surviving by not more than force of habit, but without others being born which correspond better to the new aspirations of the moral conscience.

Notes

1. The term used by Durkheim is *Dwidjas*, which refers to any members of the three higher castes, i.e., the twice-born. [Translators' note]
2. 'The Eleven' refers to a committee of eleven people charges with making sure that punishments prescribed by the Athenian courts were carried out. [Translators' note]
3. Three laws of the second century BCE which stated that no Roman citizen should be put to death without trial. [Translators' note]

CHAPTER 5

Crime and Punishment

Introduction

The texts in this chapter outline Durkheim's provocative theory of crime and punishment, set out first in The Division of Labour *and then more explicitly in* The Rules of Sociological Method. *We also reproduce here the critique these ideas elicited from Gabriel Tarde alongside Durkheim's response to Tarde. This debate gives a revealing glimpse of Durkheim's polemical side and displays both the strengths and weaknesses of his mode of reasoning.*

Tarde was a distinguished magistrate, statistician, criminologist and sociologist with views sharply opposed to Durkheim's. Fifteen years Durkheim's senior, Tarde rose to fame in the 1890s, published many books, was elected to the Collège de France and the Academy of Moral and Political Sciences in 1900 and was, in effect Durkheim's most prominent and celebrated intellectual and professional antagonist. Their increasingly vehement disagreements culminated in a famous debate at the Ecole des Hautes Etudes in 1903. There has been something of a revival of interest in Tarde in the last decade, inspired by, among others, Bruno Latour. This is discussed in a recent book edited by Matei Candea entitled The Social after Gabriel Tarde, *which offers a reconstruction of the 1903 debate and indicates the range of the disagreements between the two principals, which embraced 'the relationship between sociology and other sciences, the role of comparison, the nature of imitation, the relationship between parts and wholes, the role of contingency and rule in history and science, and the moral import of sociology' (Candea 2010: 16–17). These wider areas of disagreement are in evidence in their more specific disagreements which are on display here over the nature of crime and punishment.*

Tarde perceptively noted that, according to Durkheim's thesis, it is not strictly crime, but the coupling of crime and punishment that is healthy and socially normal, a point which Durkheim explicitly accepted. In effect, Durkheim's thesis is a complex one, embodying three distinct claims. The first, which we may call the functional to integration claim, is that crime and punishment are both functional to social integration in so far as crime elicits punishment which in turn (as the passage from The Division of Labour *explicates) reaffirms and reinforces collective beliefs and sentiments and, thus, social solidarity. The second claim, which we may label the counterfactual claim, asserts that a certain level of crime is normal and a crime-free society impossible since, if (counterfactually) all existing crime disappears, society would re-invent it – that is, new crimes would appear, for the very reason that the common conscience would 'denounce more severely acts which it previously would have judged more leniently; and that, in consequence, criminality, having disappeared under one form, would reappear under another' (this vol.: 92). The third claim, which we may call the functional to change claim, asserts that crime (though in this case not punishment) has a utility, generally indirect, but sometimes direct, in bring about moral change: indirect, as an index, so to speak, of social flexibility, 'because crime could only cease to exist if the* conscience collective *dominated individual consciences with such an ineluctable authority that all moral change would be rendered impossible; direct, in that occasionally, but only occasionally, the criminal has been the harbinger of a morality to come' (133). In debate with Durkheim, Tarde took on only the second and third of these claims, and he also attacked the evidence on which Durkheim relies and some of the underlying assumptions of his argument.*

Against the counterfactual claim, Tarde simply denied that the abolition of crime would lead to greater punitive severity, particularly towards currently venial faults, arguing, on the contrary, first that a decline in crime would lead to less severity, especially towards venial faults, and secondly that increased public severity results rather from crime waves. Behind this disagreement, of course, lies a deeper difference with Durkheim as to the sources of crime. Durkheim stressed (in a very modern way) the social construction of deviance by the defining of certain acts as criminal. Tarde (1895) was content to suggest that a radical and energetic reform of the judicial and prison system (125) would suffice to eradicate crime; Durkheim, by contrast, pointed to (some of) the ways in which society creates crime. There is, needless to say, much more that can be said about this counterfactual argument, its presuppositions and plausibility. In particular, the question remains: why did Durkheim suppose that in the absence of crime, society would always recreate it? The answer presumably lies in two underlying assumptions: that all social orders involve the institution and enforcement of collective norms (with corresponding sanctions); and that no society would ever attain that degree of social homogeneity that would preclude their violation.

As far as the functional to change claim, Tarde partly misconstrued what Durkheim wrote in The Rules, *as Durkheim indicated in his reply. He, Durkheim, did not say that there is any psychological affinity between crime and genius, and so Tarde's comments about the different causes of crime and genius and the different social backgrounds from which they allegedly stem are quite beside the point, or at any rate Durkheim's point. More pertinent is Tarde's claim that there is no connection between the violations of laws which constitute crimes and the sources of moral invention, such that eradicating the former would dry up the latter, and also, Tarde's further speculative suggestion that such eradication might open up unforeseen possibilities of moral development. Here Durkheim's response was simply to reiterate his claim that crime is to be seen as an index of social diversity and flexibility, that moral reformers are by their very nature criminals, and that, viewed more widely still, morality itself, including law, must adjust to the exigencies of social expediency. But this does not really deal with Tarde's denial of a connection; that challenge could only be met by a more precise and detailed exploration of the linkages proposed. Nor, incidentally, did Durkheim sustain the claim of the indirect functionality of crime to moral change: the most his argument as stated suggests is that the presence of crime is an indicator of the existence of other factors that in turn allegedly facilitate moral change.*

In addition, Tarde (inconsistently) offered both statistical evidence against the thesis that the contemporary rise in crime was normal (which Durkheim did not assert), and an argument against the reliability of such statistics in the first place. He also made two telling and general criticisms of Durkheim's presuppositions. First, he questioned the soundness of Durkheim's distinction between the normal and the pathological, suggesting (controversially) that such a distinction requires a teleological assumption, such as the goal of adaptation, and arguing (persuasively) that Durkheim, in linking normalcy by definition to a society's 'conditions of existence', smuggled in some normative assumptions of his own. How else could one account for Durkheim's claim that the contemporary rise of religion and the growth of anomie *were abnormal? Second, Tarde, rather rhetorically, questioned Durkheim's claims for science, arguing, like Max Weber, that science cannot prescribe values that guide the will: its role is, rather, negative, showing the limits of the possible and 'the unrealizable and contradictory character or many of our desires' – which are 'given preferences', generated outside science. To neither of these more deep-lying criticisms did Durkheim here offer any real answer.*

Extract from Durkheim, *The Division of Labour in Society*

In the first place, punishment constitutes a passionate reaction. This characteristic is all the more apparent the less cultured societies are. Indeed primitive peoples punish for the sake of punishing, causing the guilty person to suffer solely for the sake of suffering and without expecting any advantage for themselves from the suffering they inflict upon him. The proof of this is that they do not aim to punish fairly or usefully, but only for the sake of punishing. Thus they punish animals that have committed the act that is stigmatized, or even inanimate things which have been its passive instrument. Although punishment is applied solely to people, it often extends well beyond the guilty person and strikes even the innocent – his wife, children or neighbours, etc. This is because the passionate feeling that lies at the heart of punishment dies down only when it is spent. Thus if, after having destroyed the one who was its most immediate cause, some strength of feeling still remains, quite automatically it reaches out further. Even when it is sufficiently moderate in intensity to attack only the guilty person it manifests its presence by its tendency to exceed in seriousness the act against which it is reacting. From this there arose refinements of pain that were added to capital punishment. In Rome the thief had not only to give back the object stolen but also to pay a fine of double or even quadruple its value. Moreover, is not the aim of the very widespread punishment of talion to assuage the passion for vengeance?

Nowadays, however, it is said that punishment has changed in nature. Society no longer punishes to avenge, but to defend itself. In its hands the pain it inflicts is only a systematic instrument for its protection. Society punishes, not because the punishment of itself affords some satisfaction, but in order that the fear of punishment may give pause to the evilly inclined. It is no longer wrath that governs repression, but well premeditated foresight. Thus the preceding remarks cannot be generally applied: they may only concern the primitive form of punishment and cannot be extended to cover its present-day form.

Yet, in order to justify legitimately so radical a distinction between these two sorts of punishment it is not enough to demonstrate that they are employed for different ends. The nature of a practice does not necessarily alter because the conscious intentions of those implementing it are modified. Indeed it could already have fulfilled the same role in former times without this having been perceived. In that case why should it be transformed by the mere fact that we realize more fully the effects that it produces? It adapts itself to the new conditions of existence created for it without thus undergoing any essential changes. This is what happened in the case of punishment.

It would indeed be mistaken to believe that vengeance is mere wanton cruelty. It may very possibly constitute by itself an automatic, purposeless reaction, an emotional and senseless impulse, and an unreasoned compulsion to destroy. But in fact what it tends to destroy was a threat to us. Therefore in reality it constitutes a veritable act of defence, albeit instinctive and unreflecting. We wreak vengeance only upon what has done us harm, and what has done us harm is always dangerous. The instinct for revenge is, after all, merely a heightened instinct of self-preservation in the face of danger. Thus it is far from true that vengeance has played in human history the negative and sterile role attributed to it. It is a weapon of defence, which has its own value – only it is a rough and ready weapon. As it has no conception of the services that it automatically renders it cannot be regulated accordingly. It strikes somewhat at random, a prey to the unseeing forces that urge it on, and with nothing to curb its accesses of rage. Nowadays, since we are better aware of the purpose to be achieved, we also know better how to use the means at our disposal. We protect ourselves more systematically, and consequently more effectively. But from the very beginning this result was achieved, although less perfectly. Thus between the punishment of today and yesterday there is no great gulf, and consequently it had no need to change to accommodate itself to the role that it plays in our civilized societies. The whole difference lies in the fact that punishment now produces its effects with a greater awareness of what it is about. Now, although the individual or social consciousness does not fail to influence the reality it highlights, it has no power to change the nature of that reality. The internal structure of the phenomena remains unchanged, whether these are conscious or not. We may therefore expect the essential elements of punishment to be the same as before.

And indeed punishment has remained an act of vengeance, at least in part. It is claimed that we do not make the guilty person suffer for the sake of suffering. It is nevertheless true that we deem it fair that he should suffer. We may be wrong, but this is not what is at issue. We are seeking for the present to define punishment as it is or has been, and not how it should be. Certainly the term 'public vindication', which recurs incessantly in the language of the law-courts, is no vain expression. If we suppose that punishment can really serve to shield us in the future, we esteem that above all it should be an *expiation* for the past. What proves this are the meticulous precautions we take to make the punishment fit the seriousness of the crime as exactly as possible. These precautions would be inexplicable unless we believed that the guilty person must suffer because it is he who has done the injury, and indeed must suffer in equal measure. In fact this gradation is unnecessary if punishment is only a defence mechanism. It would undoubtedly be dangerous for society if the gravest criminal undertakings were placed on the same level as mere minor offences. Yet in most cases there could only be advantage in placing the minor ones on the same level as the serious ones. One cannot take too many precautions against one's enemy. Can we say that the perpetrators of the most trivial offences possess natures any less perverse and that, to counteract their evil instincts, less onerous punishments will suffice? But although their tendencies may be less tainted with vice, they are not thereby less intense. Thieves are as strongly disposed to thieving as murderers to homicide. The resistance shown by the former category is in no way weaker than that of the latter. Thus, to overcome it, we should have recourse to the same means. If, as has been said, it was solely a matter of repelling a harmful force by an opposing one, the latter's intensity should be merely commensurate with that of the former, without the quality of the harmful force being taken into consideration. The scale of punishments should therefore comprise only very few gradations. The punishment should vary only according to whether the subject is more or less hardened a criminal, and not according to the nature of the criminal act. An incorrigible thief should be treated like an incorrigible murderer. But in fact, even when it had been shown that the guilty person is definitely incurable, we would still feel bound not to mete out excessive punishment to him. This demonstrates that we have remained true to the principle of talion, although we conceive of it in a more lofty sense than once we did. We no longer measure in so material and rough terms either the gravity of the fault or the degree of punishment. But we still consider that there should be an equilibrium between the two elements, whether we derive any advantage or not in striking such a balance. Thus punishment has remained for us what it was for our predecessors. It is still an act of vengeance, since it is an expiation. What we are avenging, and what the criminal is expiating, is the outrage to morality.

There is above all one form of punishment where this passionate character is more apparent than elsewhere: it is shame that doubles most punishments, and that increases with them. Very often it serves no purpose. What good does it do to disgrace a man who is no longer to live in the society of his peers and who has more than abundantly proved by his behaviour that more fearful threats have failed to deter him? To disgrace him is understandable when there is no other punishment available, or as a supplement to some comparatively trivial material penalty. Where this is not the case punishment is redundant. One may even say that society only resorts to legal punishments when others are inadequate. If this is so, why continue with the latter? They are a form of additional torment that serves no purpose, or one whose sole reason is the need to repay evil with evil. They are so much the result of instinctive, irresistible feelings that they often spread to innocent objects. Thus the scene of the crime, the tools used in it, the relatives of the guilty person – all sometimes share in the opprobrium that we heap upon him. The causes that give rise to this diffused repression are also those of the organized repression that accompanies it. Moreover, we need only observe how punishment operates in the law-courts to acknowledge that its motivating force is entirely emotional. For it is to the emotions that both prosecuting and defending counsel address themselves. The latter seeks to arouse sympathy for the guilty person, the former to stir up the social sentiments that have been offended by the criminal act, and it is under the influence of these opposing passions that the judge delivers sentence.

Thus the nature of punishment has remained essentially unchanged. All that can be said is that the necessity for vengeance is better directed nowadays than in the past. The spirit of foresight that has been awakened no longer leaves the field so clear for the blind play of passion; it contains it within set limits, opposing absurd acts of violence and damage inflicted wantonly. Being more enlightened, such passionate action spreads itself less at random. We no longer see it turn upon the innocent, in order to have satisfaction come what may. Nevertheless it lies at the very heart of the penal system. We can therefore state that punishment consists of a passionate reaction graduated in intensity.

From where, however, does this reaction spring? Is it from the individual or from society?

We all know that it is society that punishes. But it might be that it does not do so on its own behalf. Yet what places beyond doubt the social character of punishment is that once it is pronounced, it cannot be revoked save by government, in the name of society. If it were a satisfaction granted to individuals, they would always be the ones to decide whether to commute it: one cannot conceive of a privilege that is imposed and which the beneficiary cannot renounce. If it is society alone that exerts repression, it is because it is harmed even when the harm done is to individuals, and it is the attack upon society that is repressed by punishment.

Yet we can cite cases where the carrying out of the punishment depends upon the will of individuals. In Rome certain offences were punished by a fine that went to the injured party, who could waive it or make it the subject of bargaining: such was the case for covert theft, rapine, slander and malicious damage. These offences, termed private offences (*delicta privata*), were contrasted with crimes proper, repression of which was carried out in the name of the city. The same distinction is found in Greece and among the Jews. Among more primitive peoples punishment seems occasionally to be a matter even more completely private, as the practice of the vendetta tends to show. Such societies are made up of elementary aggregates, almost of a family nature, which may conveniently be designated *clans*. When an attack is committed by one or several members of a clan against another clan, it is the latter that itself punishes the offence committed against it. What at least apparently gives even more importance to these facts, with respect to legal doctrine, is that it has been frequently maintained that the vendetta was originally the sole form of punishment. Thus at first punishment may have consisted of private acts of vengeance. But then, if today society is armed with the right to punish, it seems that this can only be by virtue of some sort of delegation by individuals. Society is only their agent. It is their interests that it looks after in their stead, probably because it looks after them better. But they are not properly those of society itself. In the beginning individuals took vengeance themselves; now it is society that avenges them. Yet since the penal law cannot have changed its nature through this simple transfer, there is thus nothing peculiarly social about it. If society appears to play a predominant role it is only as a substitute for individuals.

Yet however widely held this theory may be, it runs counter to the best established facts. We cannot instance a single society where the vendetta was the primitive form of punishment. On the contrary, it is certain that penal law was essentially religious in origin. This is clearly the case of India and Judaea, since the law practised there was considered to be one of revelation. In Egypt the ten books of Hermes, which contained the criminal law and all other laws relating to the governance of the state, were called sacerdotal, and Elien asserts that from earliest times the Egyptian priests exercised judicial power. The same holds true for ancient Germany. In Greece justice was considered to be an emanation from Zeus, and the passion as a vengeance from the god. In Rome the religious origins of the penal law are made clear by ancient traditions, by archaic practices which subsisted until a late date, and by legal terminology itself. But religion is something essentially social. Far from pursuing only individual ends, it exercises constraint over the individual at every moment. It obliges him to observe practices that are irksome to him and sacrifices, whether great or small, which cost him something. He must give from his possessions the offerings which he is constrained to present to the divinity. He must take from his work or leisure time the necessary moments for the performance of rites. He must impose upon himself every kind of privation that is commanded of him, and even renounce life itself if the gods so decree. The religious life is made up entirely of abnegation and altruism. Thus if criminal law was originally religious law, we may be sure that the interests it served were social. It is offences against themselves that the gods avenge by punishment, and not those of individuals. This is because the offences against the gods are offences against society.

Thus in lower societies the most numerous offences are those that are injurious to the public interest: offences against religion, customs, authority, etc. We have only to see in the Bible, the laws of Manu, and the records surviving of ancient Egyptian law, how slight in comparison is the importance given to prescripts that protect individuals. This is in contrast to the abundant growth of repressive legislation concerning the various forms of sacrilege, failure to observe the various religious obligations, and the requirements of ceremonial, etc. At the same time these crimes are those most severely punished. Among the Jews the most abominable crimes are those committed against religion. Among the ancient Germans two crimes alone were punished by death, according to Tacitus: treason and desertion. According to Confucius and Meng Tseu, impiety is a more grievous transgression than assassination. In Egypt the slightest act of sacrilege was punished by death. In Rome, at the top of the scale of criminality was to be found the *crimen perduellionis*.

But what then are these private punishments, instances of which we have noted earlier? They are of a mixed nature, partaking of both a repressive and a restitutive sanction. Thus the private offence in Roman law represents a kind of intermediate stage between real crime and the purely civil wrong. It has features of both and hovers on the bounds of both domains. It is an offence, in the sense that the sanction prescribed by the law does not consist merely in putting matters to rights; the offender is not only obliged to make good the damage he has caused, but he owes something else in addition, an act of expiation. However, it is not entirely a crime since, although it is society that pronounces the sentence, it is not society that is empowered to apply it. This is a right that society confers upon the injured party, who alone can exercise it freely. Likewise, the *vendetta* is clearly a punishment that society recognizes as legitimate, but leaves to individuals the task of carrying out. Thus these facts merely confirm what we have stated regarding the nature of the penal system. If this kind of intermediate sanction is partly a private matter, to a corresponding extent it is not a punishment. Its penal nature is proportionately less pronounced when its social character is less evident, and vice versa. Private vengeance is therefore far from being the prototype of punishment; on the contrary, it is only an incomplete punishment. Far from crimes against the person being the first to be repressed, in the beginning they are merely situated on the threshold of the penal law. They only moved up in the scale of criminality as society correspondingly assumed control of them more completely. This process, which we need not describe, was certainly not effected by a mere act of transferral. On the contrary, the history of this penal system is nothing but a progressive succession of encroachments by society upon the individual, or rather upon the primary groupings that it comprises. The effect of these encroachments was increasingly to substitute for the law relating to individuals that relating to society.

But the characteristics outlined above belong just as much to that diffused repression which follows acts that are merely immoral as to legal repression. What distinguishes the latter, as we have said, is that it is organized. But in what does this organization consist?

When we reflect upon the penal law as it functions in present-day societies we represent it as a code in which very precise punishments are attached to crimes equally precisely defined. It is true that the judge enjoys a certain latitude in applying to each particular case these general dispositions. But in its essentials the punishment is predetermined for each category of criminal acts. This elaborate organization is not, however, an essential element in punishment, because many societies exist in which punishments are not prescribed in advance. In the Bible there are numerous prohibitions which are utterly categoric but which are nevertheless not sanctioned by an expressly formulated punishment. Their penal character, however, is not in dispute, for, although the texts remain silent regarding the punishment, at the same time they express so great an abhorrence for the forbidden act that one cannot suspect for a moment that it will remain unpunished. Thus there is every reason to believe that this silence on the part of the law simply relates to the fact that how a crime was to be repressed was not determined. Indeed many of the stories in the Pentateuch teach us that there were criminal acts whose criminality was undisputed, but where the punishment was determined only by the judge who applied it. Society was well aware that it was faced with a crime, but the penal sanction that was to be attached to it was not yet defined. Moreover, even among those punishments laid down by the legislator there are many that are not precisely specified. Thus we know that there were different forms of torture which were not all on the same footing. Yet in a great number of cases the texts speak only generally of the death penalty, without stating what manner of death should be inflicted. According to Sumner Maine the same was true of early Rome; the *crimina* were tried before the assembly of the people which, acting in a sovereign capacity, decreed what the punishment was to be by a law, at the same time as establishing the truth of the charge. Moreover, even until the sixteenth century the general principle of the penal system 'was that its application was left to the discretion of the judge, *arbitrio et officio judicis*. .... Only the judge was not allowed to devise punishments other than those that were customary.' Another consequence of this judicial power was to make dependent upon the judge's discretion even the nature of the criminal act, which was thus itself indeterminate.

So it is not the regulation of punishment that constitutes the distinctive organization of this kind of repression. Nor is it the institution of a criminal procedure. The facts we have just cited suffice to show that for a long time this was lacking. The only organization met with everywhere that punishment proper existed is thus reduced to the establishment of a court of law. In whatever way this was constituted, whether it comprised the people as a whole or only an elite, whether or not it followed a regular procedure both in investigating the case and in applying the punishment, by the mere fact that the offence, instead of being judged by an individual, was submitted for consideration to a properly constituted body and that the reaction of society was expressed through the intermediary of a well-defined organism, it ceased to be diffuse: it was organized. The organization might have been more complete, but henceforth it existed.

Thus punishment constitutes essentially a reaction of passionate feeling, graduated in intensity, which society exerts through the mediation of an organised body over those of its members who have violated certain rules of conduct.

Now the definition of crime we have given quite easily accounts for all these characteristics of punishment.

Extract from Durkheim, *The Division of Labour in Society*

The same is true of punishment. Although it proceeds from an entirely mechanical reaction and from an access of passionate emotion, for the most part unthinking, it continues to play a useful role. But that role is not the one commonly perceived. It does not serve, or serves only very incidentally, to correct the guilty person or to scare off any possible imitators. From this dual viewpoint its effectiveness may rightly be questioned; in any case it is mediocre. Its real function is to maintain inviolate the cohesion of society by sustaining the common consciousness in all its vigour. If that consciousness were thwarted so categorically, it would necessarily lose some of its power, were an emotional reaction from the community not forthcoming to make good that loss. Thus there would result a relaxation in the bonds of social solidarity. The consciousness must therefore be conspicuously reinforced the moment it meets with opposition. The sole means of doing so is to give voice to the unanimous aversion that the crime continues to evoke, and this by an official act, which can only mean suffering inflicted upon the wrongdoer. Thus, although a necessary outcome of the causes that give rise to it, this suffering is not a gratuitous act of cruelty. It is a sign indicating that the sentiments of the collectivity are still collective, that the communion of minds sharing the same faith remains absolute, and in this way the injury that the crime has inflicted upon society is made good. This is why it is right to maintain that the criminal should suffer in proportion to his crime, and why theories that deny to punishment any expiatory character appear, in the minds of many, to subvert the social order. This is because in fact such theories could only be put into practice in a society from which almost every trace of the common consciousness has been expunged. Without this necessary act of satisfaction what is called the moral consciousness could not be preserved. Thus, without being paradoxical, we may state that punishment is above all intended to have its effect upon honest people. Since it serves to heal the wounds inflicted upon the collective sentiments, it can only fulfil this role where such sentiments exist, and in so far as they are active. Undoubtedly, by forestalling in minds already distressed any further weakening of the collective psyche, punishment can indeed prevent such attacks from multiplying. But such a result, useful though it is, is merely a particular side-effect. In short, to visualize an exact idea of punishment, the two opposing theories that have been advanced must be reconciled: the one sees in punishment an expiation, the other conceives it as a weapon for the defence of society. Certainly it does fulfil the function of protecting society, but this is because of its expiatory nature. Moreover, if it must be expiatory, this is not because suffering redeems error by virtue of some mystic strength or another, but because it cannot produce its socially useful effect save on this one condition.

Extract from Durkheim, *The Rules of Sociological Method*

If there is a fact whose pathological nature appears indisputable, it is crime. All criminologists agree on this score. Although they explain this pathology differently, they none the less unanimously acknowledge it. However, the problem needs to be treated less summarily.

Let us in fact apply the rules previously laid down. Crime is not only observed in most societies of a particular species, but in all societies of all types. There is not one in which criminality does not exist, although it changes in form and the actions which are termed criminal are not the same everywhere. Yet everywhere and always there have been men who have conducted themselves in such a way as to bring down punishment upon their heads. If at least, as societies pass from lower to higher types, the crime rate (the relationship between the annual crime figures and population figures) tended to fall, we might believe that, although still remaining a normal phenomenon, crime tended to lose that character of normality. Yet there is no single ground for believing such a regression to be real. Many facts would rather seem to point to the existence of a movement in the opposite direction. From the beginning of the century statistics provide us with a means of following the progression of criminality. It has everywhere increased, and in France the increase is of the order of 300 per cent. Thus there is no phenomenon which represents more incontrovertibly all the symptoms of normality, since it appears to be closely bound up with the conditions of all collective life. To make crime a social illness would be to concede that sickness is not something accidental, but on the contrary derives in certain cases from the fundamental constitution of the living creature. This would be to erase any distinction between the physiological and the pathological. It can certainly happen that crime itself has abnormal forms; this is what happens, for instance, when it reaches an excessively high level. There is no doubt that this excessiveness is pathological in nature. What is normal is simply that criminality exists, provided that for each social type it does not reach or go beyond a certain level which it is perhaps not impossible to fix in conformity with the previous rules.

We are faced with a conclusion which is apparently somewhat paradoxical. Let us make no mistake: to classify crime among the phenomena of normal sociology is not merely to declare that it is an inevitable though regrettable phenomenon arising from the incorrigible wickedness of men; it is to assert that it is a factor in public health, an integrative element in any healthy society. At first sight this result is so surprising that it disconcerted even ourselves for a long time. However, once that first impression of surprise has been overcome it is not difficult to discover reasons to explain this normality and at the same time to confirm it.

In the first place, crime is normal because it is completely impossible for any society entirely free of it to exist.

Crime, as we have shown elsewhere, consists of an action which offends certain collective feelings which are especially strong and clear-cut. In any society, for actions regarded as criminal to cease, the feelings that they offend would need to be found in each individual consciousness without exception and in the degree of strength requisite to counteract the opposing feelings. Even supposing that this condition could effectively be fulfilled, crime would not thereby disappear; it would merely change in form, for the very cause which made the well-springs of criminality dry up would immediately open up new ones.

Indeed, for the collective feelings, which the penal law of a people at a particular moment in its history protects, to penetrate individual consciousnesses that had hitherto remained closed to them, or to assume greater authority – whereas previously they had not possessed enough – they would have to acquire an intensity greater than they had had up to then. The community as a whole must feel them more keenly, for they cannot draw from any other source the additional force which enables them to bear down upon individuals who formerly were the most refractory. For murderers to disappear, the horror of bloodshed must increase in those strata of society from which murderers are recruited; but for this to happen the abhorrence must increase throughout society. Moreover, the very absence of crime would contribute directly to bringing about that result, for a sentiment appears much more respectable when it is always and uniformly respected. But we overlook the fact that these strong states of the common consciousness cannot be reinforced in this way without the weaker states, the violation of which previously gave rise to mere breaches of convention, being reinforced at the same time, for the weaker states are no more than the extension and attenuated form of the stronger ones. Thus, for example, theft and mere misappropriation of property offend the same altruistic sentiment, the respect for other people's possessions. However, this sentiment is offended less strongly by the latter action than the former. Moreover, since the average consciousness does not have sufficient intensity of feeling to feel strongly about the lesser of these two offences, the latter is the object of greater tolerance. This is why the misappropriator is merely censured, while the thief is punished. But if this sentiment grows stronger, to such a degree that it extinguishes in the consciousness the tendency to theft that men possess, they will become more sensitive to these lesions, which up to then had had only a marginal effect upon them. They will react with greater intensity against these lesser faults, which will become the object of severer condemnation, so that, from the mere moral errors that they were, some will pass into the category of crimes. For example, dishonest contracts or those fulfilled dishonestly, which only incur public censure or civil redress, will become crimes. Imagine a community of saints in an exemplary and perfect monastery. In it crime as such will be unknown, but faults that appear venial to the ordinary person will arouse the same scandal as does normal crime in ordinary consciences. If therefore that community has the power to judge and punish, it will term such acts criminal and deal with them as such. It is for the same reason that the completely honourable man judges his slightest moral failings with a severity that the mass of people reserves for acts that are truly criminal. In former times acts of violence against the person were more frequent than they are today because respect for individual dignity was weaker. As it has increased, such crimes have become less frequent, but many acts which offended against that sentiment have been incorporated into the penal code, which did not previously include them.

In order to exhaust all the logically possible hypotheses, it will perhaps be asked why this unanimity should not cover all collective sentiments without exception, and why even the weakest sentiments should not evoke sufficient power to forestall any dissentient voice. The moral conscience of society would be found in its entirety in every individual, endowed with sufficient force to prevent the commission of any act offending against it, whether purely conventional failings or crimes. But such universal and absolute uniformity is utterly impossible, for the immediate physical environment in which each one of us is placed, our hereditary antecedents, the social influences upon which we depend, vary from one individual to another and consequently cause a diversity of consciences. It is impossible for everyone to be alike in this matter, by virtue of the fact that we each have our own organic constitution and occupy different areas in space. This is why, even among lower peoples where individual originality is very little developed, such originality does however exist. Thus, since there cannot be a society in which individuals do not diverge to some extent from the collective type, it is also inevitable that among these deviations some assume a criminal character. What confers upon them this character is not the intrinsic importance of the acts but the importance which the common consciousness ascribes to them. Thus if the latter is stronger and possesses sufficient authority to make these divergences very weak in absolute terms, it will also be more sensitive and exacting. By reacting against the slightest deviations with an energy which it elsewhere employs against those that are weightier, it endues them with the same gravity and will brand them as criminal.

Thus crime is necessary. It is linked to the basic conditions of social life, but on this very account is useful, for the conditions to which it is bound are themselves indispensable to the normal evolution of morality and law.

Indeed today we can no longer dispute the fact that not only do law and morality vary from one social type to another, but they even change within the same type if the conditions of collective existence are modified. Yet for these transformations to be made possible, the collective sentiments at the basis of morality should not prove unyielding to change, and consequently should be only moderately intense. If they were too strong, they would no longer be malleable. Any arrangement is indeed an obstacle to a new arrangement; this is even more the case the more deep-seated the original arrangement. The more strongly a structure is articulated, the more it resists modification; this is as true for functional as for anatomical patterns. If there were no crimes, this condition would not be fulfilled, for such a hypothesis presumes that collective sentiments would have attained a degree of intensity unparalleled in history. Nothing is good indefinitely and without limits. The authority which the moral consciousness enjoys must not be excessive, for otherwise no one would dare to attack it and it would petrify too easily into an immutable form. For it to evolve, individual originality must be allowed to manifest itself. But so that the originality of the idealist who dreams of transcending his era may display itself, that of the criminal, which falls short of the age, must also be possible. One does not go without the other.

Nor is this all. Beyond this indirect utility, crime itself may play a useful part in this evolution. Not only does it imply that the way to necessary changes remains open, but in certain cases it also directly prepares for these changes. Where crime exists, collective sentiments are not only in the state of plasticity necessary to assume a new form, but sometimes it even contributes to determining beforehand the shape they will take on. Indeed, how often is it only an anticipation of the morality to come, a progression towards what will be! According to Athenian law, Socrates was a criminal and his condemnation was entirely just. However, his crime – his independence of thought – was useful not only for humanity but for his country. It served to prepare a way for a new morality and a new faith, which the Athenians then needed because the traditions by which they had hitherto lived no longer corresponded to the conditions of their existence. Socrates' case is not an isolated one, for it recurs periodically in history. The freedom of thought that we at present enjoy could never have been asserted if the rules that forbade it had not been violated before they were solemnly abrogated. However, at the time the violation was a crime, since it was an offence against sentiments still keenly felt in the average consciousness. Yet this crime was useful since it was the prelude to changes which were daily becoming more necessary. Liberal philosophy has had as its precursors heretics of all kinds whom the secular arm rightly punished through the Middle Ages and has continued to do so almost up to the present day.

From this viewpoint the fundamental facts of criminology appear to us in an entirely new light. Contrary to current ideas, the criminal no longer appears as an utterly unsociable creature, a sort of parasitic element, a foreign, unassimilable body introduced into the bosom of society. He plays a normal role in social life. For its part, crime must no longer be conceived of as an evil which cannot be circumscribed closely enough. Far from there being cause for congratulation when it drops too noticeably below the normal level, this apparent progress assuredly coincides with and is linked to some social disturbance. Thus the number of crimes of assault never falls as low as it does in times of scarcity. Consequently, at the same time, and as a reaction, the theory of punishment is revised, or rather should be revised. If indeed crime is a sickness, punishment is the cure for it and cannot be conceived of otherwise; thus all the discussion aroused revolves round knowing what punishment should be to fulfil its role as a remedy. But if crime is in no way pathological, the object of punishment cannot be to cure it and its true function must be sought elsewhere.

Tarde, 'Criminality and Social Health' in *Revue philosophique*

In his *Rules of Sociological Method* which appeared in the form of articles in the *Revue philosophique,* M. Durkheim endeavours to build – vainly, I believe – a sort of sociology *in itself* and for itself, which, purged of all psychology, and likewise of all biology, would have a great deal of trouble getting off the ground without the remarkable talent of the builder. Certainly this would be an autonomous sociology, but one which purchased its independence perhaps a trifle dearly – at the price of its reality. I do not claim to criticize this system here; but, since the author has supplied some extremely logically deduced applications of his point of view, we shall apply ourselves to one of these, which particularly struck us, and which will allow us to pass judgment on the principle from which it derives. The question concerns his manner of envisaging criminality. This manner is assuredly novel; it consists in affirming that crime is a completely normal, not in the least morbid, fact of social life; that is to say 'that it is not just an inevitable, though regrettable, phenomenon, due to the incorrigible wickedness of men, but that it is a *factor in public health,* an integral part of every healthy society', even when it is increasing as at present, and when, in fifty years, as in the France we live in, it has almost tripled.

One must concede to the distinguished sociologist that this conceit is far removed from the thoughts of the 'common herd' and he himself doesn't hide from us that, when he was led to this 'surprising' conclusion from his general rule concerning the distinction between the normal and the pathological, he could not help being a little bit 'disconcerted'. But far from seeing here any reason to call in question the absolute truth of the rule in question, he appealed to all his intrepidity as a logician and resolutely embraced this corollary, which seemed to him even to illustrate and confirm the value of his theorem, by showing 'in what new light the most essential phenomena are seen, when they are treated systematically'.

But not as new as one might think. A dozen years ago, I endeavoured to refute an identical or rather very similar paradox of M. Poletti's. This writer, it is true, did not expressly conclude, as M. Durkheim does, that 'crime is necessary, it is bound up with the fundamental conditions of all social life, and, by the same token, it is *useful*'. But he asserted that if, when criminal activity doubled or tripled, industrial and financial prosperity quadrupled or quintupled, this absolute increase in criminality is tantamount to its relative decline, the only thing which matters, and, at the basis of his thought, one sees clearly that, for him too, the present coincidence of these two advances, the advance of evil and the advance of the hardworking, is not accidental and deplorable, but quite inevitable, and betokens the fact that crime and work, crime and genius, derive their vitality from the same sources. Now M. Poletti's idea had no success in his own country or outside it; which does not alter the fact that, in reality, a good portion of the public, of the public scandalized by him and, I think, also by M. Durkheim, is imbued without acknowledging it with some secret belief similar to theirs, and still more dangerous because it is vague and unconscious. These two thinkers have had the merit of expressing with much originality a very banal notion, which finds expression every day in the growing indulgence of judges and juries, in the relaxation of the fibres of indignation and of public disgust when confronted by certain kinds of criminal outrages. If this enervation of penal and social repression was only caused by a growing sense of the complicity of everyone, more or less, in the crime of a particular individual, I would be at a loss to combat it; but it also rests upon the idea, given more credit each day, that contemporary crime is bound up with contemporary civilization like the recto to the verso, that it forms 'an integral part of it'. I am afraid therefore for M. Durkheim lest he finds himself here in agreement with the common or rather vulgar sense so scorned by him. No matter, he has rendered us the great service of obliging us to pose frankly, to confront face to face this fundamental problem: is it true that *from some perspective crime, like misfortune, is good*, and that its extirpation is no more desirable than possible? Scepticism is allowable here and the need for a rigorous examination, a sort of scrutiny of the collective *conscience*, makes itself felt.

I am well aware that our author does his best to reduce or suppress the practical interest of the question. The necessity and legitimacy of punishment, following him, are in perfect accord with the utility and necessity of crime. 'If it is normal,' he says, 'that in every society, there should be crimes, it is no less normal that they should be punished.' But here, I must confess, I no longer recognize the skillfulness of his ordinary dialectic. For in truth the reasons which he urges to justify this identity of opposites would have seemed feeble to Hegel himself. He tells us, in particular, that the sentiments of aversion and 'of detestation' prompted by crime are justified because it is only beneficial in spite of itself. But since when is it permissible to detest even an involuntary benefactor? I grant that we should owe still more recognition to thieves and assassins if they work knowingly and with deliberate purpose to fulfil the noble functions which are ascribed to them, to keep us hygienically in good national health, to provide us with innovative and enterprising characters; but still, if it proved that they render us such signal service even unwillingly, I wonder by what right we may not just inflict a punishment on them, but refuse them an acknowledgement.

'A puerile objection' – agreed; yet what does one respond to it? It is not enough to compare punishment to the functions of *excretion* for the living body; and even this comparison is singularly dangerous. From the point of view of the learned professor from Bordeaux, it is rather to the functions of *secretion* that we must compare punishment; for it is the *useless* or the harmful that is excreted, never the useful, save in the case of grave and serious illness. 'Pain,' he adds, 'also has nothing desirable about it; the individual detests it as society detests crime, and yet it is dependent upon normal physiology.' Well, no, the individual is wrong to detest pain in the cases – extremely rare, however, and perhaps even imaginary – where it is really bound up with the production of a great good, and, *if it was proved* that, without a sufficient accompaniment of agonizing pains, the success of a surgical operation or of a confinement would be impossible, it would be an absurdity to *curb* these sufferings by the use of chloroform. Society thus joins folly to ingratitude in repressing crime if it is partly to this that it owes its inventions and discoveries, and if, thanks to this, besides, as we shall see below, it escapes the danger of severities, of extravagant ferocities. I recall nevertheless that the Egyptians used to detest and sometimes beat the embalmer of corpses, all while judging him eminently useful; but no one, that I know of, thought that they were proved logical in this.

What if, in order to save the argument by cutting it back, it should be alleged that it is perhaps not crime alone, but the coupling of crime and punishment, symmetrically everlasting and universal, which is healthy and socially normal? But it is precisely the unpunished and unprosecuted crime which plays a distinguished and extensive role in history, in the formation and evolution of nations; it is this triumphant crime, buried with royal or dictatorial honours, exalted in statues in the market places, immortalized, of which it might perhaps be permissible to assert, with an overwhelming appearance of justification, that this scourge is a spur, this poison a ferment necessary and indispensable to historical progress. Without it, indeed, no more violent annexation of one's neighbour, no more cruel oppression of the lower orders and the conquered, and consequently, for want of conquest and of slavery, no more Roman Empire, no more modern cosmopolitanism and democracy, no more bloody ascent towards Justice and Peace. That is what one might say – mistaking, however, and failing to appreciate the real agents of human improvement who have been not the conquerors but the missionaries, not the ravagers of provinces but the discoverers of truth, the inventors of useful things, the collectors of artistic beauties, the kindlers of ideas perceived somewhere and then radiating everywhere by the force of example and not by the force of arms; that is what one might say, nevertheless, of glorious crime, of the crime which holds its head high, like the biblical serpent, audacious seducer and corrupter of humanity and likewise of its historians. But with low and rampant crime, that is detested and despised, the only sort that M. Durkheim attends to, how is it possible to judge it to be useful to societies where it steals in like a trespasser, worker in vice, sponger on labour, a destroyer, like hailstones, of the harvest, and where it produces nothing but the contagion of its evil example? What is it good for except to be pursued by the police, which itself is only good for this sport?

What is it good for? M. Durkheim is going to show us. And, as a matter of fact, one would not easily divine it. Imagine, supposing an impossibility, a society where there is no longer a single murder, a single theft committed, nor the least offence against morality; this could only be the result, he tells us, of an excessive unanimity and intensity of the public *conscience* in the reprobation of these acts; and the deplorable consequence would be that, having become more exacting by the very fact of the satisfactions it has received, this *conscience collective* will begin to indict with an extravagant severity the slightest acts of violence, of unscrupulousness or of immorality; it will be as if one were in a cloister where, in the absence of mortal sins, one is condemned to the hair shirt and to fasting for the most venial of peccadilloes. 'For example, unscrupulousness or unscrupulously executed contracts, which only lead to public censure or civil damages, will become criminal offences... If therefore this society is armed with the power to judge and punish, it will style these actions criminal and treat them as such.'

In fact, it does not seem that the danger pointed up by our moralist has a very marked correspondence with reality; and, for the man who is acquainted with the disastrous progress of the most excessive leniency on the part of judges as well as juries, inclined to reduce crimes to misdemeanours, turn criminal into civil cases, and to acquit as many people as possible, for the man who knows this, it is doubtless not the excessive scruples of the easily alarmed public conscience, nor the irresistible tendency towards inordinate penalties for trifles, that is the peril of the hour. I take it for granted that, in such districts where certain thefts are now punished with a 16 franc fine, with the application of the Bérenger Act, the same thefts would have merited for their perpetrators, a hundred and fifty years ago, being hanged high and handsome by the executioner of these same towns, in pursuance of the sentence of their court, which, it is true, would have a mass said the next day for the repose of their souls. Between these two exaggerations, at least, I admit that I still prefer ours, if one absolutely must choose between them. But is it really so clear that, in the situation where we no longer had real offences to punish, we would return little by little to the ancient ferociousness? Rather I believe, and it seems to me more reasonable to think that, having abandoned the practice of punishment, we would likewise no longer take the trouble to punish a plain misdeed committed accidentally in accordance with the law. We would purely and simply banish the exceptional malefactor, as one restricts oneself to expelling from a circle of honest players a cheat caught in the act. Still more would we continue to remain *judicially* indulgent towards ordinary transgressions not prejudicial to society.

It is only the tribunal of *public opinion* which would become rigorous, exacting, hard to please. And where would be the harm in that? The mistake, at all events, would be to suppose that, because there was no more adultery, for example, the salons would be invaded by a ridiculous prudishness, opposed to all freedom of behaviour and conversation in the relations of the two sexes. Far from it, it is in the circles where these relations are the most secure that they are the freest, in America or in England, and, if prudishness of language was ever banished from the earth, it would be in the salon of a loose woman, of compromised reputation, that it would find refuge. The same would hold for the world of business if no swindling, no breach of trust occurred any more; people there would become less and less suspicious, less and less inclined to see fraud in slightly risky speculations. Conversely, in situations where a branch of offence thrusts forward with an alarming rapidity and vigour, it often happens that, instead of continuing to become flabby, an honest man's conscience eventually stiffens, reacts with extravagant severity against this criminal infestation; and this is quite the opposite of M. Durkheim's predictions.

Another much more serious error is to think that the production of the criminal varieties of human nature is indissolubly bound up with those of genius; that, consequently, in stamping out crime, one would in the same stroke kill off genius, two kinds of individual originality, equally distant from the 'collective type' which would become in that manner a rule without exception. In the first place, I have great difficulty in reconciling the author's thought with itself on this point. For him, we shall see presently, there is no other touchstone of normality than its generality; for him, the average type, the collective type, is the normal type; thus everything which departs from it is an anomaly. Consequently, the above proposition of his amounts to saying that criminality is a normal thing because it favours the production of anomalies, and that its suppression would be an anomaly because it would effect the absolute hegemony of the normal state...But let us pass over this contradiction. Is it true, or not, that crime and genius are solidary? There cannot be a more serious moral problem and one which touches on more burning questions. An interdependence of the same sort has also been alleged between madness and genius, but not in the least demonstrated, although it is spurious in a very different way from that linking genius to crime. But in whatever way this latter question is finally resolved by the alienists, it has little importance, when all is said and done, for the moral conscience. It is not so in the former case. It disturbs in the highest degree practical reason, to an even greater extent than another paradox, itself surely highly formidable, which crops up before it when an apologist for war, such as Field Marshal von Moltke, or Dr Le Bon recently, claims to demonstrate not only that it is not possible but also that it is not desirable to do away with warfare, that warfare, too, 'is an integral part of social health', and that, without its periodic ration of massacres, lootings, bellicose abominations, humanity would fall to pieces. Yet, passing over this efficacy of warfare, it is, after all, homicide and theft by mutual consent. But if *unilateral* homicide and theft, and rape into the bargain, are also useful, useful to the free flight of the inventive spirit, and if the theory *of block* is applicable here too, as it has indeed been invoked to absolve the September massacres,[1] inseparable, it has been said, from the revolutionary glories, then what, I ask you, remains of the old distinction between good and evil?

If, to resolve this question, one relies upon statistics, as a source of essentially 'objective' information, one deceives oneself. The oracles of this Sybil are often ambiguous and in need of interpretation. Maps, for example, show us clearly that the richest, the most civilized, the most literate *départements*, are generally (not always) the most productive of crime just as of cases of madness. Her graphs and her tables too seem at times to testify to the same effect. But there are some significant exceptions: the case of Geneva, where criminality, according to M. Cuenoud's monograph, diminishes in proportion as it becomes civilized; the case of *London*, more remarkable still, where the crime rate is half as great as in the provincial towns and lower even, extraordinarily, than that of the English countryside. I borrow this curious detail from a recent study by M. Joly, where it is demonstrated, moreover, that, for ten years, crime in England, in all its forms, especially among the young, has diminished 10 to 12 per cent. Poor England! It is in the process of becoming very sick! If the truth must be told, the official statistics are still compiled too imperfectly and for too short a time to supply the decisive data in the debate which occupies us. They do not allow us to decide whether the rise of criminality almost everywhere at the moment is owing to the lasting and essential energies of our civilization and not just to its accidental and transitory vices, to the insufficiency of its moral effort compared with its industrial and scientific effort.

I would have more confidence in special, circumscribed statistics, gathered by private individuals to examine closely the causes of crime and separately the causes of genius. Researches of the first sort are familiar to criminologists; now, every time one of them has taken it into his head to inquire into the heredity antecedents and mode of education of 100 randomly selected criminals, he has met with a great deal more debauchery and idleness, alcoholism and madness, and ignorance too, than among the ancestors and educators of 100 honest people belonging to the same races and the same classes; but more genius? Not that I know of. On the other hand, M. de Candolle has at great length, patiently and ingeniously researched into what familial and social environment was most conducive to the appearance of genius, especially of scientific genius; and he found that, among these favourable influences, must be reckoned of first importance an essentially moral home life, free of all criminal taint and of all vice, hereditarily attached to traditional honesty. In short, it is the *minimum* or rather the absence of criminality which appeared to him to be tied to the *maximum* of scientific genius. It follows from this that there is not the least connection between the causes of crime and the causes of genius; and they might with impunity have been placed side by side for centuries – they would remain no less strange and hostile to each other. This link which one would like to establish between them, let us note, appears the more untenable in proportion as, through the improvements from the repetition of the offence, contemporary European criminality becomes more professional – a profession which, assuredly, is of no use to others – and settles still more in decaying, anti-social surroundings, unfit for all healthy work.

And, indeed, let's consider a little. How, I ask you, would the greater security procured for life and property by the complete suppression of murderers and thieves, be of a sort to hinder the inspired work of inventors? How would the elimination of all spirit of extortion, of shady speculation, in journalism and finance, form an obstacle to the independence, to the power, to the free diversity of the press, to the birth and success of viable and fruitful industrial enterprises? To be sure in this case, we should not have seen constituted, with the *success* we all know about, the Panama Canal Company;[2] but, on the other hand, without *Panamanianism* and its catastrophe, how many useful and prosperous companies would have been founded which did not dare to be born in the aftermath of the discredit cast over both good and bad concerns! Beyond the direct harm, indeed, which crime produces, we must attribute to it, not just this indirect and visible evil of prisons to construct and maintain, of the criminal justice system to operate, but also, and above all, many other indirect evils which one doesn't see: in the first place, the evil of public insecurity, the evil of the mistrust which gets in the way of utilizing the things or persons whom one mistrusts, the time and money lost in securing oneself by means of revolvers, locks and safes, against the contingency of murders and thefts, or against the possibility of immoral acts by an excessive and awkward reserve in the relations of the two sexes; then, the evil of the example, the perversion of public spirit especially by the anarchist explosions, the decline of the respect owed to human life and the diminution of the rigid

probity among honest men become a little less honest following the reading of the court reports because, compared to these monstrous misdeeds,
their own transgressions take on the colour of innocent peccadilloes.

Imagine, once more, a State purged of all its families of malefactors, of
all its vagabonds, of all its neophytes and seminarians of crime. We may
not say that it is impossible, for one might have said the same thing of slavery in antiquity, and even now of pauperism, of begging in the streets. We
may not say either that for this to happen there would have to be a
complete levelling of spirits and of feelings united in a 'collective sentiment' far more intense and far more unanimous than at present, so that
individual originality would be left mortally wounded. A radical and energetic reform of our judicial and prison system would, I believe, be sufficient. Be that as it may, however, let us note that crime is the violation not
of all the rules but only of the most basic and least debatable rules of
morality. From the fact that everyone agreed to stigmatize forcibly and to
punish severely these violations, it would in no sense follow that the rich
efflorescence of individual diversity would be cut down or pruned back,
nor even that the freedom of theoretically thinking anything at all would
be diminished. It is possible, as a matter of fact, that, in what concerns the
freedom of conduct, the public conscience might become more exacting,
the sense of justice would perhaps develop to the extent that the boldest
social reforms would be enacted without bloodshed, under the pressure of
the generalized morality. Without doubt, for want of crimes of passion,
our literature would lose some of its most common inspirations; without
habitual drunkenness, equally, the drinking song would never have been.
By way of compensation, we have no idea of all the kinds of artistic and
literary beauty of which our crimes and offences, our immoralities and our
vices, deprive us; we do not dream of these delicate flora, of these new
forms of art, purer and more exquisite, which our taste would not fail to
create for itself to delight in instead of and in place of our decadent
aesthetics.

It may be objected that I am right but yet wrong to be so insistent. I don't
believe it. It is useful to refute a paradox which is only the lively expression
of muted and unavowed, even disavowed, common sense prejudice;
common sense confined in this manner is forced into enormous mistakes,
born of confused ideas, of which it has no consciousness which horrify it
when it is shown them, but which it sets in motion. It is more interesting,
nevertheless, to ask ourselves how a sociologist like M. Durkheim could be
led to the proposition which I am combating. By the most logical path in
the world, by his way of conceiving the distinction between the normal and
the pathological in the social world. Even in the biological sphere, the definition of illness and health is a difficult task, and our scholar has devoted
the most interesting pages of his book to dealing with this nice question. He
shows, or believes he shows, that the distinctive characteristic of the

morbid state consists neither in the pain which accompanies it, and which also sometimes accompanies the healthy state, nor in the shortening of life, for it is illnesses compatible with longevity and it is normal organic functions, such as childbirth, which are often fatal – nor finally in contrast to a certain specific or social ideal which one dreams up, for this final hypothesis is completely subjective and, therefore, not in the least *scientific*. Having eliminated all these characters, only one remains, and that completely objective: the normal is the general. 'We shall call normal those facts which are the most generally found and we shall call the others morbid or pathological; *the normal type is identical with the average type* and every deviation with respect to this standard of health is a morbid phenomenon.' Now, a society without a certain regular quota of crimes has never been seen, anywhere; thus, since nothing is more general, nothing is more normal.

This principle is already quite punctured by this conclusion; and there are other equally strange ones. All individuals are defective, imperfect in some respect; thus, nothing is more normal than imperfecton and defectiveness. All animals are sick at some time or another, if only with the disorder from which they die; thus nothing is more normal than illness. In a few lines, Cournot dealt justly *with* the error of confounding the normal with the average type. Imagine a small tribe, or a species of animal, and there are some, where the average lifespan is less than the age of adulthood, it would follow that in the situation where everyone truly conformed, in the length of their existence, to this average type, and did not present any anomaly in this respect, that none of them would reproduce, and that this would be normal, Take the average level of intelligence, the average level of schooling, the average level of morality in a crowd. To what level normality is going to be reduced! At the beginning of this century, the average schooling used to consist in not knowing how to read or write. Superior culture is still an anomaly, since it is what is less general and less widespread. To be sure, on this account, ignorance and immorality are healthier and more normal things than knowledge and virtue.

M. Durkheim, in studying this subject, has omitted some necessary distinctions. He says there are healthy forms of pain; so there are, in the sense that they are useful physiologically, useful to the accomplishment of a vital function, that of the generation or repair of tissue. But physiologically they are themselves deleterious, when they do not serve to prevent greater suffering on the part of the individual. Consequently, psychological and social effort strains increasingly to reduce them, often to do away with them, to render them less and less necessary and beneficent, thanks to inventions such as the use of chloroform or of morphine. What is normal for the species may be pathological for the individual. Parturition, when it kills the individual or shortens her life, is an evil and an illness for her, but a good for the species which, but for this mortal accident, might itself die.

I wonder that M. Durkheim has not borne in mind here the famous struggle for existence. Could the pathological not be defined as what diminishes the chances of the triumph of the individual – or those of the species, let us keep the distinction well in view – in this great struggle of the living? But, from this point of view, pain appears as an evil and an anomaly which, if prolonged, would fatally entail the defeat of the individual or for that matter the species. There are illnesses with which one may live *hors du combat*, but none which allow triumph in it. From this point of view, too, the utility is evident of a notion rejected too cavalierly by our author: that of adaptation. One may, indeed, define as normal that which is adapted to triumph in the struggle. Let us add that by considering *co-operation to stay alive*, as well as conflict, one readily obtains an acceptable definition: isn't the abnormal that which renders an individual unfit or less fit to enter into an association and to strengthen the ties in it?

Pasteur's theory of the origin of the most serious, the most dangerous illnesses, those most worthy of the name, gives rise to a conception of illness which might be considered as derived from a singular and original instance of the *struggle for life*, concerning which M. Durkheim says nothing either: illness, if this microbial explanation is generalized, presents itself to us as the combat between an army of cells and an army of microbes, a combat in which our organism is at one and the same time the stake and the field of battle. These two armies are composed, separately, of combatants in good health right up to the moment when they are exterminated, but it is their contact which is morbid. Nothing applies better to criminality than this notion of illness. Criminality is a conflict between the great legion of honest men and the small battalion of criminals, and the latter like the former act *normally*, given the goal which each pursues. But as the two goals are opposed, the resistance they mutually offer each other is experienced by each of them as a pathological state which, though permanent and universal, is no less distressing for all that.

M. Durkheim's prejudice against the idea of finality, *even in social science*, prevents him from discerning the truth, amidst the rather artificial obscurities of the question he poses. How can one develop an idea, however limited, of the normal and the abnormal, if one persists in proscribing what must come first and foremost here, considerations of a teleological and also of a logical sort; that is to say if one does not consider, above all, as abnormal or morbid whatever disturbs the systematic harmony of the being, or the organic constitution, the mental or social constitution – whatever prevents the harmony of goals and the harmony of judgments from being sufficient to realize their ruling purpose? So true is this that, despite a contempt for finalism which goes so far as to make him reject even the idea of utility, the distinguished professor has himself made use of it without meaning to. He has grasped that it will not do to define the normal as the general, unless one goes back to the causes of the latter, to allow of distinguishing between generality of various sorts, accepting some of them, rejecting others, and not accepting certain rather awkward consequences of his own principle. So he has looked for these causes and believes he has found them in what he terms 'the conditions of existence'. When the conditions of existence of a society chance to change, what was normal until then – for example, the religious practices, or the individual character of ownership – becomes abnormal, in spite of its persistent generality. And that is how our author, in a note, a few pages after writing that the growth of criminality in our epoch is a normal thing, could write that the decline in religious sentiment is also something normal, such that the revival of this sentiment, still the most universal of social manifestations, would be an anomaly whereas the growth of our crime rate is not! Our present economic state, he goes on to say, 'with the absence of organization that is characteristic of it' is indeed universal, but it is none the less morbid if it is proved that it is bound up 'with the old segmentary social structure' and not with the new structure which tends to take its place. Yet what are these 'conditions of existence'? M. Durkheim does not specify: let us do so. These are the ideas or the beliefs which have spread, the rights or the duties which men have assumed, or else the new goals, or rather simultaneously the new goals and the new ideas, which they have set about pursuing. The idea of finality is thus implied in that which M. Durkheim believes takes its place.

Without any doubt, 'what is normal for a mollusc is not so for a vertebrate' and each species has its own normality; but why so? Because one irresistibly ascribes to each species a fundamental necessity (to swim, to fly, etc.), a Desire, a true Purpose, the major and necessary premise of the implicit syllogism from which we deduce the conclusion 'this must be, this is normal; this ought not to be, this is abnormal'. Even better, for each individual, pursuing the goal that we know he has or suppose he has, the conditions of normality change.

'The savage,' we are told, 'who possessed the reduced digestive organs and developed nervous system of the healthy civilized man would be a sick man in relation to his environment.' *Socially* a sick man, granted, for he would be constituted in opposition to the needs and wishes of the tribe; but not individually sick if his own ideal, contrary to that of his surroundings, called for this cerebral development and this reduction in the vegetative life.

Writing these lines brings to mind a thought of (John) Stuart Mill's which is far removed from Durkheim's. The normal state, he said somewhere, is, for every individual, the highest state he can attain. Put another way: the normal is the ideal; and the morbid is most often the general, the common, the 'vulgar', this vulgar which our author scorns so deeply but which he has no right to scorn if he wants to remain faithful to his own principle. The normal, then, for a society, is peace in justice and light, the complete extermination of crime, vice, ignorance poverty, corruption. And I am well aware that the danger of this definition is of inclining too much towards a chimera, but I still prefer it to the other, however 'scientific' it flatters itself as being.

Why so? Because I cannot admit, with my subtle contradictor, and it is not my least disagreement with him, that science, or what he calls science, cold product of abstract reason, alien, by hypothesis to every inspiration of the conscience and heart, has the supreme authority over conduct which it legitimately exercises over thought. Where did the Stoics learn the abnormal character of slavery, despite its generality, its universality, in their time? Not in listening to the geometers, not to the astronomers, nor to the physicians of those days, but to their heart. Silence the heart, and slavery is justifiable for them, as it was for Aristotle. I would add that it is the *whole* man who must think, with his heart, with his soul, even with his imagination, and not just with his reason. He must often, doubtless, muffle the first strings to allow freer play to the vibrations of the latter, to the oscillations and operations of his intelligence. It is like holding one's breath, for a few moments, so as not to muddy the surface of the pure water in which one seeks to see the reflection of its banks; and reason is this pure water. But the same happens with this *subjective abstraction,* as it were, applied to our own internal reality, as with the objective abstraction to which the external realities are artificially subjected in order to arrive at a better understanding of them by analysing them successively under their diverse aspects. The latter ought no more to be prolonged indefinitely than the former, and ought not to be taken for anything but a heuristic device, a temporarily useful fiction. From time to time, the most abstract thinker, the deepest diver – especially the deepest – in order to avoid drowning, must recapture himself as a whole, come up to the light to breathe freely; and it is in these moments of relaxation of the heart, of imaginative intoxication, following a calm reflection, that it is sometimes given to him to see a little more clearly into the intimacy of things, which have also been recaptured in the plenitude of their existence – a plenitude temporarily fragmented by the analysis.

M. Durkheim believes he is honouring science in ascribing to it the power of sovereignly directing the will, i.e., not just of *pointing out* to it the most appropriate means of reaching its dominant goal, but also of *commanding* its orientation towards this pole star of conduct. Now, it is certain that science exercises an influence over our desires, but principally a negative influence: it shows the unrealizable or contradictory character of many of them and in so doing tends to weaken, if not eliminate them; but, among those which it may judge realizable in equal or even in different degrees, by what right might it forbid us to experience some and enjoin us to experience others? It only has absolute power over our intellect; and even then it only imposes its teaching on it on the basis of first-hand evidence, or of sensory data, which it has not created and which it solicits. With greater reasons, when it applies to the will, of which it is only so to speak the private counsel, it can only command or commend this or that line of conduct on the basis of given preferences, the major premises of the moral syllogism of which it is only the minor premise and the conclusion. If it has to deal with an ambitious person, why should it prescribe love for him? If it has to deal with a lover, why should it prescribe ambition for him? Why should it ordain even for the scholar his passionate thirst for truth rather than for riches or honours? We are born, as individuals or peoples, with a particular power of projection like stars, with an impulse of our own which comes from the heart, from the sub-scientific, sub-intellectual depths of our soul; this is the necessary foundation of all the (always conditional) counsel which it can offer us. And when it is a question of modifying, whether the intensity or the direction of this internal energy, it is no law of physics or physiology, or even of sociology, which has this power, but rather the individual or national encounter, in some byway of life or history, with a new object of love or hatred, of adoration or execration which, from the stirred-up depths of our heart, draws forth new energy.

It is in demanding more from science than it can give, in ascribing to it rights which exceed its compass, already vast enough, that one gives rise to the belief in its alleged *bankruptcy*. Science has never failed to keep its genuine promises, but a crowd of false promissory notes bearing its forged signature have circulated, and these it finds it impossible to honour. It is vain to add to their number.

Durkheim's Reply to Tarde in *Revue philosophique*

I beg leave to respond briefly to M. Tarde's recent article entitled 'Criminality and Social Health': for most of the propositions which my eminent critic attributes to me are not mine. I judge them false just like him.

1.   I did not say that the rise in criminality, documented by our statistics, was normal. One will not find a sentence in my book in which this idea is expressed. I agree so little with M. Poletti's theory that I publicly refuted it in a lecture of the course on the sociology of crime which I recently taught at Bordeaux. In the book I am preparing on *Suicide,* one will find a refutation of the same thesis, in so far as it is applicable to suicides. So a first point is established. After this

declaration, M. Tarde cannot doubt that on this question he has attributed to me a position which is not mine.

In any case, M. Tarde seems to have had some doubts himself: for he felt the need of adding to his text a note to demonstrate that this proposition is 'consistent with my principles'. This method of debate, which consists of making an author say what he did not say, was once in high regard; it has since been abandoned. It was realized that it was too easy to draw from a system all the inferences one liked. I think it would be just as well not to reopen the question. But at all events, is it true that, as a matter of logic, I must accept this mistake? You decide. Having established that the existence of criminality was a universal fact, and, in consequence, fulfilled the criterion of normality, I felt obliged to raise an objection. If, I said, the facts allowed us at least to believe that, the further one advances in history, the more criminality, without disappearing, approaches zero, one might suppose that this universality and, therefore, this normality are temporary. But it so happens that the only information which we possess shows us an increase instead of a decrease. We must consequently reject the hypothesis, seeing that it is without foundation in fact. But though this rising tide of crimes does not allow us to admit that they are diminishing, it does not follow that this is normal. The question remains untouched upon and it allows of many solutions. For we are not caught on the horns of the dilemma M. Tarde devises. It may be that, in fact, it is normal that some offences rise along with civilization, but that the enormous growth which has come about in our time is pathological. Finally, I am so far from ignoring what is happening that, thinking about the sad spectacle which our statistics presently furnish us with, I wrote on the same page on which the offending passage is found: 'It may be that crime itself has abnormal forms; this happens when, for example, *it attains an exaggerated level. There is no doubt, as a matter of fact, that this excess is of a morbid nature.*'

2.   I did not say that the utility of crime consisted in preventing the moral *conscience* from indicting too harshly triflingly dishonest actions, as if these were a serious evil and must be suppressed at all costs. I do not see a single word of my book which could justify such an interpretation. I simply said that, *in fact,* if the moral *conscience* were to become strong enough so that all crimes, hitherto kept in check, disappeared completely, one would see it denounce more severely acts which it previously would have judged more leniently; and that, in consequence, criminality, having disappeared under one form, would reappear under another. Hence it follows that there is a contradiction in conceiving of a crime-free society. But I did not say that this greater severity in the way of assessing moral actions would be an evil any

more than I said it would be a blessing. And if I did not ask myself the question, it is because it cannot be posed in this abstract manner. One would also need to know in what social type it occurs in order to decide whether this recrudescence of rigour is desirable or not. In the primitive Roman City-State, where social life was only possible if the individual personality was, in great measure, absorbed in the collective personality, it would have been injurious had the moral *conscience* become too sensitive to offences directed against individuals. But today, if the sentiment of deference and respect which we feel for the great contemporary religions and which still possess some juridical support in most European codes, were to pass a certain degree of intensity, we would see what would become of our freedom of thought. I only give these examples to show that the question is not so simple.

3. I did not say that, if certain crimes became rarer, the punishments imposed on them would necessarily intensify. From the fact that they would be prosecuted more strictly it does not follow that they would be punished more strictly. I spoke of prosecution, not of repression. These are two separate problems which M. Tarde seems to confound. What ensures that these two orders of facts do not vary one with the other, is that, very often, the collective sentiment which the crime offends is equally offended by the punishment. Thus a sort of balance is established which prevents the punishment from increasing along with the intensity of the blame. It is this which comes into being for all crimes which give offence to the sentiments of sympathy which we feel for mankind in general. As this sympathy becomes more lively with civilization, we become more sensitive to the least outrages which the human person can suffer. Consequently, slight offences, which not long ago were treated indulgently, now seem scandalous to us and are punished. But, from another point of view, all repression does equal violence to this same tendency, which, in consequence, stands in the way of the punishment becoming more severe. We have more compassion for the victim, but we also have more compassion for the offender. Even, for a time, it turns out, for reasons which we cannot go into here, that the offender benefits more from this transformation than the victim. This is why, *as far as this particular kind of criminality is concerned*, punishment lessens in proportion as the moral *conscience* becomes, on this same issue, more exacting.

4. I nowhere said that crime and genius were only two different aspects of the same mental state. All this part of M. Tarde's discussion is above my head. I said that it was useful and even necessary that, in every society, the collective personality did not repeat itself identically in all the individual *consciences;* among the differences which arise in

this way, there are some which make the criminal, others, the man of genius, but I have never identified the second with the first. It can happen that the criminal is a genius, as he can be below average. In any case, the reasons for which I said that crime is normal, at a certain level, are independent of the intellectual aptitudes that one attributes to the offender.

5. It is particularly incorrect to say that 'low and rampant crime that is detested and despised, is the only sort that M. Durkheim attends to'. When I tried to show how crime could even have a direct utility, the only examples which I cited were those of Socrates and the heretical philosophers of all periods, precursors of free thought; and we know they were numerous. It is on these facts and their analogues – and these are themselves legion – that it would have been necessary to bring the discussion to bear in order that it might deal with my thesis.

Facing propositions which have been incorrectly attributed to me, I want to recall briefly those I really wanted to establish; the reader will determine whether there has been a reply.

First, I said that, *useful or not,* crime in any case is normal because it is linked to the fundamental conditions of all social life; such is the case because there cannot be a society where individuals do not diverge more or less from the collective type and because, among these divergencies, there are no less inevitably some which exhibit a criminal character. A substantially complete levelling is physically impossible. I see nothing in M. Tarde's article which responds to this argument, except the following sentence: 'One should not say that it is impossible [referring to the disappearance of all criminality], for one might have said the same thing about slavery in antiquity, and even now of pauperism, or of begging in the streets.' I cannot see the connection between the disappearance of crime and of slavery, slavery not being a crime. As for pauperism, we are scarcely in a position to know if it is destined to disappear. A wish is not a fact. And besides, on this point too, what is the connection with criminality?

I went on to say that the existence of criminality had a *generally indirect* and *sometimes direct* usefulness; indirect, because crime could only cease to exist if the *conscience collective* dominated individual *consciences* with such an ineluctable authority that all moral change would be rendered impossible; direct, in that occasionally, *but only occasionally,* the criminal has been the harbinger of a morality to come.

To destroy the first part of this proposition it would have been necessary either to prove that a fixed arrangement does not rule out, or at least make very difficult, subsequent rearrangements and that, in consequence, a morality so powerfully organized and deep-seated might yet evolve further, or else to deny that there has been and must always be moral evolution. Instead of this, M. Tarde is satisfied with enumerating the untoward consequences of theft, rape, murder, extortion. Do I need to say that I am aware of these and that I would not dream of disputing them? I did not say that crime did no harm; I said that it had a useful effect which I have just recalled. The harmful effects it may have do not show that it may not have this useful one. You will ask how it can be normal, if it is in some respect injurious? But I have precisely applied myself to establishing that it was a mistake to believe that a normal fact is entirely advantageous; there is nothing which is not injurious from some viewpoint. More than that, we must recall that the social harm caused by crime is counterbalanced by punishment and that, in accordance with M. Tarde's happy phrase which I beg leave to make use of because it catches my meaning very nicely, what is normal is the inseparable pairing of crime and punishment.

To destroy the second part of my thesis it would have been necessary to prove that one could introduce changes in morality without becoming, almost inevitably, a criminal. How then is morality to change if no one deviates from it? You say that one could add new maxims without eliminating old ones? The solution would be purely verbal. The rules which one adds on necessarily drive out others. A moral code is not a mathematical scale which can increase or decrease without changing its nature; it is an organic system in which the parts are interdependent and the least change introduced into it upsets the whole organism. At all times, the great moral reformers have condemned the reigning morality and have been condemned by it.

Finally, in this discussion, it would have been necessary not to fix one's eyes exclusively on the present forms of criminality, for the feelings they arouse in all of us scarcely allow us to speak of them objectively. More than that, one cannot judge the role and the nature of crime in general on the basis of such particular examples. Let us look at the past, and the normality of crime is no longer paradoxical; for, in looking at mankind's earlier morality, we appreciate better how important it was that it was not fixed too strongly to allow of change. Granting this, in order to deny that this necessity applies equally to our present morality, one would have to allow that the era of changing morality is over. Who would ever dare to say of any one of the forms of the future that it could go no further?

In the third place, morality is a social function; it must, therefore, like any function, have only a limited degree of vitality. This is the price of organic equilibrium. If morality appropriates to itself more than its share of the vital force, other forms of collective activity will suffer. If our respect for human life were to surpass a certain intensity, we would not put up with even the idea of war; and yet in the present state of international relations, we must have the capacity to wage war.

Nothing is more moral than respect for individual dignity, and yet, past a certain point, it renders military discipline, which is indispensable, and indeed all discipline, impossible. Too much pity for the suffering of animals, in opposing the practice of vivisectionism, becomes an obstacle to the progress of science, etc., etc. The maxim *ne quid nimis* is true of morality and its authority. But if this authority has its limits, it is inevitable that, in certain cases, it should be dominated by disregarded contrary forces, and, inversely, it must be disregarded now and then in order not to be lured outside its natural limits.

Finally, if I have said of crime that it was normal, it was by the application of a general rule which I have tried to establish for distinguishing the normal from the abnormal. The discussion of this rule should perhaps have been the foundation of the debate, for, it being granted, the rest follows. M. Tarde only touches on the question very briefly. He makes two objections.

1. The normal type, he claims, cannot be confounded with the average type; for, as everyone is more or less ill, illness would then be normal. I reply: If everyone is ill, each has a different illness; these individual characteristics therefore cancel each other out in respect of the generic type, which bears no trace of them. Might it be said that one must find, if not a specific illness, at least a general liability to illness? I accept this; but let us not be taken in by mere words. In what does this liability consist? Quite simply in the fact that the average individual, like everyone, only has a limited power of resistance which, in consequence, is perpetually laid open to being conquered by antagonistic, but more powerful, forces. What is contradictory about the fact that the state of health implies only a limited vital energy? I see it as no more than a truism.
2. In the second place, M. Tarde objects, a society in which there were only average men from the physical, intellectual, and moral points of view, would be on such an inferior level that it could not survive; how can one grant that it is healthy? What a strange muddle my ingenious adversary has perpetrated here!

In the theory which I formulated, a society which only included average individuals would be essentially abnormal.

For there is no society which does not include multitudes of individual anomalies, and so universal an occurrence is not accidental. *It is thus socially normal that there should be in every society some psychologically abnormal individuals;* and the normality of crime is only a particular instance of this general proposition. Indeed, as I expressly observed in my book [*Les Règles* p. 83], the conditions of individual health and those of social health may be very different and even contrary to one another. This can be granted without difficulty, if one recognizes with me that there is a deep dividing line between the social and the psychic. But by the same token, outside any system, the facts directly substantiate this antithesis. A society can only survive if it is periodically renewed; that is to say, if the old generations give way to others; so the former must die. Thus the normal state of societies implies the sickness of individuals; a certain death rate, like a certain crime rate, is indispensable to collective health.

At all events, as M. Tarde said in summing up, the origin of our disagreement lies elsewhere. It springs above all from the fact that I believe in science and M. Tarde does not. For it is beyond all belief to reduce it to being nothing more than an intellectual amusement, at best capable of showing us what is possible and impossible, but incapable of use for the positive regulation of conduct. If it has no other practical utility, it is not worth the trouble it costs. If he expects in this way to disarm its recent adversaries, he is sadly mistaken; in reality, he surrenders his weapons to them. Unquestionably, this sort of science will no longer fall short of men's expectations; because men will no longer expect much from it. It will no longer be exposed to being accused of bankruptcy; because it will have been found of minor value and of no great use in perpetuity. I do not see what science gains and what we gain here. For sensation, instinct, passion, all the base and obscure parts are thus placed above reason. We made use of these when we could not do otherwise, having nothing better. But when they are seen as something other than a makeshift approach which must little by little give way to science, when they are granted any pre-eminence whatever, then even if one does not openly refer to a revealed faith, one is theoretically a more or less consistent mystic. And mysticism is the rule of anarchy in the practical order, because it is the reign of fantasy in the intellectual order.

Notes

1. The 'September Massacres' refer to an outbreak of mob violence in Paris in the late summer of 1792, during the initial chaotic period following the French Revolution. By the time the violence subsided, as many as half of the prisoners in the capital's prisons had been killed, many of them priests and aristocrats.
2. Following the successful construction of the Suez Canal in 1869, the French secured a concession from the Columbian government to build a sea-level canal across the Isthmus of Panama in 1878. A private company engaged de Lesseps, who had built the Suez Canal, to take charge of the new project. Large sums were raised from speculators and ordinary citizens to fund the new project. The engineering challenges proved daunting, however, and were compounded by massive mortality among the workforce from a variety of

tropical diseases. Eventually, in 1889, the company collapsed into bank-ruptcy and work was halted. The failure provoked a huge political scandal in France, with as many as 104 French legislators implicated in malfeasance, and the initial speculative enthusiasm for the project dismissed as 'Panamanianism'.

CHAPTER 6

The Legal Prohibition of Suicide

Introduction

Le suicide, *the third major monograph Durkheim published during his years in Bordeaux, appeared in 1897, five years before he moved to Paris to take up a chair in the Science of Education.*[1] *Over the course of the nineteenth century, Western nation states had collected increasingly elaborate series of social statistics. Time series data had begun to emerge for a whole series of forms of social pathology: crime, insanity, divorce, suicide, and so forth, and these social problems had attracted growing attention from a wide range of scholars and social commentators. In the last third of the nineteenth century, the consensus was that all these problems were on the rise, and the emergence of the doctrine of degeneration as an all-purpose, biologically rooted explanation of a perceived social crisis only heightened the attention that these individual pathologies attracted.*[2] *A number of efforts had been made to analyse the statistics, and to advance explanations for the apparent malaise griping industrial societies.*

In that context, it should come as no surprise that Durkheim was attracted to the notion of using sociological methods and theories to tackle the puzzle of self-murder. As he indicated in his preface, 'Suicide has been chosen as a subject ... because, since there are few that are more precisely delimitable, it seemed to us peculiarly timely ... by such concentration, real laws are discoverable, which demonstrate the possibility of sociology better than any dialectical argument'. For him, it offered the opportunity in particular to demonstrate a principle he had abstractly argued for in the Rules of Sociological Method, *that there existed 'realities external to the individual ... as definite and substantial as those of the psychologist or the biologist' (Durkheim 1897: xi; 1951: 39).*

Preliminary analyses of the official data seemed to him to display some remarkably consistent patterns:

Each people seems to have its own suicide rate, more constant than that of general mortality, that its growth is in accordance with a coefficient of acceleration characteristic of each society; when it appears that the variations through which it passes at different times of the day, month, year, merely reflect the rhythm of social life; and that marriage, divorce, the family, religious society, the army, etc., affect it in accordance with definite laws, some of which may even be numerically expressed *(Durkheim 1897: x–xi; 1951: 38–9).*

For Durkheim, such regularities constituted prima facie *evidence of the existence of 'real, living, active forces which, because of the way they determine the individual, prove their independence of him' (Durkheim 1897: xi; 1951: 39).*

The polemical attractions of the subject for someone determined to demonstrate the possibility of a science of the social were thus obvious. They were greatly heightened by a further feature of suicide that at first blush made it inhospitable to sociological explanation, but by that very fact, made the production of a compelling sociological account of the phenomenon a particularly potent demonstration of the new science's value and possibilities. Suicide was surely the most private and personal of acts, 'an individual action affecting the individual only ... which must seemingly depend exclusively on individual factors, thus belonging to psychology alone' (Durkheim 1897: 8; 1951: 46). By definition, too, it was an action an individual could not repeat. To take such a private action and to demonstrate that it was susceptible to sociological explanation would be an intellectual coup that would go far to establish the case for sociology's bona fides.

What Durkheim ultimately sought to do, of course, was not to explain individual suicides, but to assert that suicide rates constituted a stable social phenomenon, and to provide an explanation for those differential rates that rested entirely on social factors. This is not the place to assess the strengths and weaknesses of the explanation Durkheim proffered. (One of us has attempted to do so elsewhere – see Lukes 1972: 191–225.) But one should note that his explanation involved questions of social solidarity – the ties that bound people more or less tightly to society.

Significantly for present purposes, however, at the very outset of his discussion of suicide, when he sought to examine its place in society and the nature of social attitudes to people who took their own lives, Durkheim turned to a comparative and historical examination of moral attitudes and legal responses to self-murder. Not for him abstract moral reasoning about what the status of suicide ought to be, but rather an examination of how attitudes varied across time and in the present, alongside an attempt to tease out what these laws placed in the context of the societies that gave rise to them tell us about the changing basis for the prohibition of suicide. For Durkheim argues, in the pages that follow, that in the ancient city-state suicide under some conditions was permitted: not if the individual acted alone; but under appropriate circumstances with permission from the state: 'The act is immoral only when it is wholly private and without collaboration through the organs of collective life.' The situation is otherwise in more advanced societies. While the ferocious penalties once visited on the suicide are a thing of the past – something Durkheim (characteristically) claims occurred when, 'under the influence of temporary circumstances, the entire system of public repression was enforced with excessive severity' – still 'with the progress of history, the prohibition, instead of being relaxed, only becomes more strict'. In parallel with the arguments he develops in 'Two Laws of Penal Evolution', Durkheim contends that we should understand this pattern as deriving from the rise of individualism in the modern sense. With 'their new conception of the human personality [it] has become sacred, even most sacred in their eyes, something which no-one is to offend'. Thus, he concludes, 'the principle that homicide of oneself should be reproved must be maintained'.

Extract from Durkheim, *On Suicide*

RELATIONSHIP OF SUICIDE TO OTHER SOCIAL PHENOMENA

Since suicide is, in essence, a social phenomenon, we must inquire into the place that it occupies among other social phenomena.

The first and most important question that we must answer on this subject is whether it could be classified among actions that are allowed by morality or not. Should we see it as, to some extent, a criminal matter? We know how much the question has been debated through the ages. In general, in order to resolve it, writers have begun by formulating a certain concept of the moral ideal, then considered whether suicide fits this or whether it is logically contrary to it. For reasons that we have stated elsewhere, this is not the method that we can adopt. An unregulated deduction is always suspect and, apart from that, in this case it starts from a pure postulate of individual feeling, because everyone has his own conception of this moral ideal which is stated as axiomatic. So instead of proceeding in that way, we shall first of all examine how peoples through history have considered the morality of suicide; we shall then try to determine what were the reasons for these judgements. After that, we shall only have to see if and to what extent the same reasons are founded in the nature of our modern society.

I

As soon as Christians societies were established, suicide was formally banned in them. As early as AD 452, the Council of Arles declared that suicide was a crime and could only be the result of some diabolical fury. But it was only in the following century, in 563, at the Council of Prague, that a penal sanction was added to this ban. It was decided that suicides would not be 'honoured by any commemoration in the holy sacrifice of the mass, and that the singing of psalms would not accompany their bodies to the grave'. Civil law took its inspiration from canon law and added material punishments to the religious ones. A chapter in the Institutions of Saint Louis is specifically concerned with the question: the body of the suicide was tried before the authorities that would have been competent in the event of homicide, and the possessions of the deceased did not go to the ordinary heirs, but to the baron. A great number of customs went beyond confiscation and in addition laid down various physical punishments. 'In Bordeaux, the body was hanged by its feel, in Abbeville it was dragged through the streets on a hurdle, in Lille, in the case of a man, the body was hauled to the crossroads and hanged, while if it was a woman it was burned.' Even madness was not always considered an excuse. The criminal ordinance published by Louis XIV in 1670 codified these customs without greatly moderating them. A condemnation in regular form was pronounced *ad perpetuam rei memoriam*, and the body, pulled along on a hurdle, face down, through the streets and crossroads, was afterwards hanged or thrown into the refuse pit. The victim's goods were confiscated. Aristocrats were punished with demotion and were declared commoners: their woods were cut down, their châteaux demolished and their coats of arms broken. We still have a sentence of the Parlement de Paris, passed on 31 January 1749, in accordance with this legislation.

In a sudden about-turn, the Revolution of 1789 abolished all these repressive measure and removed suicide from the list of legal crimes. But all the religions practised in France continued to prohibit and to punish it, and the morality of the average person condemned it. It still inspires in the popular conscience a repulsion that extends to the places where the person carried out his decision and to all those who are closely associated or related to him. It is seen as a moral defect, even though public opinion appears to be tending towards greater indulgence on this than before. In fact, it does still retain some of its criminal character. According to the most widespread legal practice, a suicide's accomplice is liable to prosecution for homicide. This would not be the case is suicide were considered a morally neutral act.

This same legislation is found among all Christian peoples and has remained almost everywhere more strict than in France. In England, as early as the tenth century, King Edgar, in one of the laws passed by him, compared suicides to thieves, murderers and criminal of every kind. Until 1823, it was customary to drag the body of the person who had committed suicide through the streets with a stake driven through it, and to bury it on the highway with no ceremony. Even today, the burial is in a separate place. The suicide was declared a felon (*felo de se*) and his goods were forfeit to the Crown. It was only in 1870 that this provision was abolished, together with all confiscation for felony. It is true that the exaggerated nature of the punishment had made it inapplicable for some time before: the jury would usually get round the law by declaring that the suicide had acted while the balance of his mind was momentarily disturbed and that he was consequently not responsible for his action. But the act itself continued to be classified as a crime, and each time it is committed it is the object of a trial and verdict; and attempted suicide is, in principle, punished too. According to Ferri, in 1889 there were still 106 proceedings for this misdemeanour and 84 verdicts of guilty, in England alone – and even more so when there is complicity.

In Zürich, according to Michelet, the body used to be subjected to appalling treatment. If the man had stabbed himself, a piece of wood in which the knife was stuck was buried close to the body; if he drowned himself, he was buried five feet from the water, in the sand. In Prussia, until the Penal Code of 1871, burial had to take place with no ceremonial or religious service. The new German penal code still punished complicity with three years' imprisonment (Article 216). In Austria, the old canonical penalties have been retained almost unchanged.

Russian law is more severe. If the suicide does not appear to have acted under the influence of some mental disorder, whether chronic or temporary, his will is considered nul and void, together with any other provision he may have made in the event of his death. He has no right to Christian burial. A mere attempt at suicide is punished with a fine which the ecclesiastical authority is asked to determine. Finally, any person who incites another to kill himself or who helps him in any way to carry out his resolve, for example by supplying him with the necessary instruments, is treated in the same way as an accomplice to premeditated murder. The Spanish penal code, apart from the religious and moral penalties, demands the confiscation of possession and punished any form of complicity.

Finally, the penal code of the State of New York, though it is very recent in date (1881), treats suicide as a crime. Admittedly, for practical reasons, the crime goes unpunished despite this, because the punishment cannot effectively be applied to the guilty party. But an attempted suicide can result in a prison sentence of up to two years, or a fine of as much as $200, or both. The mere fact of encouraging suicide or assisting in its accomplishment is treated as complicity to murder.

Muslim societies are no less vigorous in their condemnation of suicide. According to Mohammed, 'man dies only by the will of God according to the book that fixes the term of his life'. 'When the end has come, they may not either delay nor hasten it by a single instant.' 'We have decreed that death shall strike you each in turn and none shall go ahead of us.' Indeed, nothing is more contrary than suicide to the general spirit of Muslim civilization, because the virtue that is set above all others is absolute submission to the divine will and docile resignation that make us 'bear everything with patience'. As an act of insubordination or rebellion, suicide could thus only be regarded as a serious breach of a fundamental duty.

If we go from modern societies to those that preceded them historically, that is to say the Graeco-Roman city-states, we find that they too had laws about suicide, but ones founded on quite different principles. Suicide was only considered illegal if it was not authorized by the state. Thus, in Athens, a man who killed himself was stricken with ἀτιμία [*atimia*], as one who had committed an injustice towards the city. He was refused the honours of ordinary burial and, moreover, the hand of the corpse was cut off and buried separately. With variations in detail, the same was true in Thebes and Cyprus. In Sparta, the rule was so strict that Aristodemus was subjected to it for the way in which he sought death and was killed in the battle of Plataea. But these penalties were only applied if the person killed himself without previously asking permission from the competent authorities. In Athens if, before killing himself, a man asked the Senate to permit it, giving the reasons why life had become intolerable for him, and if the request was properly authorized, his suicide was considered as a legitimate act. Libanius mentions some of these rules, without dating them, though they were really in force in Athens; and he praises these laws highly, assuring us that they had the most beneficial effect. They were expressed in the following terms: 'Let whoever does not wish to live any longer explain his reasons to the Senate and, after gaining permission, let him give up life. If you find existence hateful, then die. If luck is against you, drink the hemlock. If you are bent with pain, leave life. Let the unfortunate describe his misfortune, let the magistrate supply the remedy and his misery will end.' The same law is to be found in Keos. It was brought to Marseille by the Greek colonists who founded the town. The magistrates kept some poison in reserve and supplied the necessary amount to all those who, after bringing their reasons for wishing to kill themselves before the Six Hundred, obtained the requisite authorization.

We are less well informed about the provisions of early Roman law: the fragments of the Law of the XII Tables which have survived to not mention suicide. However, as this legal code was strongly influenced by Greek legislation, it is likely that it contained comparable rulings. In any case, Servius, in his commentary on the *Aeneid*, informs us that according to the books of the Pontiffs, anyone who had hanged himself was denied a tomb. The statutes of a religious confraternity of Lanuvium laid down the same penalty. According to the annalist Cassius Hermina, quoted by Servius,

Tarquin the Proud, in order to deal with an epidemic of suicide, ordered the bodies of the victims to be hung on crosses and left as prey to birds and wild animals. The custom of not giving funerals to suicides seems to have continued, at least in principle, because we read in the Digest: *Non solent autem lugeri suspendiosi nec qui manus sibi intulerunt, non tædio vitæ, sed mala conscientia.*

But according to the writings of Quintilian, until quite a late date Rome had an arrangement comparable to that which we have just observed in Greece, intended to moderate the rigours of previous legislation. A citizen who wished to kill himself had to submit his reasons to the Senate, which decided whether they were acceptable and even decided the kind of death. What makes it probable that such a practice really existed in Rome is that, even under the emperors, something of it survived in the army. A soldier who tried to kill himself in order to escape military service was punished by death, but if he could prove that he had been impelled by some excusable motive, he was simply dismissed from the army. Finally, if his action was due to remorse caused by some military error, his will was annulled and his property revered to the exchequer. Moreover, there is no doubt that in Rome, in every period, consideration of the motives behind the suicide played a dominant role in the moral or judicial assessment. Hence the precept: *Et merito, si sine cause sibi manus untulit, puniendus est: qui enim sibi non pepercit, multo minus aliis parcet.* The public conscience, while as a general rule condemning it, reserved the right to authorize it in certain circumstances. This principle is very close to the one that serves as a basis for the institution mentioned by Quintilian, and it is so basic a part of Roman law on suicide that it was maintained even under the emperors. However, with time, the list of legitimate excuses grew longer. In the end there was only one single *causa injusta*: the desire to escape the consequences of a criminal sentence. And even then there was a time when the law that excluded this from the benefit of tolerance seems not to have been applied.

If we leave the town and go among those primitive peoples where altruistic suicide flourishes, it is hard to say anything precise about the legislation that may be customary. However, the tolerance with which suicide is usually considered suggests that it is not formally prohibited, though it may not be entirely accepted in every case. However, the fact remains that in all societies that have advanced beyond this inferior stage, there is none that we know of in which an individual is unreservedly accorded the right to kill himself. It is true that in Greece, as in Italy, there was a period in which the ancient laws relating to suicide fell almost entirely into disuse, but this was only at a time when the city-state itself had begun to decline so this late tolerance cannot be held up as an example to imitate: it is clearly connected with the serious upheavals that these societies were undergoing. It was the symptoms of an illness.

If we except these cases of regression, such general disapproval is in itself an instructive fact and one that should give pause to those moralists who are over-inclined to indulgence. An author must have exceptional confidence in his powers of argument to dare, in the name of a theory, to oppose the conscience of humanity on this point; or else, if, judging that the prohibition was based in the past, he demands its abrogation only for the immediate present, he must, before doing so, prove that some profound transformation has taken place in recent times in the basic conditions of collective life.

A more significant conclusion, which more or less rules out the possibility of such proof, emerges from this account. If one leaves aside the difference of detail in the repressive measure adopted by various nations, we can see that legislation on suicide went through two main phases. In the first, the individual was prohibited from destroying himself on his own authority, but the state could authorize him to do so. The act was only immoral when it was entirely an individual matter and the organs of collective life played no part in it. In certain defined situations, society allowed itself, so to speak, to be disarmed, agreeing to absolve what in principle it condemned. In the second period, this condemnation becomes absolute and without any exception. The ability to dispose of a human life, except when death is the punishment for a crime, is taken away not only from the interested party, but even from society itself. Henceforth the right has been removed from collected as well as individual arbitration. Suicide is regarded as immoral, in itself and for itself, whoever takes part in it. So, the further we advance through history, the prohibition, far from being relaxed, merely becomes more radical. So if, today, public opinion seems less strict in its judgement in the matter, this state of vacillation must be the result of accidental and temporary causes, because it is most unlikely that morality, having developed in the same direction for centuries, should change tack on this point.

The ideas that gave it this direction are still current. It is sometimes said that, if suicide is prohibited and deserves to be so, this is because, by killing himself, a man evades his obligations to society. But if this were the only consideration, we should, as in Greece, leave society free to lift a prohibition that was in any case only set up for its benefit. So if we deny it this facility, this is because we do not see the suicide merely as someone who dies owing a bad debt to society: a creditor can always wipe out the debt that is owed to him. In any case, if the disapproval shown towards suicides had no other origin than this, it should be all the stricter when the individual is more subordinate to the State, so it is in inferior societies that it would reach its zenith. But we find that, on the contrary, it gains in force as the rights of the individual become greater compared with those of the State. So, if the rule has become so formal and strict in Christian societies, the cause of this change must be sought, not in the idea that these people have of the State, but in the new concept that they have of the human person. In their eyes, this has become a sacred thing – even *the* sacred thing *par excellence*, against which no one may raise his hand. Of course, in the city-state, the individual was not of as little significance as in primitive tribes. He was granted a social value, but it was felt that this value belonged entirely to the State, so the city could freely dispose of him without his having the same rights over himself. But today, he has acquired a kind of dignity which sets him above himself and society. As long as he has not forfeited his human rights by his conduct, he seems to us in some manner to participate in the nature that every religion attributes to its gods, which puts them beyond the reach of all that is mortal. He is imbued with religiosity: man has become a god for men. This is why any attack against him appears to us sacrilegious; and suicide is one such attack. It hardly matters from whose hands the blow comes: it outrages us for the sole reason that it violates the sacrosanct characters that is in us and which we must respect in ourselves as in others.

So suicide is subject to disapproval because it is contrary to this cult of the human person on which all our morality rests. The thing that confirms this explanation is that we consider it in an entirely different way from the peoples of antiquity. Formerly, it was considered as a simple civil wrong committed against the State; religion was more or less indifferent to the matter. Now, on the contrary, it has become an essentially religious act. The Councils condemned it and the lay powers, by punishing it, only followed and imitated the ecclesiastical authority. It is because we have in us an immortal soul, a fragment of the divinity, that we must be sacred to ourselves. It is because we are something of God that we do not belong entirely to any temporal being.

But if this is the reason why suicide is classified among illicit acts, should we not conclude that this condemnation is now without foundation? It seems, indeed, that scientific criticism should not accord the slightest value to these mystical concepts or accept that there is anything superhuman in man. It was with this argument that Ferri, in his *Omicidio-suicidio*, thought he could show that all prohibition of suicide is a survival of the past, destined to disappear. Considering as absurd from the rationalist point of view that an individual could have an end and purpose outside himself, he deduced that we always remain free to give up the benefits of communal life by giving up life itself. To him, the right to live logically implied the right to die.

But this argument moves prematurely from form to substance, from the verbal formulae through which we give expression to our feelings, to those feelings themselves. Of course, taken in themselves and in the abstract, the religious symbols through which we express the respect that the human person inspires in us are not adequate to reality, and this is easy to prove; but it does not follow that this respect itself is unjustified. The fact that it plays a preponderant role in our legal system and in our morality should, on the contrary, warn us against such an interpretation. So instead of fixing on the letter of this idea, let us examine it in itself and see how it arose; and we shall see that, while the common formulation is crude, this does not mean that it has no objective value.

Indeed, the sort of transcendence that we give to the human person is not a characteristic peculiar to this. It is found elsewhere. It is simply the mark left by all collective feelings of some intensity on the objects to which they relate. Precisely because they emanate from the collectivity, the goals towards which they direct our activities can only be collective ones. Society has needs that are not the same as our own. The actions that they inspire are not therefore in tune with our individual inclinations: their aim is not our personal interest, but rather consists in sacrifices and privations. When I fast, mortifying my flesh to please the Divinity or when, out of respect for a tradition the meanings and implications of which I usually do not know, I cause myself some discomfort, when I pay my taxes, and when I devote my efforts or even my life to the State, I give up some part of myself; and, from the resistance that our egoism sets up against these acts of self-denial, we can clearly see that they are demanded of us by a power to which we are subject. Even when we happily give way to its demands, we are aware that our conduct is governed by a feeling of deference towards something larger than ourselves. However spontaneously we obey the voice that dictates this sacrifice to us, we feel that it is speaking to us in imperative tones that are not those of instinct. This is why, although it is to be hard inside our consciences, it would be contradictory for us to think of it as our own. But we alienate it, as we do our sensations; we project it outside and refer it to a being which we conceive of as exterior and superior to us, since it orders us and we obey its injunctions. Of course, everything that comes to us from the same source partakes of the same character. This is why we have been driven to imagine a higher world than this one and to people it with realities of a different nature.

Such is the origin of all those ideas of transcendence that are at the base of religions and moralities: moral obligation cannot be explained otherwise. Of course, the concrete form with which we usually endow these ideas is scientifically valueless. Whether we give them a foundation in a personal being of a special nature or in some abstract force which we vaguely hypostasize under the name of moral ideal, these are always metaphorical representations that do not adequately express the facts. But the *processus* that they symbolize is none the less real. It remains true that in all these cases we are incited to act by an authority greater than ourselves, namely society, and that the ends to which it thus commits us enjoy real moral supremacy. If this is the case, all the objections that might be made to the usual concepts through which men tried to represent this felt supremacy could not diminish its reality. This criticism is superficial and does not touch on the fundamentals. If one could establish that the worship of the human person is one of the goals that modern societies do and must pursue, then all the moral rules that derive from this principle will automatically be justified, whatever the value of the method by which it is usually justified. If the reasons that satisfy the common man may be criticized, they have only to be translated into another form of speech for them to acquire all their force.

Indeed, not only is this goal one that modern societies pursue, but it is a law of history that peoples tend increasingly to relinquish all other goals. At the start, society is all, the individual nothing. Consequently, the most intense social feelings are those that attach the individual to the collective: the latter is its own end. Man is only considered an instrument in its hands; from it, he appears to derive all his rights and he has no prerogative against it, because there is no superior power. But, little by little, things change. As societies become larger and denser, they become more complex: there is division of labour and individual differences increase, and the time comes when there will soon be nothing in common between all the members of the same human group except that they are all human. In such conditions, it is inevitable that the collective sensibility should attach itself with all its strength to this sole object remaining for it and that it should, for this reason alone, attach an incomparable value to it. Since the human person is the only thing that touches all hearts and since its glorification is the only end that can be collectively pursued, it is bound to acquire exceptional importance for everyone. In this way it rises above all human aims and acquires a religious character.

This cult of man is thus something quite different from the egoistic individualism which we spoke of earlier and which leads to suicide. Far from detaching individuals from society and from every goal beyond themselves, it unites them in a single thought and makes them servants of a single task. The man who is thus offered for collective love and respect is not the feeling, empirical individual who is each one of us; it is mankind in general, idealized humanity, as each people imagines it at every moment in its history. No one of us embodies it entirely, though none of us is entirely a stranger to it. So it is a matter not of concentrating each particular subject on himself and his own interests, but of subordinating him to the general interests of the human race. Such a goal takes him out of himself; impersonal and disinterested, it soars above all individual personalities and, like any ideal, it can only be conceived as superior to reality and dominating it. It even dominates societies, since it is the goal to which all social activity is pegged. This is why these societies no longer have the power to dispose of it freely. They recognize that they, too, take their *raison d'être* from it, that they depend on it and have lost the right to fail it – even less to authorize men to do so themselves. Our dignity as moral beings is no longer the affair of the city-state, yet it has not as a result become anything else and we have not acquired the fight to dispose of it as we wish. Whence should we derive it, indeed, if society itself, this being superior to us, does not possess it?

In such circumstances, it is necessary for suicide to be classified among immoral acts, because it rejects, in its core principle, this religion of humanity. It is said that the man who kills himself injures only himself and that society has no cause to intervene, by virtue of the old axiom: *Volenti non fit injuria*. This is not so. Society is harmed, because the feeling on which its most respected moral principles rest today, and which serves as an almost unique link between its members, is violated and it would be upset if this violation could be committed quite freely. How could it maintain the slightest authority if, when it is offended, the moral conscience did not protest? As soon as the human being is and must be considered as a sacred thing which neither the individual nor the group can dispose of freely, any attack on it must be forbidden. It is irrelevant that the guilty party and the victim are one and the same: the social ill that results from the act does not go away just because the author of it also suffers. If in ourselves and in general we are repelled by the fact of the violent destruction of a man's life and see it as a sacrilege, then we cannot tolerate it in any circumstances. A collective sentiment that relaxed to that extent would soon be powerless.

However, this does not mean that we must return to the savage penalties inflicted on suicides in previous centuries. These were instituted at a time when, under the influence of passing circumstances, the whole repressive system was imposed with excessive severity. But the principle must be upheld, namely that the homicide of oneself should meet with disapproval. It remains to be seen how this disapproval should manifest itself externally. Are moral sanctions enough, or do we need juridical ones; and if so, which? This is a matter of practical policy that will be discussed in the following chapter.

Notes

1. Durkheim's chair was not renamed as 'Science of Education and Sociology' until 1913.
2. First advanced by the French psychiatrist B.A. Morel (1857), the biologically reductionist, pessimistic doctrine of degeneration was widely embraced in Europe and North America in the last third of the nineteenth century. For explorations of its influence in nineteenth-century France, see Dowbiggin (1991) and Nye (1984).

CHAPTER 7

The Moral Foundations of Modern Law: Individualism

Introduction

In this chapter we reproduce Durkheim's remarkable article, 'Individualism and the Intellectuals', written at the height of the Dreyfus Affair. This historic political scandal which divided France into two bitterly opposed camps was a moral crisis that posed, Durkheim thought, a grave issue of principle. In this powerful and ingenious polemic, which was for him a rare intervention in current politics, Durkheim provides a sociological analysis of the issues at stake. Captain Alfred Dreyfus, a young Jewish army officer, had been falsely accused of betraying military secrets to the Germans and sentenced to life imprisonment. His accuser was subsequently acquitted of lying by a military court and Dreyfus's conviction was upheld by the army on the basis of fabricated documents. At this point the writer Emile Zola published his open letter 'J'accuse' in a Paris newspaper, denouncing the injustice of the army's actions. He was soon joined in his protest by other prominent French intellectuals, including Henri Poincaré, Anatole France and Georges Clemenceau, who spoke out in defence of the Dreyfusard cause. Durkheim was from the beginning among their number and the essay we reprint here was widely read and influential at the time. Eventually, with the victory of the Dreyfusard cause and the exoneration and reinstatement of Dreyfus, laïcité, the French version of secularism, became the acknowledged official ideology of the French republic.

The very term 'intellectual' came to signify those who supported Dreyfus. They incensed the anti-Dreyfusards who saw them as enemies of social order: as threatening the authority of the Catholic Church and the army and thus the very fabric of society. Catholic polemicists attacked academics who 'who spend their lives teaching error and in corrupting souls and, in due course, society as a whole'. Maurice Barrès wrote that the great culprits, who should be punished, are the 'intellectuals', the 'anarchists of the lecture-platform', the 'metaphysicians of sociology'. A

150

'band of arrogant madmen. Men who take a criminal self-satisfaction in their intelligence, who treat our generals as idiots, our social institutions as absurd and our traditions as unhealthy...' Indeed, Barrès defined 'an intellectual' as 'an individual who persuades himself that society must be based on logic and who fails to recognize that it rests in fact on necessities that are anterior and perhaps foreign to the reason of the individual'. (Interestingly, by this definition, given the argument of 'Individualism and the Intellectuals' and Durkheim's theory of religion, with its focus on collective beliefs and sentiments, ritual and symbolism, Durkheim would not qualify as an intellectual.)

In similar vein, Ferdinand Brunetière, literary historian and critic and one of the 'immortals' of the strongly anti-Dreyfusard Académie Française, published an article vehemently defending the army and the social order. Ironically, he contended, those responsible for anti-semitism were in part scientists, because they had postulated the inequality of races; and in part the Jews themselves, because of their 'domination' in politics, law, education and administration. As for the army, 'it has made us what we are': in its blood, 'national unity has been formed, cemented and consolidated'. He saw this unity as threatened by 'individualism', which led to 'anarchy', and he poured scorn on the various 'intellectuals' who promoted it by presuming to doubt the justice of Dreyfus's trial. They were persons who, in virtue of some specialized knowledge, were taken to have special authority in all matters, including 'the most delicate questions concerning human morality, the life of nations and the interests of society'. Such an assumption was unfounded and dangerous, and the danger was only increased by their appeal to science to support their merely individual opinions. Grand phrases like 'the scientific method, aristocracy of intelligence, respect for truth' only served to conceal the pretensions of 'individualism', which was the great sickness of the present time.

Each of us has confidence only in himself, sets himself up as the sovereign judge of everything and does not even allow his opinion to be discussed. Don't tell this biologist that human affairs are not amenable to his scientific 'methods'; he will laugh at you! Don't confront this palaeographer with the judgment of three court-martials; he knows what the justice of men is, and, anyway, is he not the director of the Ecole de Chartres? And this man, the first person in the world to scan the verses of Plautus, how can you expect him to bend his 'logic' at the word of an army general? One does not spend one's life in studies of that importance in order to think 'like everyone else'; and the true intellectual could not behave just like anyone. He is Nietzsche's 'superman' or 'the enemy of laws' who was not made for laws but rather to rise above them; and we others, mediocre as we are, have only to admire and be grateful! I am merely pointing out that when intellectualism and individualism reach this degree of self-infatuation, one must expect them to be or become nothing other than anarchy; – perhaps we are not yet at this point, but we are rapidly approaching it.).

Durkheim's riposte to these claims that it was the intellectuals, with their doctrine of individualism, who were out of step with society is sharp and deadly.

Durkheim, 'Individualism and the Intellectuals' in *Revue Bleue*

The question which for the last six months has so grievously divided the country is in the process of being transformed; having begun as a simple question of fact, it has become more and more general in scope. The recent intervention of a well-known *littérateur*[1] has contributed greatly to this development. It seems to have been felt that the time had arrived to renew with a great fanfare a controversy that was dying out through repetition. That is why, instead of returning yet again to a discussion of the facts, that writer wanted, in one leap, to rise immediately to the level of principles. Thus it is the state of mind of the 'intellectuals',[2] the fundamental ideas to which they adhere, and no longer the detail of their arguments that is what has been attacked. If they obstinately refuse 'to bend their logic at the word of an army general', that is, evidently, because they have arrogated to themselves the right to judge the question; because they are putting their own reason above authority, and because the rights of the individual appear to them to be imprescriptible. It is, therefore, their individualism which has brought about their dissension. But in that case, it has been said, if one wants to restore peace to men's minds and prevent the return of similar discords, it is this individualism which must be directly confronted. This inexhaustible source of domestic divisions must be silenced once and for all. And a veritable crusade has begun, directed against this public scourge, 'this great sickness of the present time'.

We fully agree to conducting the debate in these terms. We too believe that the controversies of yesterday were only superficial expressions of a deeper disagreement; and that men's minds have been divided much more over a question of principle than over a question of fact. Let us therefore leave on one side the minutely detailed arguments which have been exchanged from side to side; let us forget the Affair itself and the melancholy scenes we have witnessed. The problem confronting us goes infinitely beyond the current events and must be disengaged from them.

I

There is a preliminary ambiguity which must be cleared up first of all. In order to facilitate the condemnation of individualism, it has been confused with the narrow utilitarianism and utilitarian egoism of Spencer and the economists. This is to take the easy way out. It is not hard, in effect, to denounce as an ideal without grandeur that narrow commercialism which reduces society to nothing more than a vast apparatus of production and exchange, and it is only too clear that all social life would be impossible if there did not exist interests superior to the interests of individuals. Nothing is more just than that such doctrines should be treated as anarchic, and with this attitude we are in full agreement. But what is inadmissible is that this individualism should be presented as the only one that there is or even that there could be. Quite the contrary: it is becoming more and more rare and exceptional. The practical philosophy of Spencer is of such moral poverty that it now has scarcely any supporters. As for the economists, even if they once allowed themselves to be seduced by the simplicity of this theory, they have for a long time now felt the need to temper the rigour of their primitive orthodoxy and to open their minds to more generous sentiments. M. de Molinari is almost alone, in France, in remaining intractable and I am not aware that he has exercised a great influence on the ideas of our time. In truth, if individualism had no other representatives, it would be quite pointless to move heaven and earth in this way to combat an enemy that is in the process of quietly dying a natural death.

However, there exists another individualism over which it is less easy to triumph. It has been upheld for a century by the great majority of thinkers: it is the individualism of Kant and Rousseau, that of the *spiritualistes*, that which the Declaration of the Rights of Man sought, more or less successfully, to translate into formulae, that which is currently taught in our schools and which has become the basis of our moral catechism. It is true that it has been thought possible to attack this individualism under cover of the first type, but that differs from it fundamentally and the criticisms which apply to the one could not be appropriate to the other. So far is it from making personal interest the object of human conduct, that it sees in all personal motives the very source of evil. According to Kant, I am only certain of acting well if the motives that influence me relate, not to the particular circumstances in which I am placed, but to my quality as a man *in abstracto*. Conversely, my action is wicked when it cannot be justified logically except by reference to the situation I happen to be in and my social condition, my class or caste interests, my passions, etc. That is why immoral conduct is to be recognized by the sign that it is closely linked to the individuality of the agent and cannot be universalized without manifest absurdity. Similarly, if, according to Rousseau, the general will, which is the basis of the social contract, is infallible, if it is the authentic expression of perfect justice, this is because it is a resultant of all the particular wills; consequently it constitutes a kind of impersonal average from which all individual considerations have been eliminated, since, being divergent and even antagonistic to one another, they are neutralized and cancel each other out.[3] Thus, for both these thinkers, the only ways of acting that are moral are those which are fitting for all men equally, that is to say, which are implied in the notion of man in general.

This is far indeed from that apotheosis of comfort and private interest, that egoistic cult of the self for which utilitarian individualism has justly been reproached. Quite the contrary: according to these moralists, duty consists in averting our attention from what concerns us personally, from all that relates to our empirical individuality, so as uniquely to seek that which our human condition demands, that which we hold in common with all our fellow humans. This ideal goes so far beyond the limit of utilitarian ends that it appears to those who aspire to it as marked with a religious character. The human person, whose definition serves as the touchstone according to which good must be distinguished from evil, is considered as sacred, in what one might call the ritual sense of the word. It has something of that transcendental majesty which the churches of all times have given to their Gods. It is conceived as being invested with that mysterious property which creates an empty space around holy objects, which keeps them away from profane contacts and which draws them away from ordinary life. And it is exactly this feature that induces the respect of which it is the object. Whoever makes an attempt on a man's life, on a man's liberty, on a man's honour inspires us with a feeling of horror, in every way analogous to that which the believer experiences when he sees his idol profaned. Such a morality is therefore not simply a hygienic discipline or a wise principle of economy. It is a religion of which man is at once both believer and God. But this religion is individualistic, since it has man as its object, and since man is, by definition, an individual. Indeed there is no system whose individualism is more uncompromising. Nowhere are the rights of man affirmed more energetically, since the individual is here placed on the level of sacrosanct objects; nowhere is he more jealously protected from external encroachments, whatever their source. The doctrine of utility can easily accept all kinds of compromises, without denying its fundamental axiom: it can allow that individual liberties should be suspended whenever the interest of the greatest number requires this sacrifice. But there is no possible compromise with a principle which is thus put above and beyond all temporal interests. There is no reason of State which can excuse an outrage against the person when the rights of the person are placed above the State. If, therefore, individualism by itself is a ferment of moral dissolution, one must expect to see its anti-social essence as lying here.

One can now see how grave this question is. For the liberalism of the eighteenth century which is, after all, what is basically at issue, is not simply an armchair theory, a philosophical construction. It has entered into the facts, it has penetrated our institutions and our customs, it has become part of our whole life, and, if we really must rid ourselves of it, it is our entire moral organization that must be rebuilt at the same time.

II

Now, it is a remarkable fact that all these theorists of individualism are no less sensitive to the rights of the collectivity than they are to those of the individual. No one has insisted more emphatically than Kant on the supra-individual character of morality and law. He sees them rather as a set of imperatives that men must obey because they are obligatory, without having to discuss them; and if he has sometimes been reproached for having carried the autonomy of reason to excess, it could equally be said, with some truth, that he based his ethics on an act of unreasoning faith and submission. Besides, doctrines are judged above all by their products, that is to say by the spirit of the doctrines that they engender. Now Kantianism led to the ethics of Fichte, which was already thoroughly imbued with socialism, and to the philosophy of Hegel whose disciple was Marx. As for Rousseau, one knows how his individualism is complemented by an authoritarian conception of society. Following him, the men of the Revolution, in promulgating the famous Declaration of Rights, made France one, indivisible, centralized, and perhaps one should even see the revolutionary achievement as being above all a great movement of national concentration. Finally, the chief reason for which the *spiritualistes* have always fought against utilitarian morality is that it seemed to them to be incompatible with social necessities.

Perhaps it will be said that this eclecticism is self-contradictory? Certainly, we do not propose to defend the way in which these different thinkers have set about combining these two aspects in the construction of their systems. If, with Rousseau, one begins by seeing the individual as a sort of absolute who can and must be sufficient unto himself, it is obviously difficult then to explain how civil society could be established. But here it is a question of ascertaining, not whether such and such a moralist has succeeded in showing how these two tendencies may be reconciled, but rather whether they are in principle reconcilable or not. The reasons that have been given for establishing their complementarity may be worthless, and yet that complementarity may be real. The very fact that they are generally to be found together in the same thinkers offers at least a presumption that they are contemporaneous with one another; whence it follows that they must depend on a single social condition of which they are probably only different aspects.

And, in effect, once one has ceased to confuse individualism with its opposite, that is to say, with utilitarianism, all these apparent contradictions vanish as if by magic. This religion of humanity has all that is required to speak to its believers in a tone that is no less imperative than the religions it replaces. Far from confining itself to indulging our instincts, it offers us an ideal which infinitely surpasses nature; for we do not naturally have that wise and pure reason which, dissociated from all personal

motives, would make laws in the abstract concerning its own conduct.
Doubtless, if the dignity of the individual derived from his individual qualities, from those particular characteristics which distinguish him from
others, one might fear that he would become enclosed in a sort of moral
egoism that would render all social cohesion impossible. But in reality he
receives this dignity from a higher source, one which he shares with all
humans. If he has the right to this religious respect, it is because he has in
him something of humanity. It is humanity that is sacred and worthy of
respect. And this is not his exclusive possession. It is distributed among all
his fellows, and in consequence he cannot take it as a goal for his conduct
without being obliged to go beyond himself and turn towards others. The
cult of which he is at once both object and follower does not address itself
to the particular being that constitutes himself and carries his name, but to
the human person, wherever it is to be found, and in whatever form it is
incarnated. Impersonal and anonymous, such an end soars far above all
particular consciences and can thus serve as a rallying-point for them. The
fact that it is not remote from us (for the very reason that it is human) does
not prevent it from dominating us.

Now all that societies require in order to hold together is that their
members fix their eyes on the same end and come together in a single faith;
but it is not at all necessary that the object of this common faith be quite
unconnected with individual natures. In short, individualism thus understood is the glorification not of the self, but of the individual in general. Its
motive force is not egoism but sympathy for all that is human, a wider pity
for all sufferings, for all human miseries, a more ardent desire to combat
and alleviate them, a greater thirst for justice. Is this not the way to achieve
a community of all men of good will? Doubtless it can happen that individualism is practised in quite a different spirit. Certain people use it for
their own personal ends, as a means of disguising their egoism and escaping more easily from their duties towards society. But this abusive exploitation of individualism proves nothing against it, just as the utilitarian
fictions of religious hypocrites prove nothing against religion.

But I now immediately come to the great objection. This cult of man has
for its first dogma the autonomy of reason and for its first rite freedom of
inquiry. Now, it will be said, if all opinions are free, by what miracle will
they then be harmonious? If they are formed without knowledge of one
another and without having to take account of one another, how can they
fail to be incoherent? Intellectual and moral anarchy would then be the
inevitable consequence of liberalism. Such is the argument, always being
refuted and always reappearing, which the perennial enemies of reason
take up periodically, with a perseverance that nothing can discourage, each
time a passing weariness of the human spirit puts it more at their mercy.
Certainly, it is true that individualism does not go without a certain intellectualism; for liberty of thought is the first of all liberties. But why has it

been seen to have as a consequence this absurd self-infatuation which would confine each within his own desires and would create a gap between men's minds? What it demands is the right for each individual to know those things that he may legitimately know. It does not sanction unlimited right to incompetence. Concerning a question on which I cannot pronounce with expert knowledge, my intellectual independence suffers no loss if I follow a more competent opinion. The collaboration of scientists is only possible thanks to this mutual deference. Each science continuously borrows from its neighbours' propositions which it accepts without verifying them. The only thing is that my intellect requires reasons for bowing to the authority of others. Respect for authority is in no way incompatible with rationalism provided that authority be rationally based.

This is why, when one seeks to summon certain men to rally to a sentiment that they do not share, it is not sufficient, in order to convince them, to remind them of that commonplace of banal rhetoric, that society is not possible without mutual sacrifices and without a certain spirit of subordination. It is still necessary to justify *in this particular case* the submission one asks of them, by showing them their incompetence. When, on the other hand, it is a matter of one of those questions which pertain, by definition, to the common judgment of men, such an abdication is contrary to all reason and, in consequence, contrary to duty. For, in order to know whether a court of justice can be allowed to condemn an accused man without having heard his defence, there is no need for any special expertise. It is a problem of practical morality concerning which every man of good sense is competent and about which no one ought to be indifferent. If, therefore, in these recent times, a certain number of artists, but above all of scholars, have believed that they ought to refuse to assent to a judgment whose legality appeared to them to be suspect, it is not because, as chemists or philologists, philosophers or historians, they attribute to themselves any special privileges, or any exclusive right of exercising control over the case in question. It is rather that, being men, they seek to exercise their entire right as men and to keep before them a matter which concerns reason alone. It is true that they have shown themselves more jealous of this right than the rest of society; but that is simply because, as a result of their professional activities, they have it nearer to heart. Accustomed by the practice of scientific method to reserve judgment when they are not fully aware of the facts, it is natural that they give in less readily to the enthusiasms of the crowd and to the prestige of authority.

III

Not only is individualism distinct from anarchy; but it is henceforth the only system of beliefs that can ensure the moral unity of the country.

One often hears it said today that only a religion can bring about this harmony. This proposition, which modern prophets feel it necessary to utter in a mystical tone of voice, is really no more than a simple truism on which everyone can agree. For we know today that a religion does not necessarily imply symbols and rites in the full sense, or temples and priests. All this external apparatus is merely its superficial aspect. Essentially, it is nothing other than a system of collective beliefs and practices that have a special authority. Once a goal is pursued by a whole people, it acquires, as a result of this unanimous adherence, a sort of moral supremacy which raises it far above private goals and thereby gives it a religious character. On the other hand, it is clear that a society cannot hold together unless there exists among its members a certain intellectual and moral community. However, having recalled this sociological truism, one has not advanced very far. For if it is true that religion is, in a sense, indispensable, it is no less certain that religions change, that yesterday's religion could not be that of tomorrow. Thus, what we need to know is what the religion of today must be.

Now, all the evidence points to the conclusion that the only possible candidate is precisely this religion of humanity whose rational expression is the individualist morality. To what, after all, should collective sentiments be directed in future? As societies become more voluminous and spread over vaster territories, their traditions and practices, in order to adapt to the diversity of situations and constantly changing circumstances, are compelled to maintain a state of plasticity and instability which no longer offers adequate resistance to individual variations. These latter, being less well contained, develop more freely and multiply in number; that is, everyone increasingly follows his own path. At the same time, as a consequence of a more advanced division of labour, each mind finds itself directed towards a different point of the horizon, reflects a different aspect of the world and, as a result, the contents of men's minds differ from one subject to another. One is thus gradually proceeding towards a state of affairs, now almost attained, in which the members of a single social group will no longer have anything in common other than their humanity, that is, the characteristics which constitute the human person in general. This idea of the human person, given different emphases in accordance with the diversity of national temperaments, is therefore the sole idea that survives, immutable and impersonal, above the changing tides of particular opinions; and the sentiments which it awakens are the only ones to be found in almost all hearts. The communion of minds can no longer form around particular rites and prejudices, since rites and prejudices have been swept away in the natural course of things. In consequence, there remains nothing that men may love and honour in common, apart from man himself. This is why man has become a god for man, and it is why he can no longer turn to other gods without being untrue to himself. And just as each of us embodies something of humanity, so each individual mind has within it something of the divine, and thereby finds itself marked by a characteristic which renders it sacred and inviolable to others. The whole of individualism lies here. That is what makes it into the doctrine that is currently necessary. For, should we wish to hold back its progress, we would have to prevent men from becoming increasingly differentiated from one another, reduce their personalities to a single level, bring them back to the old conformism of former times and arrest, in consequence, the tendency of societies to become ever more extended and centralized, and stem the unceasing growth of the division of labour. Such an undertaking, whether desirable or not, infinitely surpasses all human powers.

What, in any case, are we offered in place of this individualism that is so disparaged? The merits of Christian morality are extolled to us and we are subtly invited to rally to its support. But are those who take this position unaware that the originality of Christianity has consisted precisely in a remarkable development of the individualist spirit? While the religion of the Ancient City was entirely made up of material practices from which the spiritual element was absent, Christianity expressed in an inward faith, in the personal conviction of the individual, the essential condition of piety. It was the first to teach that the moral value of actions must be measured in accordance with intention, which is essentially intimate, escapes all external judgments and which only the agent can competently judge. The very centre of the moral life was thus transferred from outside to within and the individual was set up as the sovereign judge of his own conduct having no other accounts to render than those to himself and to his God. Finally, in completing the definitive separation of the spiritual and the temporal, in abandoning the world to the disputes of men, Christ at the same time opened the way for science and freedom of thought. In this way one can explain the rapid progress made by scientific thought from the date that Christian societies were established. Let no one therefore denounce individualism as the enemy that must be opposed at all costs! One only opposes it so as to return to it, so impossible is it to escape. Whatever alternative is offered turns out to be a form of it. The whole question, however, is to know how much of it is appropriate, and whether some advantage is to be gained by disguising it by means of symbols. Now, if individualism is as dangerous as people say, it is hard to see how it could become inoffensive or salutary, by the mere fact of having its true nature hidden with the aid of metaphors. And, on the other hand, if that restricted individualism which constitutes Christianity was necessary eighteen centuries ago, it seems probable that a more developed individualism should be indispensable today; for things have changed in the interval. It is thus a singular error to present individualist morality as antagonistic to Christian morality; quite the contrary, it is derived from it. By adhering to the former, we do not disown our past; we merely continue it.

We are now in a better position to understand the reason why certain people believe that they must offer an unyielding resistance to all that seems to them to threaten the individualist faith. If every attack on the rights of an individual revolts them, this is not solely because of sympathy for the victim. Nor is it because they fear that they themselves will suffer similar acts of injustice. Rather it is that such outrages cannot rest unpunished without putting national existence in jeopardy. It is indeed impossible that they should be freely allowed to occur without weakening the sentiments that they violate; and as these sentiments are all that we still have in common, they cannot be weakened without disturbing the cohesion of society. A religion which tolerates acts of sacrilege abdicates any sway over men's minds. The religion of the individual can therefore allow itself to be flouted without resistance, only on penalty of ruining its credit; since it is the sole link which binds us one to another, such a weakening cannot take place without the onset of social dissolution. Thus the individualist, who defends the rights of the individual, defends at the same time the vital interests of society; for he is preventing the criminal impoverishment of that final reserve of collective ideas and sentiments that constitutes the very soul of the nation. He renders his country the same service that the ancient Roman rendered his city when he defended traditional rites against reckless innovators. And if there is one country among all others in which the individualist cause is truly national, it is our own; for there is no other whose fate has been so closely bound up with the fate of these ideas. We gave the most recent expression to it, and it is from us that other people have received it. That is why we have hitherto been held to be its most authoritative exponents. We cannot therefore renounce it today, without renouncing ourselves, without diminishing ourselves in the eyes of the world, without committing real moral suicide. Lately it has been asked whether it would not perhaps be convenient for us to agree to a temporary eclipse of these principles, so as not to disturb the functioning of a system of public administration which everyone, anyway, recognizes to be indispensable to the security of the state. We do not know if the antinomy really presents itself in this acute form; but, in any case, if a choice really must be made between these two evils, we would choose the worst of them were we to sacrifice what has hitherto been our historical *raison d'etre*. A public institution, however important it may be, is only an instrument, a means that relates to an end. What is the point of so carefully preserving the means if one abandons the end? And what a deplorable calculation to make – to renounce, in order to live, all that constitutes the worth and dignity of living,

Et propter vitam vivendi perdere causas!

IV

In truth, it is to be feared that this campaign has been mounted with a certain lack of seriousness. A verbal similarity has made it possible to believe that *individualism* necessarily resulted from *individual,* and thus egoistic, sentiments. In reality, the religion of the individual is a social institution like all known religions. It is society which assigns us this ideal as the sole common end which is today capable of providing a focus for men's wills. To remove this ideal, without putting any other in its place, is therefore to plunge us into that very moral anarchy which it is sought to combat.[4]

All the same, we should not consider as perfect and definitive the formula with which the eighteenth century gave expression to individualism, a formula which we have made the mistake of preserving in an almost unchanged form. Although it was adequate a century ago, it is now in need of being enlarged and completed. It presented individualism only in its most negative aspect. Our fathers were concerned exclusively with freeing the individual from the political fetters which hampered his development. Freedom of thought, freedom to write, and freedom to vote were thus placed by them among the primary values that it was necessary to achieve, and this emancipation was certainly the necessary condition for all subsequent progress. However, carried away by the enthusiasm of the struggle, solely concerned with the objective they pursued, they ended by no longer seeing beyond it, and by converting into a sort of ultimate goal what was merely the next stage in their efforts. Now, political liberty is a means, not an end. It is worth no more than the manner in which it is put to use. If it does not serve something that exists beyond it, it is not merely useless: it becomes dangerous. If those who handle this weapon do not know how to use it in fruitful battles, they will not be slow in turning it against themselves.

It is precisely for this reason that it has fallen today into a certain discredit. The men of my generation recall how great was our enthusiasm when, twenty years ago, we finally succeeded in toppling the last barriers which we impatiently confronted. But alas! disenchantment came quickly; for we soon had to admit that no one knew what to do with this liberty that had been so laboriously achieved. Those to whom we owed it only made use of it in internecine strife. And it was from that moment that one felt the growth in the country of this current of gloom and despondency, which became stronger with each day that passed, the ultimate result of which must inevitably be to break the spirit of those least able to resist. Thus, we can no longer subscribe to this negative ideal. It is necessary to go beyond what has been achieved, if only to preserve it. Indeed, if we do not learn to put to use the means of action that we have in our hands, it is inevitable that they will become less effective. Let us therefore use our liberties in order to discover what must be done and with the aim of doing it. Let us use them in order to alleviate the functioning of the social machine, still so harsh to individuals, in order to put at their disposal all possible means for developing their faculties unhindered, in order, finally, to work towards making a reality of the famous precept: to each according to his works! Let us recognize that, in general, liberty is a delicate instrument the use of which must be learnt, and let us teach this to our children; all moral education should be directed to this end. One can see that we will not be short of things to do. However, if it is certain that we will henceforth have to work out new objectives, beyond those which have been attained, it would be senseless to renounce the latter so as to pursue the former more easily; for necessary advances are only possible thanks to those already achieved. It is a matter of completing, extending, and organizing individualism, not of restricting it or struggling against it. It is a matter of using and not stifling rational faculties. They alone can help us emerge from our present difficulties; we do not see what else can do so. In any case, it is not by meditating on the *Politique tirée de l'Ecriture sainte* that we will ever find the means of organizing economic life and introducing more justice into contractual relations!

In these circumstances, does not our duty appear to be clearly marked out? All those who believe in the value, or even merely in the necessity, of the moral revolution accomplished a century ago, have the same interest: they must forget the differences which divide them and combine their efforts so as to hold positions already won. Once this crisis is surmounted, it will certainly be appropriate to recall the lessons of experience, so that we may avoid falling once more into that sterile inaction for which we are now paying; but that is the task of tomorrow. As for today, the urgent task, which must be put before all else, is that of saving our moral patrimony; once that is secure, we shall see that it is made to prosper. May the common danger we confront at least help us by shaking us out of our torpor and giving us again the taste for action! And already, indeed, one sees initiatives awakening within the country, men of good will seeking one another out. Let someone appear who can combine them and lead them into the struggle: perhaps victory will then not be long in coming. For what should, to a certain extent, reassure us is that our adversaries are only strong by virtue of our weakness. They have neither that deep faith nor those generous enthusiasms that sweep people irresistibly to great reactions as well as to great revolutions. Of course, we would not dream of doubting their sincerity; yet who can fail to notice the improvised quality of all that they believe? They are neither apostles who allow themselves to be overwhelmed by their anger or their enthusiasm, nor are they scholars who bring us the product of their research and their deliberations. They are literary men seduced by an interesting theme. It seems therefore impossible that these games of dilettantes should succeed in keeping hold for long of the masses, providing that we know how to act. Moreover, what a humiliation it would be if, having no stronger opponents than these, reason were to end by being defeated, even if only for a time.

Notes

1. See the article by M. Brunetière: 'Après le procès', in *Revue des Deux Mondes* of 15 March 1898.
2. Let us note in passing that this word, which is most appropriate, does not properly have the pejorative meaning that has so maliciously been attributed to it. The intellectual is not a person who has a monopoly of understanding (intelligence); there are no social functions where understanding is unnecessary. But there are those in which it is at once both the means and the end, both the instrument and the goal. Here understanding is used to extend understanding, that is to say, to enrich it with knowledge, ideas, and new experiences. It is thus the basis of these professions (the arts and the sciences) and it is in order to express this peculiarity that it has come to be natural to call those who practise them intellectuals.
3. See *Contrat social*, vol. II, Chap. III.
4. This is how it is possible, without contradiction, to be an individualist while asserting that the individual is a product of society, rather than its cause. The reason is that individualism itself is a social product, like all moralities and all religions. The individual receives from society even the moral beliefs which deify him. This is what Kant and Rousseau did not understand. They wished to deduce their individualist ethics not from society, but from the notion of the isolated individual. Such an enterprise was impossible, and from it resulted the logical contradictions of their systems.

CHAPTER 8

The Origins of Law

Introduction

One often overlooked medium through which Durkheim and the Durkheimians sought to construct the boundaries of the new discipline of sociology, to organize it into sub-fields, and to contribute to a sense of an emerging collective enterprise that was in the process of developing a cumulative science, was through book reviews, a strategy we mentioned briefly in the introduction to Chapter 1. Writing to his fellow-editor and disciple Célestin Bouglé in June of 1897 as they were planning the first volume of the Année sociologique, *Durkheim spoke of the need to 'reject the current methods of criticism, which are too concerned with seeing the author behind the work, and with ranking talents instead of noting results and their importance. In matters of science, shouldn't the ranking of men be a simple consequence of ranking what one owes them, whether it be insights or information?' (Durkheim to Bouglé, 20 June 1897, cited in Lukes 1972: 290).*

The following year, in the opening pages of his new journal, Durkheim expounded at some length about their decision to allocate a substantial portion of the Année *to book reviews, and the seriousness with which he and his colleagues planned to approach this task. 'Our role as critics,' he explained, 'must be to extract from the works we study the objective residue, that is, the suggestive facts and the fruitful insights – whether they be intrinsic value or because of the discussions they evoke' (cited in Lukes 1972: 290). At this early stage in the development of sociology, surveying the universe of potentially useful publications required an ecumenical but disciplined approach. Since 'many [of the works with which we have to deal] are not explicitly sociological, we could be satisfied with giving their contents, with merely expounding, as it were, the materials they contain; as far as possible, we had to submit them to a preliminary elaboration which would indicate to the reader what information contained in them is useful to the sociologist' (Durkheim 1898: vi–vii).*

This reviewing strategy was one Durkheim consistently followed wherever his critical essays appeared. In the pages of the Année, *however, it was supplemented by a further set of editorial interventions. A consistent effort was made to ensure that 'all analyses of works which refer to the same question have been grouped together in such a way that they complement and illuminate each other. By themselves, these groupings already constitute comparisons which may be useful' (Durkheim 1899: vii). Nor were these subdivisions static, a priori groupings. On the contrary, as his and his colleagues' conception of the field evolved and became more complex, so the categories under which the reviews were grouped were refined and extended. Reviewing was for Durkheim and the Durkheimians a vital and creative part of their attempt to create a distinctive sociological science. As Bouglé put it, the aim was 'to develop lasting frameworks for future analyses and syntheses, which follow the essential relations between social phenomena, the truths accumulated by the historical sciences, and thus to organize the latter, no longer from the outside, imposing on them the conclusions of detached speculations, but from within by assimilating their conquests (Bouglé 1907: 166). As an index of the significance the Durkheimians attached to law and morality, however, two of the six sections of the first volume of the* Année *were devoted to this general area of sociology, the third section, on the sociology of morality and law (subdivided into eight subsections); and the fourth section on the sociology of crime.[1]*

Both reviews reprinted in this chapter demonstrate how Durkheim sought to put these principles into action. The first, which antedates the appearance of the Année sociologique *by five years, is a review of Gaston Richard's 'Essay on the Origin of the Idea of Law' that appeared in the pages of the* Revue philosophique. *Richard was at this stage of his career a convinced Durkheimian, and he would contribute to each of the first ten volumes of the* Année *before breaking decisively with Durkheim around 1908, and (ironically) launching fierce critiques of Durkheim's theory of morality and his social realism. In the early 1890s, however, Richard and Durkheim had very similar perspectives on the sociology of law, and on the competing perspectives adopted by philosophers. Richard's critiques of utilitarian and metaphysical approaches to understanding law, and his search for its social roots naturally draw approving comments from Durkheim, as does his insistence on the primacy, in a historical sense, of the criminal law, with the law of contract being derivative and coming later. What draws Durkheim's criticism is an over-reliance on dialectical argument, and Richard's emphasis on the genesis of the* idea *of law, rather than the genesis of the law, which for Durkheim gets things precisely backwards: The idea of the law 'results from the law. It dimly reflects the juridical life itself, it does not create it; in just the same way as our idea of the world is only a reflection of the world in which we live.'*

The second part of this chapter contains one of the many reviews Durkheim contributed to the Année, *in this instance from the eighth volume. It is an example of Durkheim reviewing an article from a neigh-bouring discipline, on this occasion by a German author publishing in a journal of comparative law. The topic of Kulischer's paper is one Durkheim considers of great significance, the origins of punishment and penal law, and we can see here how he sifts through the work of a legal scholar, endorsing portions of his argument, while raising doubts about others.*

Durkheim's review of Richard, 'Essay on the Origin of the Idea of Law' in *Revue Philosophique*

It is still quite generally believed in France that there are and can only be two sorts of ethics, between which the moralist is compelled to choose; that the only means of escaping utilitarianism is to resort to the apriorism of the metaphysicians. It seems that from the moment that one employs the observational method, one is necessarily condemned to denying the reality of duty and that of disinterestedness, that is, to making pure illusions of both of them. The book under review is above all else a protest against this preconception; it is a vigorous effort to open a new pathway in legal ethics and legal philosophy and it is this which makes for the novelty and interest of the work. M. Richard, indeed, combats with the same fervour both the utilitarians' and the metaphysicians' doctrines; both seem to him equally incapable of explaining the law as a duty, and for the same reason. For these two hostile brethren are less far apart from each other than is ordinarily believed; both teach as a matter of fact an almost identical individualism. The utilitarian is an individualist since he makes self-interest the sole end of conduct; but the metaphysician is no less so, since his ethics consist in an apotheosis of the individual personality. Perhaps, it is true, one might reproach the author for passing too lightly over some great metaphysical doctrines, like Hegelianism, which if anything have erred by excess of the opposite sort. Even Kantianism, which M. Richard has more particularly in mind, partly escapes individualism, because it subjects the individual to a law which the individual did not make, to an objective rule, to an imperative and impersonal order. However, it is incontestable that this impersonal ideal is nothing else than the individual in abstract and idealized form. Now, following M. Richard, an individualistic doctrine could not then be the basis of law; for judicial practice cannot dispense with charity. The dogma of egoism, whether it be that of the utilitarians or that of the metaphysicians, deprives the notion of duty of all content; for duty above all consists of giving oneself, sacrificing oneself, resigning oneself. Consequently, by the same token, it is the ruination of law which can only be the logical and even physical condition of duty (p. xii).

What gave birth to the individualist error, was that empiricists and apriorists studied the idea of law in the abstract, detaching it from the circumstances which had determined its formation and development. They did not see that it was the act of living in society which led men to define their juridical relations, to fix 'what all may require from each and what each may expect from all'. In a word, the philosophy of law cannot be separated from its sociology. The problem as our author poses it may therefore be formulated in this way: What are the social influences which gave rise to the idea of the law and in terms of which it has evolved historically? Now, when the question is posed in these terms, one thing is immediately obvious: the idea of law is not a simple one. It is made up of elements, each of which must be studied in turn.

The first of these elements is the idea of arbitration. As a matter of fact, the first codified customs are only collections of arbitration awards; it is moreover easy to understand how the institution of arbitration must have developed very early on, as soon as societies came into being. In every individual *conscience* there exist two muted states of consciousness, susceptible, when the opportunity offers, of being transformed into clear ideas. 'One is the conception of social goals, i.e., of a mutual protection against the causes of destruction' (p. 4) whether they have a human or a material origin; the other is the sense of a committed struggle between the individual appetites of the very members of the group. These two propensities are opposed to one another. Consequently, if the first is strong enough, it will keep the second in check and ward off its excesses. It will prevent conflicts from degenerating into open warfare, inducing men to refer the object of their disagreement to an arbiter; the latter, moreover, will be determined to intervene for the same reason, i.e., under the pressure of the suffering which his sympathetic feelings occasion him at the sight of the conflict which has arisen. Arbitration is thus an immediate result of sociability, and even a quite rudimentary sociability suffices to produce it.

But for law to exist, it is not enough for there to be arbitration, this arbitration must also be guaranteed to the victim, i.e., he must always have the right to have recourse to it without the guilty party being able to abridge it. This guarantee is distinct from arbitration, for it has not always accompanied it historically. 'Primitive societies' courts of justice do not give executory force to their judgments; the parties are not even obliged to refer their litigation to them' (p. 25). We are therefore in the presence of a new component of the idea of law, the idea of guarantee.

But what could have led me to arrange this guarantee? This question, according to M. Richard, has, until now, wrecked the applied philosophy of law. These philosophers, as a matter of fact, have generally believed that only an external apparatus of coercion of conventional origin could have produced this result. Thus a self-interested calculation would have taught humanity to prefer the evil of submission and discipline to the more formidable evils of universal and interminable warfare. But it is not true that man is a utilitarian being. 'Calculation is not the author of history.' Besides, the state of anarchy has never been the object of horror for mankind that Hobbes assumes; for many races have never left it. We must pursue the opposite approach. It is within the *conscience* and not outside it, it is in the sympathetic and altruistic states of mind and not in the selfish feelings that we must look for the solution to the problem. Society compels the defendant to yield and protects the victim, because it feels itself responsible for the latter. The broad sympathy which it feels for each of its members does not allow it to witness unmoved damage suffered by one of them; moreover, it is conscious that the harm which he suffers could not be spread without danger for society itself. It therefore espouses quite naturally a cause which is its own. For this to happen, it need not be organized as a State; it suffices that the individuals who compose it feel linked together in the struggle for existence. It is this quite internal feeling which secures the *guarantee* and not, as the utilitarians have believed, an external and artificial coercion. The State, once constituted, can render more regular the carrying out of this guarantee; but it does not create it. It has its roots in the very *conscience* of societies.

But the idea of arbitration and that of guarantee imply that of offence; for the guarantee is a protection and, in consequence, presupposes a threat or an assault. It follows then from the preceding analysis that the idea of offence is one of the elements which serve to make up the idea of law and, consequently, is anterior to it. This conclusion, to begin with, upsets received ideas. We are used to considering an offence as the violation of the law and, in consequence, the law as anterior to the offence. But this is, according to M. Richard, to invert the real order of facts. If, he says, the mind suppresses the offence, then charity and sympathy will hold sway unimpeded and unalloyed; there will consequently be nothing to guarantee and the law will not be born. For the law to be possible, sociability must exist, but it must also be disturbed in a partial and intermittent manner. If it is entirely absent, a state of war exists; if it is perfect, there is no conflict.

The only thing is, if the notion of law depends upon that of offence, where does the latter come from and upon what does it rest? The author rejects both the theory which makes the offence the creation of the legislator, and that which simply sees it as a particularly harmful action. The offence is a natural thing which has its roots in the very constitution of society and not in the fickle will of statesmen; on the other hand, offence and harm are distinct things. A false deed, a bankruptcy are often more terrible calamities than a murder and yet do not have the same criminological importance. What constitutes the offence is that it manifests the absence of altruistic dispositions. 'The radical crime is absolute selfishness, the desire to live for oneself alone, to take cognizance only of one's own goals in the world.' (p. 68) We can see that this solution is not very far from the one M. Garofalo has proposed; it is distinct from it, however. By altruistic dispositions, M. Richard comprehends not only honesty and justice, but filial piety, national feeling, sense of decency, the sentiment of honour, etc. His definition is thus wider than that of the Italian criminologist, and accounts better for the facts. Then again, it permits the linking up of the offence with the fundamental conditions of social life; for, in order for egoism to be detested, there is no necessity that the legislator intervene, it is sufficient that there is a coherent society conscious of its unity. If, among primitive peoples, the conception of offence is more obscure than among civilized nations, this is because altruism is more imperfect there; but it does not have a different character and does not depend upon other causes.

Thus we see forming little by little the idea of law. The starting point is society's intervention in the settlement of conflicts; from there come arbitration and the guarantee. The definition of offence has shown us what rule society follows in the settlement of conflicts; it fights against egoism, it represses insociability. But by what means? It is necessary to answer this question for the notion of the law to be completely specified.

In point of fact, society makes use of two methods to attain its goal. It obliges the culprit to make amends for the harm he has caused; beyond this, at least in some instances, it imposes a punishment on him. The idea of punishment and that of reparation seem, at first sight, very different; but the author reduces them to a unity; he sees here only two different forms of the idea of debt. Penal repression and compensation appear to him, indeed, to be both derived from the custom of the composition which was the original practice. Now composition is compensation for the damage caused by the crime; it is a debt contracted by the criminal, simply by virtue of his offence. When the custom of composition disappeared, it was replaced by the obligation on the part of the culprit to make amends for the harm he had done. Even the obligations which are born of the contract were derived from the same source. In an interesting passage, the author shows that the law of contract, far from having been the primordial fact of juridical life, as certain theorists have claimed, is, on the contrary, a simple extension of the criminal law. We believe it is beyond all question, indeed, that the latter has been the germ from which issued all of the law.

As for punishment, it too is a debt, but in another sense. It corresponds to the debt of security which society owes to its members. On the one hand, crime gives rise to a resentment on the part of the whole community against the criminal and, consequently, to a need for vengeance. Now collective vengeance is no less contrary than private vengeance to the notion of guarantee; it is a disturbance of order. Society is therefore obliged to protect the criminal himself against its own anger. But on the other hand, it is no less obliged to protect itself against aggression. Hence there

arises the institution of punishment. We see the connections which it
sustains with the composition: the one is the substitute for private
vengeance; the other, for public vengeance.

These are the four elements which united, fused together, form the
notion of the law. This notion appears to the layman to be perfectly simple
and indivisible. We see that, in reality, it is extremely complex. This illusion stems from the fact that the parts of which it is formed have aggluti-
nated, that some of them have even disappeared from the field of
consciousness; a whole chapter, the eighth, is devoted to describing the
psychological process from which this simplification arises. But however
complex this idea may be, it still possesses a unity in this sense: that all the
elements of which it is composed are impressed with the same character,
derived from the same source, namely the idea of social solidarity. This is
why the parties submit their conflicts to an arbitrator and why society
espouses the cause of the victim; crime is nothing else than an outrage
against solidarity, and it is to protect it against individual and collective
vengeance that punishment and civil reparation have been instituted. It is
thus in truth the soul of the law.

Such is the conclusion of this work where the spirit of observation is
assuredly far from absent, but which still seems to us to be distinguished
above all by a remarkable dialectical ingenuity. It is not just in the entirety
of the account, but better still, in the details of the argumentation that the
author's logical qualities are deployed most comfortably. His arguments
hang together, hurry along at so rapid a rate that the reader is swept away,
even despite himself. Far from avoiding objections, he seeks them out,
raises them against himself with a sort of coquetry; one has the feeling that
he takes pleasure in this fencing. Perhaps he even dallies a little and at
times pushes ingenuity to the point of affectation. Thus the whole discussion which he institutes to establish the priority of the notion of offence
over that of the law seems to us a little over-subtle. In historical reality, the
law and violations of the law constitute two orders of concomitant and
contemporaneous facts and, in consequence, it is not possible to say that,
chronologically, one preceded the other. It can thus only be a question of
logical priority; and this is of quite minor importance for the sociologist.
What matters for sociology is to know what are the connections which
really exist between things, and not those according to which the concepts
must be logically arranged. Besides, is the line of argument itself very rigorous? Let us suppose that there are no offences; pure charity holds sway. So
be it! But even then, a compulsory form of charity exists, defined by some
imperative rules of conduct to which are attached more or less definite
sanctions. These rules are therefore juridical; the fact that they are not
deviated from does not imply that they do not exist.

This preponderance of the dialectical point of view affects moreover the
general design of the book. What the author looks for indeed – as the title

already witnesses – is the genesis not *of the law,* but *of the idea of the law.* He seems therefore really to consider the law not as a set of things, of given realities the laws of which must be sought according to the method of the natural sciences, but rather as a system of concepts linked logically among themselves and subordinated to a master concept which in large part contains them. As a matter of fact, such is indeed the nature of the solution propounded. We have seen, indeed, how the idea of debt was involved in that of offence, this in turn in the idea of guarantee, and, finally, the idea of guarantee and arbitration in the idea of solidarity. Doubtless, M. Richard does not suppose that any of these notions, nor accordingly the one which envelopes them, is given to us ready-made. It is built up gradually. But in whatever fashion it takes shape, once it exists, it would be this which, in developing, would have given birth to the law. The law would only be its realization out of the different conditions of experience. But nothing justifies our believing that the law has been realized in this manner. In order that one might postulate the existence of an idea *of the law, the law,* or what exists in reality, the laws, which is to say the indeterminate multitude of juridical rules, must have existed. Each of these is subject to particular causes and answers to special purposes. Far from a single idea having presided at their elaboration, they were born more often than not of fortuitous causes and in an altogether unconscious manner. Collective activity has congealed itself in diverse forms which they determine, without men having been aware of the social necessities to which they were responding. Doubtless, in one sense, this idea has an origin, but there is nothing very obscure about it. It stems, in fact, from the very spectacle of the juridical rules which takes place before our eyes; so far from having pre-existed it, it results from the law. It dimly reflects the juridical life itself, it does not create it; in just the same way as our idea of the world is only a reflection of the world in which we live. It does not express, therefore, the essence of the things it represents. It is permissible, it is true, to search for this essence. There are, at least one may believe, among the varieties of juridical rules, some common, and in consequence, essential characteristics. But only an already advanced knowledge of the law could furnish us with the conception of it. It is thus not this conception which could have been the germ from which the law emerges.

But if we rid the doctrine of this logical apparatus, an extremely interesting idea emerges which, we think, ought to be retained. It is customary to distinguish justice, that is to say the law, from charity. The first would be the elementary basis of morality and the second would be like the crowning point. M. Richard shows that on the contrary, these theories reverse the natural order of things, and that charity is the foundation of the law. Perhaps, it is true, the reason he gives for this is not completely convincing. Charity, he says, is the soul of the law, because the law is born of our feeling of solidarity against war. But we only feel this solidarity towards the unjust war, towards the attack which injures recognized rights. This solidarity thus presupposes that there already exists a form of justice, that the constitution of the law had been previously determined. Could this determination develop independently of all sentiment of solidarity, and could the latter only arise to assure the defence of rights, once they were established? Then the old theory would be in large part correct and would account for the most important facts. But none of this is so. The rights of each have only been defined thanks to mutual concessions and sacrifices; for what is in this fashion accorded to some is necessarily given up by others. The right which I concede to others of keeping the fruits of their labour implies that I renounce the option of seizing these. The law thus results from a mutual limitation of our natural powers, a limitation which can only develop in a spirit of understanding and harmony.

Durkheim's review of Kulischer's 'Research on Primitive Penal Law' in *L'Année sociologique*

In our analysis of this article, we can only deal with doctrines, and we must leave aside the numerous and well studied facts on which they are based. However, it should be pointed out that the article is given additional interest by its happy use of Russian sources. The author wishes to correct on two points the common theory that sees the origin of punishment in vengeance:

1. The vengeance of one group against another only indirectly contributed to the formation of penal law. Vengeance is not a punishment; it is modern warfare that it resembles. It was not able to transform itself into punishment since everywhere it tends to give rise to composition, that is, to damages. The offender's group always takes up the cudgels on his behalf, and this precludes any judgment of the legitimacy or illegitimacy of his act. If perchance some groups do not make common cause with those of their members who have harmed other groups under certain conditions, this can only be a secondary phenomenon. Indeed, for them to derive any advantage from this, the State must already have relieved them of all responsibility, having stipulated that they break all links with those of their members who have committed acts of aggression and that they abandon them to the vengeance of their victims. In the absence of such an intervention from above, the principle of joint responsibility would expose them to vengeance, whatever their attitude might be towards the real authors of the aggression. It is only when independent groups have been forced, in particular to defend themselves against a common enemy, to come together and to maintain peace amongst themselves, that a

group has been able to repress an attack by one of its members against another group or consider as alegitimate punishment the vengeance exercised by the latter. It is not the attack in itself that it condemns, it is the 'breaking of the peace', which would involve it in a dangerous war against its neighbour or would oblige it to pay composition [compensation] if it wished to avoid this. For the murder of a stranger to be evaluated as a crime, this murder had to be injurious to the sole good that was common to several groups, that is to say established peace.

2. The reaction by which a group responds to crimes committed by one of its members does not have the character of vengeance. These crimes, quite distinct from acts of war which evoke blood vengeance, are principally treason, incest, sacrilege and the murder of kin, which is in no way a form of murder in general, but something quite different: they never entail either vengeance or composition. If the most ancient legal documents do not mention them, this is not however because they were tolerated: but the most ancient codes are veritable international treaties, concluded by sovereign groups in order to ensure peace; they are therefore only concerned with those acts which involve the relations of one group to another and which in consequence could threaten peace; the administration of justice within each group did not interest them. The sanction for crimes committed within a group and against it consists in proscription, or in excommunication. All the members of the group are united amongst themselves by a close sympathy: that is the necessary condition of success in the constant struggle for existence. Thus is explained the fact that, in certain less advanced societies, the murder of a kinsman remains unpunished: sympathy for the murderer himself is too strong there for him to be touched. But in most cases it is partially neutralized by the sympathy the victim inspires and even more by the feeling of danger which is aroused by internal dissensions, in a groups always menaced by the enemy from without. It remains, nonetheless, too intense for the murderer to be killed as one kills a stranger; but it is sufficiently diminished for one no longer to wish to have anything to do with him and thus no longer tolerate his presence.

Proscription manifests at the same time the horror which the murder arouses and the fellow-feeling which is still attached to the murderer. Texts show us that very often one does not believe oneself authorized to kill him, as an enemy; one would regard oneself as committing a fresh crime. And when one makes up one's mind to do this, one seeks by a sort of fiction to avoid it being a crime. For example a mode of execution is chosen which brings about death only indirectly, or which does not allow the offence to fall on one person alone (stoning); the execution is entrusted to a slave; it is preceded by an excommunication which renders the guilty party a stranger, an enemy. But in all these cases, as well as in those where the proscribed person, in the absence of protection and resources, necessarily dies, what essentially characterizes the social reaction is that it consists in a proscription. The group which reacts does not in most cases have the intention of killing the guilty party, and it never considers itself as having a duty to do so. Capital punishment has historically derived from the *Friedloslegung;* nevertheless the latter is in no way, in principle, a capital punishment, a mode of execution. What is essential to it is the violent and definitive expulsion of the guilty party from residence within the group and all relations with its members are henceforth forbidden. This is why it very generally involves the destruction of the house of the proscribed party and of his property. It is probably to the crime of treason that capital punishment, properly so-called, in substitution for proscription, has been applied. For the traitor in effect proscription does not entail the need to live outside all society without any protection, since he naturally receives the hospitality of the enemy group which has profited from his crime: it therefore does not affect him. Only in the case of treason would primitive societies therefore have been led to put to death one of their members themselves.

We have serious reservations about the theories of M. Kulischer, notably on two points. In the first place, all the difficulties which the study of the sanction of murder within the group raise are far from being clarified: how can one explain that, in societies of apparently closely related types, the murder of a kinsman sometimes entails a rigorous proscription and sometimes remains without any sanction? The skill with which M. Kulischer groups together facts must not let us forget that the problem has aspects which he neglects. In the second place, we believe that crimes properly so-called – acts which provoke a reaction by the group against one of its members – have an essentially religious character which determines the equally religious sanction, namely excommunication. In this respect alone, M. Kulischer's theory, which explains proscription by a diminution of sympathy appears to us as retrograde when compared with the more complex conceptions of the religious origins of punishment which are in the process of being established.

With these reservations, however, M. Kulischer's article still shows powerfully that punishment has its origins, not in vengeance, but in the reaction of the group against its members, and that he undertakes, with more care than anyone to date has shown, the study of this reaction. It is from the same principle that the ideas that we have expressed in the *Année sociologique* since its origins are derived. But although this principle has already inspired studies which we have reviewed (*Année sociologique*, I,

p. 353; V, p. 400) M. Kulischer's work is in this respect the most important which we have had to report.

Note

1. The other sections were General Sociology, the Sociology of Religion, Economic Sociology, and a miscellaneous section devoted to the relationships between sociology and neighbouring social sciences, Anthropology, Social Geography and Demography.

CHAPTER 9

The Basis and Evolution of Contract

Introduction

In the fourth year of his time at Bordeaux, Durkheim began to lecture on the topic of law and social norms ('Physique générale du droit et des mœurs'). After an interval of five years, during which he gave courses on the sociology of the family, the sociology of crime, the sociology of religion, and the history of socialism, he returned to the subject in 1896–97, and in one form or another it was a staple of his teaching for the rest of his career, even down to his penultimate year of lectures at the Sorbonne, in 1914–15. He was at work on revising the portion of the course devoted to morality in the autumn of 1916 when he suffered the stroke that essentially ended his intellectual career, and from whose after-effects he died a year later, on 15 November 1917.

Much of Durkheim's unpublished work subsequently vanished, though the text of a version of these lectures was eventually deposited in the Musée de l'Homme in Paris. Their first appearance in print, however, was in Istanbul, as a consequence of an odd historical accident. In 1934 a young Turkish legal scholar, H.N. Kubali, who was working on his doctoral thesis on the concept of the state among the pioneers of French sociology, visited Paris and made the acquaintance of Durkheim's nephew, Marcel Mauss. Mauss showed him Durkheim's unpublished lecture notes on law and morality, and later gave Kubali a typed copy of the portions most relevant to his thesis topic. Kubali took them back with him to Turkey, and after the war, following some correspondence with Durkheim's daughter, Marie Halphen, he obtained copies of the remaining lectures, and published them. In 1957, these texts were then translated into English by Cornelia Brookfield and published as Professional Ethics and Civic Morals *(Durkheim 1957).*

A good portion of this posthumously published book is taken up with a discussion of property law considered as a social phenomenon. Durkheim examines there, in characteristic fashion, the questions of the nature and origins of property rights, what we should understand by the term 'property rights', and how such things came into existence. What can be appropriated as property, he points out, is socially and historically contingent. It is not given in the physical nature of things – and indeed, for much of human history, it extends beyond the category of things to include the ownership of human beings, via the institution of slavery. It is public opinion in every society, he contends, that makes some objects regarded as liable to appropriation and others not: it is not their physical nature as natural science might define it, but the form their image takes in the public mind. And even incorporeal things may, under some circumstances, be subject to appropriation. (Consider, for example, the ability to appropriate ideas, central to intellectual property law in our own time.)

Property, Durkheim argues, is something withdrawn from general circulation. Ownership implies exclusive possession. It shares this feature with sacred religious objects, which likewise are set apart, constituting a set of things surrounded by prohibitions and requiring ordinary individuals to keep their distance. Hence, he argues and proceeds to try to demonstrate, the origins of property are to be found in the nature of certain religious beliefs. Likewise, property is property only if it is respected, that is to say, held sacred. It begins as something collective, and only subsequently is transformed into something individual, through social processes whose long-term origins and historical development Durkheim attempts to analyze in the closing section of his discussion of property in Professional Ethics and Civic Morals *(not included here).*

The dichotomy between the sacred and the profane forms, in many ways one of the crucial (and problematic) elements of Durkheim's later work (Lukes 1972: 24–8), is one of the central themes of his last great monograph, The Elementary Forms of Religious Life. *'Sacred things,' he contends there, 'are things isolated and protected by prohibitions; profane things are those things to which the prohibitions are applied and that must keep at a distance from what is sacred' (Durkheim 1912: 56; translation Durkheim 1995: 38). In that later work, he would claim to have shown that the most essential notions of the human mind, notions of time, of space, of genus and species, of force and causality, of personality, those, in a word, which the philosophers have labelled categories and which dominate the whole of logical thought, have been elaborated in the very womb of religion (Durkheim 1913: 35–6). Property rights, Durkheim seems to have concluded many years before, could properly be added to that list.*

In our view, however, it is the second major theme that Durkheim discusses in Professional Ethics and Civic Morals *that is of more sustained contemporary relevance. This is his renewed attempt to grapple with the sociological significance of contract law. The question of contracts and their relationship to the social order had fascinated Durkheim from the very beginning of his attempt to construct the new discipline of sociology.*

One of the key elements of that early analysis, Durkheim's remarkable discussion of the non-contractual basis of contract, is reprinted here. Read together with the reflections on contract law presented in his lectures and then appearing posthumously in Professional Ethics and Civic Morals *(also reprinted here in a new translation), they constitute a sustained argument that remains an original and highly relevant contribution to social theory, one whose significance we attempt to highlight in the remainder of this introduction.*

'Who now reads Spencer?' is the memorable phrase with which Talcott Parsons opened his synthetic study of European social theory, The Structure of Social Action. *But, as Parsons well knew, the answer in Durkheim's time was 'almost everyone'. It was all very well to conclude in the late 1930s that 'Spencer is dead', in both the literal and the metaphorical senses of the term. But Spencer's argument had been – and continued to be – profoundly influential. It contrasted 'the automatic and spontaneous solidarity' of mutual exchange in the market with the 'conscious pursuit of social ends'. It expressed the view that industrial society is made up of individuals, who are viewed atomistically (that is, severally, or one by one) as entering freely into contracts and thereby inhabiting a social system that coheres as a result of the unhindered play of individual interests that require neither conformity to shared beliefs and norms nor state regulation. One of Durkheim's central intellectual achievements was and remains his devastating critique of the deficiencies of such a worldview, an intellectual perspective that continues in our own time to exercise an enormous influence. In one or another form, it underlies much of mainstream neoclassical and welfare economics and the disciplines influenced by and modelled on them. And Durkheim's critique of it can readily be redirected,* mutatis mutandis, *at the writings of the Austrian economists such as Carl Menger, Ludwig von Mises and Friedrich von Hayek. For Hayek the very idea of social justice is a 'mirage' and economics the study of the market order which spontaneously forms itself out of voluntary exchanges between individuals in pursuit of their respective interests, turning enemy into friend, as opposed to the deliberate arrangement or organization of resources in the service of a unitary hierarchy of ends – a form of social order that for Hayek can only be a stage along the 'road to serfdom'. Thus Durkheim's argument has no less relevance as a critique of the basic assumptions of the libertarian and neoliberal thinking of our times.*

For Durkheim, contracts ultimately and necessarily rest upon something more than simple self-interest. As Parsons perceived, Durkheim's critique began from the thought that 'in a contract not everything is contractual'. The two texts reproduced in this chapter spell out the key elements of that critique.

In the first, taken from the chapter on 'Organic Solidarity and Contractual Solidarity' in The Division of Labour in Society, *Durkheim first claims that the sphere of social regulation throughout society 'continues to grow' and become 'ever more weighty and complex' and then shows that the growth of 'spontaneous agreements between individual interests', of which contracts are 'the natural expression' – which so impressed Spencer – require such regulation: that liberty, as he wrote elsewhere, is 'the fruit of regulation'. He was here articulating the idea of legal and moral rules as bearing a* constitutive *relation to what they regulate (an idea much elaborated in our time by John Searle), rendering it possible and giving it recognizable form. Thus, as he rightly contends, contract law, alongside informal moral rules imposing professional obligations, 'constitutes the foundation of our contractual relationships'. It 'confers rights and imposes duties upon us' and thereby 'exercises over us a regulatory action of the utmost importance, since it determines in advance what we should do and what we can demand'. Thus it is an illusion – fully exhibited by Spencer and still very much alive today – to reduce 'the role of society' to a 'passive one of seeing that contracts are carried out'. For social regulation is needed to 'determine in what conditions they are capable of being executed and, if the need arise, restore them to their normal form'. It follows that agreement between the parties 'cannot make a clause fair which is itself unfair' according to the rules which specify what counts as fair and unfair.*

Durkheim here illustrates this argument by referring to the contractual relations of marriage and adoption, which, he shows, are increasingly 'taking on a public character', but then develops his critique into a completely general argument against what has been called 'the illusion of free markets' (see Harcourt 2011) and, more generally still, the idea of voluntary exchange as the basis of social order. 'We co-operate,' he writes, 'because we have wished to do so, but our voluntary co-operation creates for us duties that we have not desired' – a 'network of obligations from which we have no right to disengage ourselves' that is 'not our handiwork'. Mere mutual adjustment of self-interests could, in any case, never produce more than 'transitory links and associations of a fleeting kind'; indeed, on inspection, 'every harmony of interests conceals a latent conflict, or one that is simply deferred'. The legal and moral norms that constitute contractual relations establish the conditions for voluntary co-operation under 'organic solidarity'. And this is the kernel of Durkheim's critique of the 'atomistic' view expressed by Spencer: society 'does not resolve itself into a myriad of atoms juxtaposed together, between which only external and transitory contact can be established'. Such a view allows neither for the ways in which the minds of individuals 'interpenetrate' and 'cleave closely to one another' nor for 'the ties that extend beyond the very moment when the act of exchange is being accomplished'. In this sense, he writes, '[e]very society is a moral society'.

This selection is especially rich and rewarding in revealing Durkheim's sociological vision or perspective at work. It also contains (as does the next

passage we reprint) a hint at the theory of 'mediating organs' or 'second-
ary associations' based on occupation that he foresaw as interposed
between individual citizens and the state (a theory he was to develop and
expound in the Preface to the second edition of The Division of Labour*).*
And it includes a rather inexplicit paragraph in which he observed that 'a
whole school of thought' (he was referring to laissez-faire economists)
failed to realize that a contract (he meant the labour contract) could be
unjust, citing the fact that 'a whole section of the population cannot aban-
don their function', since they lack the 'freedom of mobility' (to secure
better wages and conditions).

This last thought and the political standpoint from which it derived is
rendered much more explicit in the second text we have selected for inclu-
sion in this chapter. This comes from his book Professional Ethics and
Civic Morals, *based on the lectures on law and social norms (Physique*
générale du droit et des mœurs), referred to at the beginning of this intro-
duction. Here Durkheim offered a summary history of the evolution of
contract as a sequence of stages. First there was real *contract, in which*
debt is incurred by the actual transfer of a thing, giving rise to the obliga-
tion to pay. The second stage was the ritual *verbal contract, where the*
parties are bound by a magico-religious solemn agreement that gives 'an
objective character to the word and to the resolve of the promissor'. The
third stage is the consensual *contract where, although words are used, they*
no longer have a sacred character and simply 'give expression to the will
they reveal and where what binds is consent that is freely given by the
parties'. What counts as being free from constraint is variable across soci-
eties ('the incidence of force or constraint by fear is … quite relative'),
becoming less and less severe. And this leads into the fourth stage, namely,
the just *contract (since what counted as being 'under the pressure of obvi-*
ous constraint' was, evidently, shaped by a sense of justice: it amounted to
suffering injury or being subject to 'extortion'). This fourth stage of
contract measures the validity of a contract by 'its consequences for the
contracting party' and invokes the idea of 'fairness' in the idea of exchang-
ing goods and services at their 'true or normal', that is, just, value.

At this point Durkheim entered a discussion (here all too brief) of a topic
familiar to Marxists, namely, exploitation. Observing that '[w]e disapprove
any contract … that favours one party unduly at the expense of another',
he did not offer any adequate account of how one determines a 'fair price'
other than suggesting that there is 'in every social group a state of opinion
that fixes its normal value at least roughly' and that with the extension of
markets this becomes more determinate over time. But he commented that
the notion of the just contract was as yet largely 'moral' and had not greatly
affected the law, other than the law against contracts of usury. But he
plainly saw this idea as informing regulations introduced into industrial law
to prevent employers from exploiting workers, proposals for a minimum

wage, the development of social insurance against sickness, old age and accidents and reforms of labour law to protect workers' interests.

The last pages of this section reveal the egalitarian basis of Durkheim's 'socialism': his belief that class consciousness would 'tend gradually to fade away' as the demand for 'greater justice in contracts' prevails and his principled objection to the institution of inheritance – the principle being that 'the distribution of things amongst individuals can be just only if it is made relative to the social deserts of each one'. And so he foresaw 'the recasting of the morals of property' to bring about a world in which 'the sole economic inequalities dividing men are those resulting from the inequality of the services'. Yet he recognized that prohibiting the voluntary bequeathing of property through 'testamentary inheritance' would violate 'certain family customs that are very deeply rooted' and so envisioned a progressive elimination of the right to dispose of property by will, which would in any case be of far less concern in a more egalitarian world.

Durkheim's thoroughgoing egalitarianism is here on full display in all its late nineteenth-century evolutionary optimism. It is in part reminiscent of Marx's conception of the 'lower stage' of communism in which the principle of distributive justice was to be 'to each according to his contribution'. But in part it is also meritocratic. Thus he envisaged the growth of a moral sentiment that 'tends to eliminate or strip away from all social sanctions every kind of physical and material inequality – all inequalities that derive from the accident of birth or from family status, leaving only those of merit'. But, foreshadowing the Rawlsian critique of this idea, he plausibly asked: 'are not these inequalities of merit fortuitous too? For these all men are born with – by temperament, and it seems hardly just to make them bear responsibility for them.' To ignore and deny 'any special merit in gifts or mental capacity acquired by heredity' was, he thought, 'the very acme of justice'. Here, he wrote, begins the domain of charity – 'the feeling of human sympathy that we can see becoming clear even of these last remaining traces of inequality'. For the foreseeable future, there would be a need to 'put a tentative price on merit' through incentives until the day when charity 'in its true meaning' becomes 'a strict obligation, that may be the spring of new institutions'.

Extract from Durkheim, *The Division of Labour in Society*

I

The conception of the social contract is today therefore very difficult to defend, because it bears no relation to the facts. The observer does not, so to speak, meet with it in his path. Not only are there no societies that have had such an origin, but there are none whose present structure bears the slightest trace of a contractual organization. Thus it is neither a fact derived from history nor a trend that emerges from historical development. Consequently in order to instil new life into this doctrine and to give it fresh credibility, it has been necessary to term the contract the acceptance on the part of each individual, once he has become an adult, of the society into which he is born, by the mere fact that he continues to live in it. But then one must term contractual any step taken by men that is not determined by constraint. On this reckoning there is no society, whether present or past, which is not, or has not been, contractual, for there is not one that can continue to exist through constraint alone. We have stated the reason for this earlier. If it has occasionally been believed that constraint was once greater than it is today, it is by virtue of the illusion that the small importance accorded to individual liberty in lower societies has been attributed to a coercive regime. In reality social life, where it is normal, is spontaneous; if it is abnormal, it cannot last. The individual abdicates spontaneously, and it is not even fair to talk of abdication when there is nothing to be abdicated. If therefore we give the word this wide and somewhat distorted meaning, there is no distinction to be made between the different social types. And if we only mean by this the well-defined legal bond that this expression designates, we may be assured that no link of this kind has ever existed between individuals and society.

But if higher societies do not rest upon a basic contract which has a bearing on the general principles of political life, they would have – or tend to have – according to Spencer, as their sole basis the vast system of special contracts that link individuals with one another. Individuals would only be dependent upon the group to the extent that they depended upon one another, and they would not depend upon one another save within the limits drawn by private agreements freely arrived at. Thus social solidarity would be nothing more than the spontaneous agreement between individual interests, an agreement of which contracts are the natural expression. The type of social relations would be the economic relationship, freed from all regulation, and as it emerges from the entirely free initiative of the parties concerned. In short, society would be no more than the establishment of relationships between individuals exchanging the products of their labour, and without any social action, properly so termed, intervening to regulate that exchange.

Is this indeed the nature of societies whose unity is brought about by the division of labour? If this were so, one might reasonably doubt their stability. For if mutual interest draws men closer, it is never more than for a few moments. It can only create between them an external bond. In the fact of exchange the various agents involved remain apart from one another and once the operation is over, each one finds himself again 'reassuming his self' in its entirety. The different consciousnesses are only superficially in contact: they neither interpenetrate nor do they cleave closely to one another. Indeed, if we look to the heart of the matter we shall see that every harmony of interests conceals a latent conflict, or one that is simply deferred. For where interest alone reigns, as nothing arises to check the egoisms confronting one another, each self finds itself in relation to the other on a war footing, and any truce in this perpetual antagonism cannot be of long duration. Self-interest is indeed the least constant thing in the world. Today it is useful for me to unite with you; tomorrow the same reason will make me your enemy. Thus such a cause can give rise only to transitory links and associations of a fleeting kind. We see how necessary it is to examine whether such is effectively the nature of organic solidarity.

Nowhere, as Spencer admits, does industrial society exist in a pure state: it is a type that is partly ideal, one that develops more and more in the course of evolution, but which has not yet been completely realized. Consequently, in order to have the right of attributing to it the traits we have just set out, we should establish methodically that societies exhibit them the more completely the more evolved they are, with the exception of those cases where regression has occurred.

In the first place it is asserted that the sphere of social activity continues to diminish more and more in favour of that of the individual. But in order to demonstrate this proposition by a valid experiment it is not enough to do as Spencer does and cite some cases where the individual has effectively emancipated himself from collective influence. No matter how numerous such examples are, they can only serve as illustrations and in themselves lack any power of proof. It is very possible that in one respect social action has regressed whilst in others it has been enlarged, so that in the end we mistake transformation for disappearance. The sole way of proving this objectively is not to quote a few facts as they occur to one, but to follow the history from its origins down to most recent times of the mechanism through which social action is essentially exerted, and to see whether over time it has grown or diminished in volume. We know what is the legal position. The obligations that society imposes upon its members, however slight in importance and duration, take on a legal form. Consequently the relative dimensions of this mechanism allow one to measure precisely the relative extent of social action.

It is abundantly clear that, far from decreasing, this mechanism is continuing to grow, becoming more complex. The more primitive a legal code is, the smaller it is in size. On the other hand, the more recent it is, the more considerable it becomes. Of this there is no possible doubt. But it assuredly does not follow that the sphere of individual activity is growing smaller. We must indeed not forget that if life is more regulated it is also generally more abundant. This is nevertheless adequate proof that social discipline is not continually growing more lax. One of the forms that it assumes tends, it is true, to regress, as we have ourselves established. But other forms, much richer and more complex, are developing in its place. If repressive law is losing ground, restitutive law, which in the beginning did not exist at all, is continually growing. If social intervention has no longer the effect of imposing certain uniform practices upon everybody, it consists more in defining and regulating the special relationship between the different social functions, and this is not less because it is different.

Spencer will answer that he did not assert that every kind of control had decreased, but only positive control. Let us accept this distinction. Whether positive or negative, this control is nevertheless social, and the main question is to know whether it is extended or contracted. But whether it is for decreeing something to happen or for prohibiting it, for saying *Do this* or *Do not do that,* if society intervenes more we have no right to say that individual spontaneity is increasingly adequate for all purposes. If the rules that determine conduct are multiplied, whether their commands are positive or negative, it is not true to say that it springs more and more completely from private initiative.

But is the distinction itself well-founded? By positive control Spencer means one that constrains a person to act, whilst negative control constrains him only to abstain from action. For example, a man has a piece of land; I cultivate it for him either wholly or in part, or I impose upon him, either partially or entirely, the mode of cultivation he must employ: this is a positive control. On the other hand, I give him no help or advice about his farming; I merely prevent him from touching his neighbour's crop or from tipping his rubbish there: this is negative control. The difference is fairly clear-cut between taking it upon oneself to pursue in the place of another citizen some goal which is properly his or to intervene concerning the means that this citizen employs to pursue it, and on the other hand to prevent him harassing another citizen who is pursuing his own chosen goal.[7] If this is the meaning of the terms, positive control is far from disappearing.

We know indeed that restitutive law is continually growing. In the vast majority of cases it either indicates to the citizen the aim that he should pursue or it intervenes in the means that this citizen is employing to attain his chosen goal. For each juridical relationship it resolves the two following questions: (1) In what conditions and in what form does the relationship normally exist? (2) What are the obligations to which it gives rise? The determination of the form and conditions is essentially positive, since this forces the individual to follow a certain procedure in order to attain his goal. As for obligations, if in principle they came down to a prohibition not to disturb another in the exercise of his functions, Spencer's thesis would be true, at least in part. But more often than not these obligations consist in the performance of services of a positive nature.

But let us go into the detail.

II

It is absolutely true that contractual relationships that originally were rare or completely missing are multiplied as labour in society is divided up. But what Spencer seems to have failed to perceive is that non-contractual relationships are developing at the same time.

Let us first examine that section of the law that is wrongly termed private and that, in reality, regulates the relationships between diffused social functions or, to put it differently, the innermost life of the social organism.

In the first place we know that domestic law, from being originally simple, has become increasingly complex, that is, the different species of legal relationships that give rise to family life are much more numerous than formerly. On the one hand, the relationships that result from them are pre-eminently of a positive kind; it is a reciprocity of rights and duties. On the other hand, they are not contractual, at least in their typical form. The conditions upon which they depend are related to our personal status, which itself depends upon our birth, our blood relationships, and consequently upon facts independent of our will.

However, marriage and adoption are sources of domestic relationships and these are contracts. Yet it so happens that the closer we come to the highest types of society, the more these two legal relationships also lose their strictly contractual character.

Not only in lower societies, but in Rome itself right up to the end of the Empire, marriage remained an entirely private matter. It was generally a type of sale, a real one among primitive peoples, a fictitious one later, but which was valid only by sole consent of the parties, duly attested. Neither solemn forms of ceremony of any kind, nor the intervention of any authority whatsoever were then necessary. It is only with Christianity that marriage took on a different character. Early on, Christians got into the habit of having their union blessed by a priest. A law of the emperor Leo the Philosopher converted this usage into a law for the East; the Council of Trent did as much for the West. Henceforth marriage was no longer freely contracted, but only through the mediation of a public authority, that is, the Church. The role of the Church is not only that of a witness, but she it is and only she that forges the legal bond that up to then the will of private individuals had sufficed to establish. We know how at a later stage the civil authority became the substitute for the religious authority in fulfilling this function and how, at the same time, the role of social intervention and of the necessary formalities was extended.

The history of the adoption contract is still more cogent.

We have already seen how easily and on how large a scale adoption was practised among the Indian clans of North America. It could give rise to every form of kinship. If the person adopted was of the same age as the person adopting him or her, they became brothers and sisters. If the former was a woman who was already a mother, she became the mother of the person adopting her.

Among the Arabs, before Mahomet's time, adoption was often used to found real families. It frequently happened that several persons adopted one another; they then became brothers and sisters, and the relationship that united them was as strong as if they were of common descent. The same kind of adoption is to be found among the Slavs. Very often members of different families took one another as brothers and sisters, and formed what is called a confraternity (*probatinstvo*). These societies were contracted freely and without formality: an agreement was sufficient to establish them. However, the bond that united these siblings by election was even stronger than that which springs from a natural sibling relationship.

Among the Germans adoption was probably as easy and frequent. Very simple ceremonies sufficed to constitute it. But in India, Greece or Rome it was already subject to conditions that were laid down. The person adopting had to be of a certain age, had not to be related to the person adopted in a degree that would not have allowed him to be the natural father. Finally this change of family became a very complex legal operation that necessitated the intervention of a magistrate. At the same time the number of those who enjoyed the right of adoption became more limited. Only the father of a family or a bachelor *sui juris* could undertake adoption, and the former could only do so if he had no legitimate children.

Under our present law restrictive conditions have multiplied. The person adopted must be of the age of majority, the person adopting must be over fifty and have treated the adopted person for a long time as his child. Even so we must add that within such limitations adoption has become a very rare event. Before the drawing up of our legal code it had even fallen almost completely into disuse and still today certain lands such as Holland and Lower Canada do not allow it at all.

At the same time as adoption was becoming rarer, it was losing its effectiveness. In the beginning the adoptive parental relationship was in every respect similar to that of natural parenthood. In Rome the similarity was still very great, yet it was no longer perfectly identical. In the sixteenth century it no longer gave any right to the inheritance *ab intestat* of the adoptive father. Our legal code has re-established this right, but the kinship to which adoption gives a right does not extend beyond that of the adopting and the adopted persons.

We see how defective is the traditional explanation that attributes this custom of adoption among ancient societies to the need to ensure the perpetuation of the cult of one's ancestors. The peoples who have practised it most widely and freely, such as the American Indians, the Arabs and the Slavs, did not know of this cult. On the contrary, it is Rome and Athens, that is, in countries where the domestic type of religion was at its height, where this right was subjected for the first time to control and restrictions. Thus if it has been able to satisfy these needs, it was not because of them that it was established. Conversely, if it tends to disappear it is not because we are less eager to ensure the perpetuating of our name and race. It is in the structure of present-day societies and in the place that the family occupies in them that we must seek the cause that determined this change.

A further proof of this truth is that it has become even more impossible to leave a family by a private act of authority than to enter it. Just as the bond of kinship is not the outcome of a binding contractual relationship, it cannot be broken through an undertaking of a similar kind. Amongst the Iroquois we occasionally see part of the clan depart to swell the ranks of the neighbouring clan. Among the Slavs a member of the Zadruga who is tired of the life in community can separate himself from the rest of his family and become legally a stranger to it, as in the same way he can be excluded by it. With the Germans a not very complicated ceremony allowed every Frank who so desired to free himself completely from the obligations of kinship. In Rome a son could not renounce his family of his own volition, and from this trait we can recognize a higher social type. But the bond that the son could not break could be broken by the father. It was this operation that constituted emancipation. Today neither father nor son can modify the natural condition of domestic relationships: they remain as determined at birth.

To sum up: at the same time as domestic obligations are becoming more numerous they are taking on, so to speak, a public character. In principle they not only have no contractual origin, but the role played by contract is continually decreasing. On the other hand the social control over the way in which obligations are entered into and dissolved is modified, and is continually increasing. The reason for this lies in the progressive disappearance of the segmentary organization. The family was indeed for a long while a true social segment. Originally it was mixed together in the clan. If it later became distinct from it, it was as a part of the whole. It is the product of a secondary segmentation of the clan, identical to that which gave rise to the clan itself. When the latter has disappeared it still retains that same capacity. But everything that is segmentary tends increasingly to be absorbed into the mass of society. This is why the family is obliged to transform itself. Instead of remaining an autonomous society within the larger one, it is drawn increasingly into the system of organs of society. It becomes one of these organs itself, invested with special functions. Consequently all that takes place within it is capable of having general repercussions. It is this that brings about the need for the regulatory organs of society to intervene, to exercise a moderating effect over the way in which the family functions or even, in certain cases, one that acts as a positive stimulus.

But it is not only outside the sphere of contractual relationships, but also on the interplay between these relationships themselves that social action is to be felt. For in a contract not everything is contractual. The only undertakings worthy of the name are those that are desired by individuals, whose sole origin is this free act of the will. Conversely, any obligation that has not been agreed by both sides is not in any way contractual. Wherever a contract exists, it is submitted to a regulatory force that is imposed by society and not by individuals: it is a force that becomes ever more weighty and complex.

It is true that the contracting parties can agree to dispense in certain respects with the arrangements laid down in the law. But firstly, their rights in this respect are not unlimited. For example, an understanding between parties cannot validate a contract that does not satisfy the conditions for validity laid down by the law. It is certain that in the vast majority of cases the contract is no longer now constrained to employ set forms, but we must not forget that in our legal codes there still exist 'solemn contracts'. Yet if the law generally does not prescribe the formalist requirements that once it did, it subjects the contract to obligations of another kind. It denies any binding power to undertakings entered into by one incapacitated mentally, or those that lack a purpose, or whose reasons are illegal, or made by a person who has no right to sell, or relating to a thing that cannot be sold. Among the obligations that the law decrees must flow from the various forms of contract, there are some that cannot be changed by any stipulations whatsoever. Thus the seller cannot shirk the obligation to indemnify the buyer against any eviction which results from an action which is his (the seller's) responsibility (Art. 1628), nor to reimburse the price of the sale in the case of an eviction, whatever the cause, providing that the buyer was unaware of the risk he was running (Art. 1629) nor to explain clearly what the buyer is binding himself to do (Art. 1602). Likewise, to a certain extent at least, he cannot be dispensed from giving a guarantee against hidden defects (Arts 1641 and 1643), particularly if he (the seller) was aware of them. If it concerns real estate, it is the buyer who has a duty not to profit from the situation by offering a price appreciably far below the real value of the thing, etc. (Art. 1674). Moreover, concerning all matters of proof, the nature of the actions to which the contract assigns a right, the time scale within which they must be performed – these are all entirely removed from the sphere of individual negotiation.

In other cases the action of society is manifested not only in the refusal to recognise a contract drawn up in contravention of the law, but by positive intervention. Thus, regardless of the terms of the agreement, the judge in certain circumstances may grant the debtor a stay of execution (Arts 1184, 1244, 1655, 1900), or oblige a borrower to return to the lender the latter's property before the date agreed upon, if he has pressing need of it (Art. 1189). But what demonstrates even more clearly that contracts give rise to obligations that have not been contracted for is that 'they commit one not only to what is expressed in them, but also to all the consequences that equity, usage and the law impart to the obligation incurred, according to its nature' (Art. 1135). By virtue of this principle there must be ascribed, in addition to the contract, 'the clauses which are customary to it, although not expressed' (Art. 1160).

Yet even when social action is not stated in this express form, it does not cease to be real. Indeed this possibility of dispensing with the law, which seems to reduce contractual law to the role of a possible substitute for contracts proper, is in the vast majority of cases purely theoretical. To convince ourselves of this we have only to represent to ourselves what it consists of.

Undoubtedly when men bind one another by contract it is because, through the division of labour, whether this be simple or complex, they have need of one another. But for them to co-operate harmoniously it is not enough that they should enter into a relationship, nor even be aware of the state of mutual interdependence in which they find themselves. The conditions for their co-operation must also be fixed for the entire duration of their relationship. The duties and rights of each one must be defined, not only in the light of the situation as it presents itself at the moment when the contract is concluded, but in anticipation of circumstances that can arise and can modify it. Otherwise, at every moment there would be renewed conflicts and quarrels. Indeed we must not forget that if the division of labour makes interests interdependent, it does not mix them together: it leaves them distinct, and in competition with one another. Just as within the individual organism each organ is at odds with the others, whilst still acting in concert with them, each contracting party, whilst having need of the other, seeks to obtain at least cost what he needs, that is, to gain the widest possible rights in exchange for the least possible obligations.

Thus it is necessary for the allocation of both rights and obligations to be prescribed in advance, and yet this cannot take place according to some preconceived plan. There is nothing in the nature of things from which we can deduce that the obligations of either party should attain any particular limit. But every decision of this kind can only be the result of a compromise, one that steers a middle course between the interests that are in competition and their solidarity with one another. It is a position of equilibrium that can only be found by a more or less laborious process of trial and error. It is very clear that we cannot begin this process again, or restore after fresh effects this equilibrium, every time that we enter into a contractual relationship. We lack all the elements for doing this. It is not at the moment when difficulties arise that they should be resolved. Yet we cannot foresee the variety of possible circumstances that may arise during the period our contract will run, nor fix beforehand, by means of a simple mental calculation, what will be in every case the rights and duties of each person, save in matters of which we have very special practical experience. Moreover, the material conditions of life prevent a repetition of such operations. For at every instant, and often unexpectedly, we find we bind ourselves in this way, either in what we buy or sell, or in travelling, hiring out our services, and putting up at a hotel, etc. Most of our relationships with others are of a contractual nature. If therefore we had each time to launch ourselves afresh into these conflicts and negotiations necessary to establish clearly all the conditions of the agreement, for the present and the future, our actions would be paralysed. For all these reasons, if we were only bound by the terms of our contract as they had been worked out, only a precarious solidarity would emerge.

But contractual law exists to determine the legal consequences of those of our acts that we have not settled beforehand. It expresses the normal conditions for attaining equilibrium, as they have evolved gradually from the average case. Epitomizing numerous, varied experiences, it foresees what we could not do individually; what we could not regulate is regulated, and this regulation is mandatory upon us, although it is not our handiwork, but that of society and tradition. It constrains us to respect obligations for which we have not contracted, in the precise meaning of the term, since we have not deliberated upon them or, on occasions, even been aware of them beforehand. Undoubtedly the initial action is always a contractual one. But it entails consequences, even immediately, that more or less go beyond the limits of the contract itself. We co-operate because we have wished to do so, but our voluntary co-operation creates for us duties that we have not desired.

Viewed in this light, the law of contract appears very differently. It is no longer a useful supplement to individual agreements, but their basic norm. It imposes itself upon us with the traditional authority of experience, it constitutes the foundation of our contractual relationships. We can only depart from it in part, and by chance. The law confers rights and imposes duties upon us as if they derived from a certain act of our will. In particular cases we can renounce some rights and relieve ourselves of some duties. Both nevertheless represent the normal type of rights and duties that the circumstances entail, and deliberate action must be taken if we wish to modify them. Thus modifications are comparatively rare; in principle, it is the rule that is applied, and innovations are exceptional. The law of contract therefore exercises over us a regulatory action of the utmost importance, since it determines in advance what we should do and what we can demand. It is a law that can be changed only by the agreement of the parties concerned. Yet so long as it has not been repealed or replaced, it retains an entire authority. Moreover, we can only act in the capacity of legislator very periodically. Thus only a difference in degree marks the law that regulates the obligations arising from contract and those that prescribe the other duties of citizens.

Finally, beyond this organized, precise pressure exerted by the law, there is another that arises from morals. In the way in which we conclude and carry out contracts, we are forced to conform to rules which, although not sanctioned, either directly or indirectly, by any legal code, are none the less mandatory. There are professional obligations that are purely moral but that are nevertheless very strict. They are particularly apparent in the so-called liberal professions. If perhaps they are less numerous in other occupations, we may, as we shall see, have grounds for asking whether this is not the result of some unhealthy state. Although this kind of action is more diffuse than the legal one, it is just as much a social matter. Moreover, it is necessarily more extensive the more contractual relationships are developed, for like contracts its action has many ramifications.

Summing up, therefore, the contract is not sufficient by itself, but is only possible because of the regulation of contracts, which is of social origin. The former implies the latter, firstly because the function of contract is less to create new rules than to diversify pre-established rules in particular cases; secondly, because it has not, and cannot have, any power to bind save under certain conditions that need to be defined. If in principle society confers upon it a power of obligation it is because generally the agreement of individual wills is sufficient to ensure – excepting the reservations made above – harmonious collaboration between the diffused social functions. But if it runs contrary to its own purpose, if it is such as to disturb the regular working of the social organs, if, as has been said, it is not fair, then, since it lacks social value, it must needs be stripped of all authority. Thus in any case the role of society cannot be reduced to a passive one of seeing that contracts are carried out. It has also to determine in what conditions they are capable of being executed and, if the need arise, restore them to their normal form. Agreement between the parties concerned cannot make a clause fair which of itself is unfair. There are rules of justice that social justice must prevent being violated, even if a clause has been agreed by the parties concerned.

Thus some regulation is necessary, but its extent cannot be delimited in advance. A contract, states Spencer, has the purpose of ensuring for the workman expenditure on his behalf equivalent to what his labour has caused him. If this is really the role of contract, it can never fulfil it unless it is regulated much more meticulously than it is today. For it would indeed be a miracle if it sufficed to guarantee to produce such equivalents. It is because sometimes gain outweighs the outlay, sometimes the opposite – and the disproportionality is often glaring. Yet – and this is the retort of a whole school of thought – if the gains are too low, the function will be abandoned for other functions; if they are too high, the function will be much sought after and competition will reduce the gain. They forget that, a whole section of the population cannot abandon their function in this way, since no other is available to them. Even those possessing more freedom of mobility cannot immediately take advantage of it. Such revolutions are always long drawn-out before being accomplished. Meanwhile unfair contracts, unsocial by definition, have been executed with the co-operation of society, and when equilibrium has been established in one respect there is no reason for it to be upset in another.

We need not demonstrate that this intervention, in its various forms, is of an eminently positive kind, since its effect is to determine the manner in which we should co-operate together. It is true that it is not the act of intervention that sets off the functions that co-operate with one another. Yet it regulates their cooperation once it has begun. As soon as we have taken the first step towards co-operation, we are committed and the regulatory action of society exerts itself upon us. If Spencer termed this action negative it is because for him contract consists solely in exchange. Yet even from this standpoint the expression he employs is inexact. Undoubtedly, after having taken delivery of an article or had a service performed for me, when I refuse to provide the agreed equivalent I am taking from another what belongs to him, and it may be said that society, in obliging me to keep my promise, is merely preventing the occurrence of some prejudice or indirect act of aggression. But if I have merely promised a service without having received in advance the recompense for it, I am nonetheless bound to fulfil my undertaking. However, in that case I am not enriching myself at the expense of others. I am merely refusing to be of service to them. Moreover, exchange, as we have seen, is not the whole of contract; there is also the harmonious working of the functions that are co-operating. These are not only in contact in the brief time when things pass from one person to another. More extensive relationships necessarily result from them, in the course of which it is important that their solidarity should not be disturbed.

Extract from Durkheim, *The Division of Labour in Society*

IV

The following propositions sum up this first part of our work.

Social life is derived from a dual source, the similarity of individual consciousnesses and the social division of labour. In the first case the individual is socialized because, lacking any individuality of his own, he is mixed up with his fellows in the same collective type. In the second case it is because, whilst his physiognomy and his activities are personal to him, distinguishing him from others, he depends upon them to the very extent that he is distinguished from them, and consequently upon the society that is the result of their combining together.

The similarity of consciousnesses gives rise to legal rules which, under the threat of repressive measures, impose upon everybody uniform beliefs and practices. The more pronounced the similarity, the more completely social life is mixed up with religious life, and the closer economic institutions are to communism.

The division of labour gives rise to legal rules that determine the nature and relationships of the function thus divided up, but the infringement of the rules entails only measures of reparation lacking any expiatory character.

Each set of legal rules moreover is accompanied by a set of rules that are purely moral. Where penal law is very voluminous shared morality is very extensive. This means that there are a host of collective practices placed under the protection of public opinion. Where restitutive law is very developed, for each profession a professional morality exists. Within the same group of workers a public opinion exists, diffused throughout this limited body, which, despite the lack of any legal sanctions, is nevertheless obeyed. There are customs and usages common to the same group of functionaries which none can infringe without incurring the reprimand of the corporation. Yet this morality is distinguished from the previous one by differences analogous to those that separate the two corresponding species of laws. This morality is in fact localized within a limited area of society. Moreover, the repressive character of the sanctions attached to it is appreciably less severe. Professional faults give rise to a disapproval much weaker than attacks upon public morality.

However, the rules of professional morality and law are categorical, like the others. They force the individual to act in accordance with ends that are not his own, to make concessions, to agree to compromises, to take into account interests superior to his own. Consequently even where society rests wholly upon the division of labour, it does not resolve itself into a myriad of atoms juxtaposed together, between which only external and transitory contact can be established. The members are linked by ties that extend well beyond the very brief moment when the act of exchange is being accomplished. Each one of the functions that the members exercise is constantly dependent upon others and constitutes with them a solidly linked system. Consequently the nature of the task selected derives from duties that are permanent. Because we fulfil this or that domestic or social function we are caught up in a network of obligations from which we have no right to disengage ourselves. There is above all one organ in regard to which our state of dependence continues to grow: this is the state. The points where we come into contact with it are multiplied, as well as the occasions when it is charged with reminding us of the sentiment of our common solidarity.

Thus altruism is not destined to become, as Spencer would wish, a kind of pleasant ornament of our social life, but one that will always be its fundamental basis. How indeed could we ever do without it? Men cannot live together without agreeing, and consequently without making mutual sacrifices, joining themselves to one another in a strong and enduring fashion. Every society is a moral society. In certain respects this feature is even more pronounced in organized societies. Because no individual is sufficient unto himself, it is from society that he receives all that is needful, just as it is for society that he labours. Thus there is formed a very strong feeling of the state of dependence in which he finds himself: he grows accustomed to valuing himself at his true worth, viz., to look upon himself only as a part of the whole, the organ of an organism. Such sentiments are of a kind not only to inspire those daily sacrifices that ensure the regular development of everyday social life but even on occasion acts of utter renunciation and unbounded abnegation. For its part society learns to look upon its constituent members no longer as things over which it has rights, but as co-operating members whom it cannot do without and towards whom it has duties. Thus it is wrong to oppose a society that derives from a community of beliefs to one whose foundation is co-operation, by granting only the first a moral character and seeing in the latter only an economic grouping. In reality, co-operation also has its intrinsic morality. There is only reason to believe, as we shall later see more clearly, that in our present-day societies this morality has still not developed to the extent which from now onwards is necessary for them.

But this morality is not of the same nature as the other. The latter is strong only if the individual is weak. Made up of rules practised by all without distinction, it receives from this universal, uniform practice an authority that makes it something superhuman, removing it more or less from argument. The other, by contrast, develops as the individual personality grows stronger. However regulated a function may be, it always leaves plenty of room for individual initiative. Even many of the obligations that are subject to penalties in this way have their origin in a choice by the will. It is we who choose our profession and even certain of our domestic functions. Doubtless once our resolve has ceased to be internal and been translated externally into social consequences, we are bound by it: duties are imposed upon us that we have not expressly wished. Yet it is through a voluntary act that they arose. Finally, because these rules of conduct relate not to the conditions of ordinary life but to different forms of professional activity, they have for this reason a more temporal character which, so to speak, whilst retaining all their obligatory force, makes them more accessible to the actions of men.

There are thus two great currents in social life, to which correspond two types of structure that are no less different.

Of these currents, the one that has its origin in social similarities flows at first alone, and has no competition. At that time it mingles with the very life of society. Then gradually it becomes channelled and becomes less apparent, whilst the second continues to grow bigger. Likewise the segmentary structure is more and more overshadowed by the other, but without ever disappearing completely.

Extract from Durkheim, *Professional Ethics and Civil Morals*

A contract is commonly taken to be such a simple operation that it has been believed possible to make it the elementary fact from which all other social facts would be derived. The theory of the 'social contract' rests on this very idea. According to this theory, the social bond *par excellence*, that which unites the individuals within one and the same community, has been or ought to be a contract. If the contract is understood as an elementary phenomenon, either chronologically or, as Rousseau understands it, logically, it is because as a concept, it seems clear in itself. Apparently, it does not need to be linked to another notion that would clarify it. Jurists have often operated on the same principle: thus, they have reduced all the obligations in personal action to either torts or contracts. Yet all the other obligations that do not expressly have their source in a tort or a contract strictly speaking are considered as variations of these. This is how the concept of the quasi-contract has been formed, under which, for example, we explain the obligations arising out of the management of other people's business, or the fact that a creditor has received more than his due. The idea of the contract seemed so clear in itself that the originating cause of these various obligations became clear as soon as this cause was assimilated to the contract proper, or to a species of the contract. Yet nothing is more deceptive than this seeming clarity. Far from being primal, the institution of the contract did not appear and above all did not develop until a very late date. Far from being simple, this institution is extremely complex and it is not easy to understand how it was formed. What matters most is that we understand this very clearly. In order to do so, let us begin by defining the nature of the contractual bond.

To begin with, and more generally, what does a legal moral bond consist of? We define it as a relation that the public consciousness conceives between two subjects, individual or collective, or else between these subjects and a thing, and by virtue of which one of the parties involved has at least one definite right over the other. In most cases, there exists a right on both sides.

This reciprocity, however, is not necessary. A slave is legally bound to his master, and yet he has no right over him. Now, this kind of bond can have two different origins. (1) Either it expresses an actual state of things or of persons in a relation, such that, chronically or durably, the terms in relation are of a certain nature, in some particular setting, and are held by public consciousness to have inherited certain acquired characteristics. (2) Or they express a not yet current state of things or of persons that is simply wished for on both sides. In this case, then, it is not the intrinsic nature of the state of affairs but the fact that this state of affairs is wished for that generates the right. In this case, the right consists simply of bringing about the state of affairs just as it has been desired. Thus, because I was born in a certain family, because I bear a certain name, I have certain duties towards individuals who happen to be my relatives or towards individuals of whom I may have to be the legal guardian. Because a certain thing has been added to my property by legal means, I have property rights over this thing. Because I own a certain building located in a certain way, I have a certain right of easement over the neighboring estate, etc. In all these cases, it is a fact, established or completed, that gives birth to the right I exercise. But I may come to an agreement with the owner of a house for him to lease his property to me in exchange for a certain amount of money to be paid over to him every year on certain agreed terms. In this case, there exists simply, on the one hand, my desire to occupy this estate and to pay the promised amount, and on the other hand, the desire of the other party to give up his rights in exchange for the promised amount. There are only volitions or states of will involved, and yet the state of wills in question may suffice to give rise to obligations and, as a consequence, to rights. We should reserve the label 'contractual' only for the bonds that originate in either of these two ways. Without doubt, there exist many intermediate bonds between these two opposing types. However, the main thing is to contrast these extremes with one another, so that the comparison high-lights their distinctive features. Nothing is more clear-cut than their oppo-sition, as it has appeared to us: on the one hand, legal relationships that originate in the status of persons or of things, or in prior modifications contained in this status; on the other hand, legal relationships that origi-nate in an agreement aimed at modifying this status.

Now, this definition directly implies that the contractual bond cannot be primal. Indeed, parties can only agree to contract obligations if these obli-gations do not result from a legal status, whether of things or of persons, that is already acquired; they can only modify this status, and add on new relationships to the pre-existing ones. The contract, then, is a source of variations which presupposes another legal basis, one that has another origin. The contract is the instrument *par excellence* via which the changes are carried out. The contract itself cannot constitute the original founda-tion upon which the law rests. It implies that two legal entities at least are already constituted and organized, that these entities enter into relations with one another, that these relations change their constitution; and that something belonging to the one passes to the other, and vice versa. For example, there may be two families, A and B. A woman leaves A to live with a man from B and becomes, in some respects, integrated as a member of his group. There has been a change in the extent of these families. If this transfer happens peacefully, with the consent of the two families involved, we then get a more or less elementary form of marriage. It follows that marriage, being necessarily a contract, presupposes a pre-existing organi-zation of the family that has nothing contractual about it. This is another proof that marriage rests on the family, and not the family on marriage.

Let us suppose now that incest has not been prohibited, and that every man has been united with a woman of his own family, then the sexual union would not have involved any real transfer either of persons or things. The matrimonial contract would not have come into existence.

Not only is the contractual bond not primal, but it is easy to see why men foresaw its possibility only at a late stage in history. Indeed, where do these bonds (i.e the rights and obligations arising from the state either of persons or of things) arise? They result from the sacred nature of these persons and things, from the moral prestige they are endowed with, whether directly or indirectly. If early man holds himself beholden to his own group, it is because this group is in his eyes sacred. If he also acknowledges his obligations towards the individuals forming this group, it is because the sanctity of the whole spreads to its parts. All the members of the same clan bear within them, as it were, a fragment of the divine being of which the clan is supposedly the offspring. Thus, they all bear a religious mark, and this is why they are bound to be defended and their death is to be avenged, etc. We have seen too that the rights which have their origins in things derive from the religious nature of these things – there is no need to return to this point. Therefore, all the moral and legal relations that arise from status, real or personal, arise from some virtue *sui generis* intrinsic to a thing or to a person, and which commands respect. But how could a virtue of this kind be comprised of mere inclinations? What is there and what could there be about the fact of willing some thing or some relation that may compel such a relation to actually take place? If we think about it, we can see that the idea that an agreement about the same purpose could bind these two parties was a great legal innovation that presupposed a very advanced stage in history. If I have resolved to act in a certain way or another, I can always go back on my resolution. Why then would two resolutions made by two different parties be more binding just because of their agreement? It is perfectly understandable that I should pause in the presence of a person whom I deem sacred, and that I should refrain from touching him or modifying his present state because of the characteristics that I attribute to him and the respect that I therefore owe to him. It is the same with things to which I attribute the same qualities. But an act of the will or a resolution is nothing more than a possibility; by definition, it is not carried into effect. How is it, then, that a thing should be able to compel me to that degree, a thing that does not exist, or at least exists only ideally? We think that all kinds of factors must have intervened to give our volitions an obligatory force that the mere concept of volition does not include of itself. Therefore the legal notions of contract and the contractual bond, far from being immediately self-evident, must have been constructed with a great deal of effort.

It was, indeed, only after a very long time that societies succeeded in moving past the initial phase of the merely statutory right and superimposing a new right. It was only by successive modifications in the former that they progressively got closer to the latter. This evolution came about in different ways. The main ones are as follows.

It is a general rule that new institutions start off by modelling themselves after older ones and detach themselves from the latter only by degrees in order to develop their own nature freely. The function of the contractual right was to modify personal status, and yet, in order for this purpose to be achieved, it was first based on the model of the statutory right. The bonds between persons that arise from their acquired and completed state, depend on this very state. They derive from the fact that these persons share one common characteristic that commands mutual respect. More precisely, the members of the same clan, or of a same family, have mutual duties because they are supposed to be of the same flesh and blood. Not that this physical consubstantiality has moral efficacy in itself. But it means that the blood conveys a sacred principle from which it indistinguishable: to have the same blood is to share a same god, and the same religious characteristic. Very often, therefore, the adoption rite consists in introducing a few drops of the clan's blood into the veins of the adoptee. That being said, when men felt the need to create bonds other than those resulting from their status, that is to create bonds that were willed, they designed them quite naturally after the sole bonds that were before their eyes. Two distinct individuals or groups, between whom there are no natural ties, agree to accomplish something in common. In order to be bound by their agreement, they must achieve this material consubstantiality deemed to be the source of every obligation. They mingle their blood. For example, two contracting parties may dip their hands in a vase into which they have poured some of their blood, and suck up a few drops of this mixture. This operation, which is today common knowledge, was studied by R. Smith under the name of 'blood covenant'. In this way, the two parties were under an obligation to each other. In some respects, this relation was the result of their intention – there was something contractual about it, however it became wholly efficacious only by taking the form of a contractual relationship. The two individuals formed, as it were, a kind of artificial group resting upon links analogous to those found in the natural groups to which each of these individuals belonged. For that matter, there were other means leading to the same results. Food makes blood and life: to eat the same food is therefore to commune together with the same source of life, it is to acquire the same blood. This is the source of the great role played by the rite of food communion in every religion, from the most ancient ones to Christianity. The same sacred thing is eaten in common in order to partake of the same god. People taking part in this ritual are thereby bound to one another. Two contracting parties were also able to bind each other by drinking from the same glass, or by eating the same dish, or even by eating together. The act of drinking out of the same glass is still to be found in many wedding customs. The practice of sealing a contract by drinking together presumably has presumably no other origin, as does that of shaking hands.

In these examples, the bonds derived from personal status serve as a model for new contractual links. However, the bonds derived from *real* status were also used to the same end. The duties and obligations that I have in respect of a thing depend on the state of that thing, and on its legal situation. If this thing is the property of another, I must respect it; if, nevertheless, this thing should come into my possession, I have to return it or the equivalent of it. This being so, let us suppose that there are two individuals or groups who want to engage in a transaction, for example, the exchange of one thing for another, or for a sum money. One of the parties hands over the thing; by this act alone, the one who receives it finds himself contracting an obligation, that of restoring the equivalent of the thing in question. This is the origin of what has been called the real contract, that is, a contract that derives only from the actual transaction of a thing. Now, we know the role that real contracts have played not only in Roman law and in Germanic law, but also in our own ancient French law. There still remain very clear traces of it in the law of the present day. It is indeed from this that the custom of earnest payment comes. Instead of giving the object of the exchange itself, only part of its value, or another object was given. Often, a valueless thing sufficed, such as the wisp of straw or the glove used in Germanic Law. The object received made the one who received it a debtor to the other party. In the course of time, the gesture of handing over the object came to suffice.

However, as we see, neither the blood covenant, nor the real contract were contracts properly speaking. For in these two types of cases, the obligation does not result from the efficacy of the agreement. This would be, of itself, powerless to bind. It must moreover express a state, of persons or things, and it is this state and not the agreement that is the real originating cause of the link thus created. If, on the strength of a blood covenant, I find myself under an obligation towards my allies, and vice versa, this is not by virtue of the consent given, but because, through the process that has been undertaken, we find ourselves sharing the same blood. If, in a *real* contract, I owe the price of the object received, it is not because I have promised to pay it, but because this object has come into my possession, and because it is thereby in a certain legal situation. All these practices are just so many devices to achieve almost the same ends as a contract, but by means other than the contract proper. For, we must repeat, what constitutes the contract is the declaration of agreement involved. Now, there must be something more than this: a state of things or persons must have been created without any intermediary, of a kind to bring about effects in law. As long as an intermediary exists, there can be no proper contract.

There is, however, another way by means of which we get closer to the true contract. The parties cannot be bound unless they assert themselves. This affirmation is made in words. Now, words are something that are real, natural, and complete, something that can be vested with a religious power to bind and compel those who have uttered them. For this to be so, they have to be pronounced according to ritual forms and in ritual conditions. When this is the case, they become sacred. One means of giving them this sacred character is the oath, that is, the invocation of a divine being. Through this invocation, the divine being becomes the guarantor of the promise exchanged; and the promise henceforth (and even before its performance) becomes binding under threat of religious penalties of known gravity. For example, each contracting party pronounces a word that binds him or a formula that calls some divine curse on his head should he fail to honour his commitment. Very often sacrifices and magical rituals of all kinds reinforce still further the coercive power of the words thus pronounced.

This was the origin of formal and solemn contracts. Their main characteristic is that they are binding only if the parties have committed themselves according to a definite and solemn formula, from which divergence is not allowed. It is the formula that binds. It is the distinctive characteristic of magical and religious formulas. The legal formula is only a substitute for religious formalism. When some definite words, put in a specific order, come to have a moral influence which is lost if they are different or uttered in a different sequence, we can be assured that they have or have had a religious meaning, and that their special power comes from religious causes. For it is only the religious word that can have this power over things and men. With the Romans in particular, there is a phenomenon showing how much at first contracts were endowed with a sacred power: it is the custom of the *sacramentum*. When two contracting parties disagreed about what their respective rights and duties were, they deposited a sum of money in a temple, which varied according to the importance of the dispute: this was the *sacramentum*. The one who lost his case also lost the sum he had deposited. This meant that he was fined by the deity, which implies that his undertaking was considered as an offence against the gods. The gods were, then, parties to the contract.

We can now see how slowly the notion of contract has emerged. Neither the blood covenant nor *real* contracts are true contracts. The solemn contract is closer to it. This is because, as soon as the parties have asserted themselves, the commitment is sacred. However, even in this case, it is not from the agreement that the moral value of the commitment arises, but from the formula used. Should the solemn ritual be lacking, there is no contract. In the next lecture, we shall see the other stages that contract law had to go through to reach its present state.

As we saw in the last lecture, societies have arrived at the notion of contract with much difficulty. All rights and duties derive from an actual state of persons or of things; but, in the contract *proper*, it is a state only conceived and not yet in being that is the source of the obligation. The only thing given and granted has been a declaration of intention. How can such a declaration bind the party making it? Should we say that in the contract, two parties are involved and that they bind each other somehow; that they have become in some way interdependent, and that this solidarity does not leave them wholly free? Assuming that the other contracting party has promised to fulfil an obligation, and that I, for my part, have promised something in return, how can these two promises mutually bind us to our obligations? It is not because the other has pledged himself towards me that my commitment to him is more or less compelling. Both pledges are of the same nature; and if neither of them has in itself the moral force to bind the parties, their agreement will not implement such a bond. Moreover, for a contract to come into existence, there is no need for an agreement on reciprocal performances. It may also be a unilateral contract. For example, donation contracts, as well as pledge contracts, do not involve any reciprocity. If I declare, in certain given circumstances, that I will give a certain amount of money or a certain thing to a certain person, I am bound to fulfil my promise, although I have received nothing in exchange. Therefore in this case it is solely the affirmation of my intention, without any other reciprocal declaration, that binds me. How does it come to have this special power?

It took peoples a very long time to imbue the mere expression of intention with such legal and moral effect. When exchanges became more frequent, the need for contractual links made itself felt, and expedients were used to meet this need. Without creating new law, an attempt was made to adapt Statute Law to these new needs. The principle was as follows. As soon as the contracting parties reached an agreement, a state of things or of persons was immediately brought into being, which then became the source of subsequent obligations. For example, one of the contracting parties would carry out the service he agreed on. From then on, there was something acquired and brought into being, that bound the other party. The vendor delivered the thing, which came into the possession of the purchaser according to the terms of the contract. Thus, the latter was bound to perform his part of the contract, by virtue of the rule (universally accepted, albeit differently sanctioned by various societies), that one may not get richer at the expense of others. Or else, once the terms of the contract were agreed upon, the contracting parties consented to an operation that created a kind of kinship *sui generis* between them; this acquired kinship then created a whole system of rights and duties. By these two processes, Statute law was adapted because an agreement, and the links created thereby, were genuinely contractual in nature. But these links do not result from an agreement, and in this respect there is still no contract *proper*. In both cases, the consent is not binding in itself; in fact, it generates no rights, except through an intermediary. It is the acquired state, either of things or of persons, immediately following the agreement, which alone gives legal effect to that agreement. As long as the contract has not been performed, at least in part, as long as the contracting parties have not mingled their blood or sat at the same table, they remain free to go back on their decision. The declaration of intention alone is ineffective. Statute law has been used to arrive at the same results as contract law, but for the moment, the latter has still not come into existence.

There is, however, another method by which men have succeeded in getting nearer to it. In any case, parties cannot agree unless they declare their intentions outwardly, or unless they project them externally. Their intentions have to become known, so that the society may attach a moral meaning to them. This declaration or outward expression is couched in words. Now, words are something real and tangible that can be vested with religious force that, once they are uttered, gives them the power to bind and to compel those who pronounce them. For this to happen, they must merely be uttered according to certain formulas and in certain religious forms. They become sacred. Now, we can well imagine that, once endowed with this sacred meaning, such words command the respect of those who have uttered them. They carry the same prestige as those things and persons which are the object of rights and duties. They too, therefore, may be a source of obligations. One means of rendering them thus and hence, conferring this binding force, is the oath, that is, the invocation of a divine being. By this invocation, the being becomes the guarantor of the pledges made or exchanged; he inheres in them and imbues them with his nature and the feelings he inspires. To breach the oath is to offend the divine being, to be exposed to his revenge, that is, to the religious penalties that appear to the faithful as certain and inevitable as those meted out by courts later in history. Thus, as soon as the words are spoken by the contracting party, they no longer belong to him, they have become exterior to him, for they have changed in nature. They are sacred, and he is profane. As a consequence, they fall outside his control: even though they come from him, they are no longer dependent on him. He can no longer change them and he is bound to carry them out. The oath is also a means of giving words, that is, the direct manifestations of the human will, the kind of transcendence that all moral things have. The oath also strips the words, as it were, from the individual who utters them and changes them into something new that imposes itself on his will.

Such is presumably the origin of formal and solemn contracts. Their distinctive feature is that they are not valid unless certain special formulas have been uttered. This cannot be evaded, or else the contract will have no binding force. Now, this, too, is an essential characteristic of magical and religious formulas. When the special words, put in a certain defined sequence, are held to have a force which would be lost should the slightest modification be made, we can be sure that they have or have had a religious meaning and that they derive their special force from a religious source. This is because only religious words can have this effect upon men and things. Legal formalism is only a substitute for religious formalism. Moreover, in Germanic, the word referring to the fact of making a solemn contract is *adhramire* or *arramire*, which has been translated as: *fidem jurejurendo facere*. It is sometimes associated with *sacramentum*: '*Sacramenta quae ad palatium fuerunt adramita.*' *Adramire* is to make a solemn promise on oath. It is extremely probable that originally, the Roman *stipulatio* had the same character. It was a contract made *verbis*, that is, by means of a special formula. Now, for those who know to what degree the principles of Roman law were religious and pontifical, there is no doubt that these *verba* were at first ritual formulas intended to consecrate the commitment. It is certain that they were pronounced before priests and possibly in sacred places. Were not solemn words, moreover, called sacramental words?

However, it is probable that, if not always, at least very often, verbal rituals did not suffice to consecrate the words exchanged and make them irrevocable; manual rites were also used. Such was probably the source of God's penny (*denier à Dieu*). God's penny was a coin that one of those contracting gave to the other once the bargain was struck. It was neither a deposit, nor a kind of down payment, for it was supplied by one of the parties as an additional payment that was not charged to the amount finally paid. It does not therefore seem possible to see it as a partial performance such as we see in real contracts. But it must have a meaning. It was generally used in religious practices, as shown by its name: God's penny. Might it not rather be a vestige of some offering intended to interest the deity in the contract, as it were, and to make him party to the agreement? This is quite as effective a means of invoking the deity as the utterance of words, and thus, of sanctioning the agreement.

The same probably applies to the rite of the wisp of straw. In the last lecture we read this ritual as a survival of the real contract. But this was a mistake. There are in fact no grounds for believing that the former predates the latter; hence, there is no proof that it derives from the real contract. Another reason for not believing this is that the wisp of straw, or *festuca*, delivery of which consecrated the undertaking, was not handed over by the future creditor, but by the future debtor. Unlike the transfer in real contract, it was not a completed or partly completed performance, since the debtor still had to perform his entire side of the agreement. The effect of such an operation did not bind the creditor to the debtor, but rather bound the debtor to the creditor. Finally, the solemn contract of the Romans, which was made *verbis*, that is, by means of consecrated formulas, was called *stipulatio.* Now the word *stipulatio* comes from *stipula,* which also means wisp of straw. And '*Veteres, quando sibi aliquid promettebant, stipulam tenentes frangebant.*' The *stipula* was still widely used until a late stage in history. It means, therefore, that it was closely linked to the verbal solemn contract. The two processes seem inseparable. As for the exact meaning of this rite, it is difficult to say. Obviously, it meant a kind of liege homage from the debtor towards the creditor, binding the former to the latter. It transmitted part of the debtor's legal personality and part of his rights to the creditor. What makes me think it has this meaning is the nature of the operation that replaced it in the later Middle Ages. Indeed, the *festuca* did not survive after the Frankish period. It was replaced by a gesture of the hand. When it was matter of an undertaking that had to be given to a definite person, the future debtor placed his hands in those of the creditor. When it was just a unilateral promise or an affirmatory oath, the hand was laid on relics, or raised to the sky (was it to call it as witness ?). Here, the sacred, if not mystic, character of the gestures is clearer, and indeed they can still be found in our present customs. On the other hand, there is no doubt that their purpose was to create a bond. This is particularly noticeable in the two main kinds of contract. First, there was the feudal contract that bound men to their lord. In order to plight fealty and homage, the vassal knelt down and put his hands in those of the lord, and pledged loyalty to him. The same practice can be found in plighting troth. It was by joining hands that the fiancés promised to marry each other, a practice that has left a trace in the ritual of Catholic marriage. We also know that the betrothal contract was obligatory.

We are no longer in a position to say precisely what the religious beliefs underlying these practices were. However, the comparisons we have just made suggest some general indications. The laying on of hands or the joining of hands are a substitute for the ritual of *festuca.* As a consequence, both must have the same meaning and the same purpose. Now, the ritual of laying on of hands is very well known; all religions use it. When it is to bless or consecrate some object, the priest lays his hands upon it; when an individual seeks absolution for his sins, the priest lays his hands on the victim he is about to sacrifice. Whatever was unclean in him or in his personality comes out of him and is passed on to the animal and destroyed with it. In a different example, the victim, sacrificed by a similar process to pay tribute to some divinity, becomes a substitute for the person who sacrifices it, or has it sacrificed. Thus, men imagined the personality as a communication, either total or in determined parts; and it is obvious that the purpose of these rituals was to bring about such a communication. Doubtless, when we study them in hindsight, we are inclined to see them only as symbols or ways of giving allegorical form to the bonds contracted. It is nevertheless a general rule that customs never take a symbolic form to start with; symbolism only occurs when they degenerate and lose their primary meaning. Customs are originally not symbols but effective causes of social relations; they bring these into existence and it is not until later that they degenerate into mere external and material signs. The transfer that gave rise to the real contract is well known to be a real transfer; it is what makes the contract and what gives it its binding quality. It is only much later that it becomes merely a means of giving material evidence of the contract. The same applies to the customs we have just described. They should be seen in the same way as the *blood covenant*. They too have the effect of binding the contracting parties by affecting their legal personality. Perhaps the handshake or *Handschlag* has the same origin?

Thus, contracts of this kind are made up of two parts: a verbal core (the formula), and concrete rituals. As such, they are already closer to the true contract than to the real contract. For although intermediate practices are still needed to give legal effect to the agreement, at least these practices directly bind the parties involved. This is because these intermediate practices were not the actual performance, either wholly or even in part, of the object of the contract. Whatever the solemn ritual employed, the undertakings made by each party must still be met in full, even once the solemn ritual has been completed. On both sides, there are only promises, and yet these promises commit the two parties. This is not the case with the real contract, since one of the contracting parties has already performed his undertaking, wholly or in part; thus one of the parties has gone past the state of intention, since he has fulfilled his promise. It is true that the blood covenant had the same advantage. It is easy to see, however, that such an excessively complex ritual could only serve on special occasions, and not in the small matters of everyday life. It could not be used in ordinary day-to-day trading. It was hardly ever used except to create an enduring association.

Moreover, the solemn contract was easy to improve and indeed this occurred in due course. The material rites cloaking it, as it were, gradually faded away into nothing. In Rome, this improvement was as early as the classical era. The outward formalities of the *stipulatio* became a distant memory; only scholars find traces of it in popular customs and in the folklore of the distant past, or in the actual form of the word. But the formalities were no longer needed for the *stipulatio* to be valid. The latter consisted exclusively of the consecrated formula which had to be pronounced with scrupulous exactitude by the contracting parties. The same phenomenon has occurred in modern societies under the influence of Christianity. The Church tended more and more to make the oath the necessary and sufficient condition for the validity of the contract, without further formality. Thus, the intermediate practices between the agreement and the obligation to fulfil this agreement gradually fell away. Since words are the direct expression of the will, there only remained, as conditions external to the consent itself, the definite character of the formula intended to express this consent, and the particular power and character of the formula. When these powers were brought to naught and there was no longer any required formula for the contracting parties, then the contract proper or consensual contract was born.

That is the fourth stage of its evolution. How then did the contract reach the point where it freed itself of this last extrinsic and accidental feature? Several factors contributed to this result.

First, as trade developed, it became much commoner and more varied, which made it difficult to maintain the cumbersome formalism of the solemn contract. New relationships were created by means of contracts which the consecrated, stereotyped formulas did not suit. Legal operations themselves needed to become more flexible to be able to conform to social life. When exchanges become incessant, when trade continues without respite, it is impossible to require every buyer or seller to take an oath, or use such or such precise formula, and so on... The workaday continuity of these relations inevitably ruled out all solemn ritual and it was only natural to seek the means to curtail, simplify, or even get rid of this formalism. But this explanation is not enough. Just because these means were needed, it does not mean that they were found. We still need to explain how they appeared to the public mind when they were found to be necessary. Just because an institution is useful does not mean it will appear from nowhere as required. It must come from something, that is, the ideas of the time must allow it to appear, and existing institutions must not be an obstacle to it but rather be the material from which it will come. Thus it was not enough for economic progress to call for the consensual contract; it still had to be conceived of as possible by public opinion. Until then, it had seemed that contractual obligations could only result from specific ceremonials or from the actual delivery of the thing. That is why there needed to be a change in the public mindset that would allow them to originate differently. Thus we can picture how this last transformation occurred.

What was the initial obstacle to the idea of the consensual contract? It was the principle that any legal obligation could only result, it seemed, from an actual state of persons or of things. In itself, this principle is indisputable. Every right has a justification, and this justification can only be something definite, that is, an established fact. Is it impossible for mere declarations of intention to meet this requirement? Not at all. It is true that they cannot do so if the party making the undertaking is free to forswear. In this case, the intention would not constitute an established fact, since we do not know which way it will finally go; we cannot know for certain what it was, or what it will become. Therefore, nothing definite can result from it, nor can any right arise from it. But let us imagine that the intention of the contracting party is asserted in such a way that it cannot forswear. In that case, it will have all the features of an established and actual fact, which is likely to bring about similar consequences, since it is irrevocable. If I undertake to sell or let to you a certain item, in such a way that once this commitment is taken, I no longer have the right or the means to break it I elicit an equally clearly defined mental state in you, based on your certainty of what I am about to do. You rely, reasonably enough, on the promised performance: you are entitled to take it for granted, and you act accordingly. You decide something, you buy or sell something because of this justifiable certainty. If I then suddenly withdraw and deprive you of this certainty, I cause as much trouble to you as if I had taken back, after its delivery, the thing that I had handed over to you when forming the real contract with you. I change your mental state, and I annihilate all the transactions you may have started on faith of the given word. We can see that this unjustified wrong is immoral.

Now, in the solemn contract, the condition we have just set out is met: the irrevocability of the intention is guaranteed. It is the solemn nature of the commitment that gives it this characteristic, by consecrating it, and by making of it something that no longer depends on me, despite coming from me. The other party is thus justified in relying on my word (and vice versa if the contract happens to be bilateral). He has a moral and legal right to consider my promise as binding. If, then, I break that promise, I am committing a twofold breach of duty: (1) I am committing sacrilege, since I am violating an oath, I am profaning a sacred thing, I am committing an act forbidden to me by religion, I am encroaching upon the realm of sacred things. (2) I am disturbing another in his possession just as I if I were a neighbour encroaching upon his land, I am harming him or am liable to harm him. Now, inasfar as the right of the individual is sufficiently recognized, it is forbidden to harm another unjustifiably. Thus, in a solemn contract, the formal tie that binds the contracting parties is twofold: I am bound to the gods by my oath, I am compelled by them to fulfil my promise. But I am also bound to another because my oath, by alienating my word and exteriorizing it, allows him to possess it for good, as if it were a thing. There is then, a twofold resistance to the violation of such contracts, in ancient and religious law on the one hand, and in modern and human law on the other.

We can now glimpse how these things must have happened. It is the second of these two elements which, entirely freed from the fetters of the former (e.g. of the solemn formalities), has become the consensual contract. The demands of a more active life tended to reduce the importance of ceremonials. At the same time, indeed, shrinking faith made people value them less, and little by little, the meaning of many disappeared. If then there had been in the solemn contract no more than the legal ties generated by the solemn formalities, such an evolution would have inevitably led to actual regression in contract law, since the undertaking would have lacked any basis. But we have just seen that there was another tie which would survive, that which is rooted in individual rights. It is true that this second type of tie stems from the first; for if there is already an established fact, if the word becomes objective and cannot be forsworn by the contracting party, it is because an oath has been taken. Now, could this result, which used to be obtained in this way, be arrived at otherwise? It is enough to establish that the mere declaration of intention, unreserved, unequivocal and unconditional, in all aspects irrevocable, is indeed irrevocable. Therefore, it could affect individuals just as it had when it was couched in solemn ritual, it had the same binding force. This proved the existence of the consensual contract, which built up from the solemn contract. The latter had taught men that commitments could be made for good, except that the definitive character was the result of formal or liturgical ceremonies. The definitive characteristic became separate from the cause that had brought it about in the first place, and was linked to another cause, thus giving birth to a new kind of contract, or rather, the contract *proper*. The consensual contract is a solemn contract whose useful effects are kept but brought about by other means. Had the solemn contract not existed, the idea of the consensual contract would not have been formed, nor would there have been any idea that a word of honour, which is fleeting and breakable by anyone, could be thus fixed and substantialized. However, whereas the solemn contract was fixed by means of magical or religious operations, in the consensual contract the given word acquired the same fixity and objectivity through the effect of the law alone. To understand this new kind of contract, we cannot start from the nature of the will or from the words that express it; there is nothing in the given word to bind the individual pronouncing it. The obligatory force and the acts come from without. It is religious beliefs that synthesized them; once achieved, this synthesis was sustained by other causes, because it was useful.

Of course, this explanation simplifies things, to make these matters more intelligible. Formalism was not abolished and replaced by a new principle in one day. On the contrary, it was only very slowly that the solemn formalities lost ground, under the dual influence we mentioned: the new demands of economic life and the blurring of the notions that lay at heart of these solemn formalities. It was, too, only very slowly that the new rule emerged from the formalist practices obscuring it. This occurred as the need became more and more pressing, and the old traditions offered increasingly less resistance. The conflict between the two principles lasted a very long time. Both the real contract and the solemn contract remained the basis of Roman contractual law, which was preserved only for certain particular cases. Until very late in the Middle Ages, very distinct traces of the old legal concepts could be found.

Moreover, the solemn contract has not disappeared. There are vestiges of its application in all codes of law. The foregoing account helps us understand what these vestiges correspond to. The solemn contract binds men in two ways: it binds them to one another, and it binds them either to the deity (if the deity participates in the contract), or to the society (if the society takes part in the contract through its representatives). Now, we know that the deity is only the symbolic form of the society. The solemn contract is therefore more binding than any other contract. This is why it is required every time that the bonds to be contracted are of great importance, such as in marriage. Marriage is a solemn contract, not only because the solemn ritual makes it easier to prove its existence, recording the dates, etc., but also because it invokes high moral values and cannot be changed freely by the contracting parties. The purpose is to involve a higher moral authority in the relationship being formed.

In sum, the consensual contract is in fact the culmination, the point where the real contract on the one hand, and the verbal solemn contract on the other hand, have converged in the process of their development. In the real contract, there is the transfer of a thing and it is this transfer that gives birth to the obligation: because I have received the object that you have handed over to me, I become your debtor. In the solemn contract, there is no actual performance; everything is accomplished through words, usually accompanied by certain ritual gestures. However, these words are uttered in such a way that, as soon as they leave the mouth of the promisor, they become, so to speak, exterior to him; they are *ipso facto* separated from his will, he no longer has power over them, they are what they are and he can no longer change them. They have thus become a thing in the true sense of the word. But then, they too are subject to transfer; they too can be alienated in some way or handed over to another, just like the material objects that make up our possessions. Those expressions still in current use: to give one's word, to pledge one's word, are not mere metaphors but signify a real transfer. Once given, our word does not belong to us any longer. In the solemn contract, this transfer had already been performed, but was subject to the magical and religious operations we have mentioned and which alone made this transfer possible, since they objectivized the word and the resolution of the promisor. When this transfer freed itself of the rituals on which it used to depend, and alone came to constitute the whole contractual act, the consensual contract was born. Now, once the solemn contract had come into existence, this reduction and simplification were bound to happen naturally. First of all, the verbal and other rituals declined, owing to a kind of spontaneous degeneration and the pressure of social needs that demanded faster transactions. Then, the useful effects of the solemn contracts could be attained sufficiently by means other than these rituals; it sufficed for the law to declare irrevocable any declaration of intention stated as such. This simplification was all the more easily accepted as in the natural course of things, the less used practices had lost a great deal of their meaning and initial authority. No doubt this reduced contract could not have the same binding force as the solemn contract, since in the latter the parties are, as it were, doubly bound – bound to the moral authority invoked in the contract, and bound to one another. But the economic needs of the time required contractual ties to lose some of their rigidity; if they were to be made more easily, they had to take on a more secular character, and the act designed to create this tie had to lose its religious solemnity. It sufficed to reserve the solemn contract for cases where the contractual relationship was of particular importance.

Such is the principle of the consensual contract: in the final analysis, it substitutes a simple verbal transfer or even, to be more exact, a mental and psychological transfer, for the material transfer of the real contract as we shall see. Thus, once it was established, it entirely replaced the real contract, which then no longer had any reason to exist. Its obligatory force was no greater, and moreover its forms were pointlessly complex and vague. This is why it has left no trace in contemporary law, whereas the solemn contract survives in it, alongside the consensual contract which was born from it.

As this principle became established, it caused various changes in the institution of contract, and these changes would little by little alter its entire appearance.

The system of the real contract and of the solemn contract corresponds to a stage in social evolution where the right of individuals was still little recognized. The consequence was that the individual rights involved in every contract were only poorly protected. Certainly it happened quite often that a recalcitrant debtor was sentenced to a penalty such as whipping, imprisonment or a fine. For example, in China, he would receive a certain number of strokes of the bamboo; the same custom is to be found in Japan; and in ancient Hindu law, the penalty was monetary. But the rule whereby the true sanction was to compel the contracting party either to keep his word, or to compensate for the wrong he may have caused to the other party by failing to meet his undertaking – this rule was at the time still unknown. In other words, at that time a contract gave rise to penal sanctions only when it appeared as an offence against the public authority, and the way in which it affected individuals was not taken into account. No provision was made for the private wrongs it might cause. As a consequence, the creditor had no guarantee that his debt would be paid. It is surely this situation that gave rise to a curious custom to be observed in different societies, but especially in Ireland and in India – this is probably why it is generally known under its Indian name: the *dhârna*. In order to constrain the debtor to pay his due, the creditor installs himself at his doorstep and threatens to let himself die of hunger unless the debt is repaid. And, of course, the threat could not have been considered as serious if the man on hunger strike had not been determined to go all the way if necessary, that is, if he was not ready to commit suicide. Marion, when listing the legal means to enforce the payment of a debt, says that 'In the fourth place, there was the hunger strike, when the creditor installed himself at the doorstep of the debtor and let himself die of hunger'. The efficacy of this strange procedure comes from the beliefs and feelings attached to the dead. We know how dreaded they were. They are powers from which the living cannot escape. Thus it happened often in early societies that suicide was committed as a means of revenge. It was believed that killing oneself better ensured revenge than killing one's enemy. It was, above all, a means of revenge that the weak could use against the strong. Someone who, given the circumstances of his life, would be defenceless against some high-placed person, would still have the power to replace the earthly revenge that he could not take on his enemy with a revenge from beyond the grave that was held to be more terrible, and above all, infallible. It might even be possible, in the case of the *dhârna* proper, that suicide often aimed at immuring the debtor in his house whilst giving a magical character to the threshold, thus rendering it impassable. It is indeed on the threshold that the creditor settles, and there that he dies; it is therefore there that his spirit, once released from the body, will return. The spirit will keep watch over this threshold and prevent the actual owner of the house from crossing it. At least, he will be in great danger if he crosses it. This constitutes, as it were, a seizure of the house by the dead, a kind of posthumous distraint.

Such a custom obviously shows that, in order to obtain his due, the creditor was left to his own devices. Besides, even in Germanic law, he was the one who had to perform the distraint. It is true that the law commands the debtor to allow it to happen, but the authorities do not intervene on behalf of private individuals, and they do not even help them. It is because the specific bond established by the contract did not have a strong moral character: it became so only in the consensual contract, for in here the relationship created by the contract alone constitutes its authority. As a result, the essential purpose of the sanctions applying to the contracts is not to avenge the disregard of the public authority, as in the case of the defaulting debtor, but to ensure for both parties the full and direct fulfillment of the rights they had acquired.

It is not, however, only the sanctions – that is, the outward organization of the contractual right – that have been altered. Its internal structure too was entirely transformed.

At first the solemn contract, like the real contract, could only be unilateral. The unilateral character of the latter resulted from the fact that one of the parties performed indirectly; he could therefore not be bound to the other. There was only a debtor (the one who had received) and a creditor (the one who had delivered the thing). In the solemn contract, it was the same, for it involves an individual who promises and one who receives the promise. For example, in Rome, someone would ask: 'Do you promise to do or give this or that?' And the other would reply 'I do promise.' In order to create a bilateral bond, that is to say, in order for an exchange to take place in the course of the contract, and for each contracting party to be both debtor and creditor, there needed to be two separate contracts, independent of each other, for the roles assigned to each were entirely different. There was necessarily a true inversion: the one who spoke first as stipulator or creditor later on spoke as debtor and promisor, and vice versa. The independence of the two operations was such that the validity of the first was entirely distinct from the validity of the second. Let us suppose, for example, that I have solemnly promised to pay a certain sum to Primius as the price of a murder that he on his part has promised to commit: under the terms of a solemn contract, this reciprocal obligation will take shape by means of two unilateral and successive contracts. I shall begin by solemnly promising a sum of money to Primius, who will accept – at this stage, I am the promisor and he is the stipulator and there is no mention of any murder to commit. Then, in another contract, he will promise to commit this murder, at my request. Now, the second contract is unlawful, because its cause is immoral. The first contract, however, is perfectly legal. As a consequence, Roman law used to consider the promise to pay the sum of money as valid in itself, and a legal loophole was used to escape the consequences. Such a system did not lend itself easily to operations of exchange or to bilateral or synallagmatic relations. In fact, in Germanic law, synallagmatic contracts, if not unknown, were only used in cash transactions, and cash transactions are not truly contractual. Only the consensual contract was able simultaneously to create the twofold network of bonds constituted by any bilateral agreement. It is because the greater flexibility of the system allows every contracting party to play both the role of the debtor and of the creditor, of the stipulator and of the promisor. Since contracting parties are no longer under obligation to scrupulously follow a definite formula, reciprocal obligations can be contracted simultaneously. Both parties declare at the same time that they consent to the exchange, on the conditions they have agreed on.

Another innovation of great importance resulted from the fact that consensual contracts became of necessity *bona fide* contracts. This name is given to contracts whose scope and legal effects must be exclusively determined by the intent of the parties.

It was impossible for the real and for the consensual contracts to show such a characteristic, or at least, only very imperfectly. This is because in both cases the obligation derived not purely and simply from the consent given or from the manifestation of intent. There needed to be another factor for the contracting parties to be bound. Thereafter, this factor, which was even decisive, inevitably changed the nature and the form of both these contracts. It was therefore impossible for these two types of contract to depend exclusively or even mainly on what might be called the psychological factor, that is, the will or intention. In the case of the real contract, there was the thing transferred; since it constituted the binding force of the act, it contributed to a large extent to determining the scope of the obligation. In the Roman *mutuum,* or simple loan, the borrower owed things of the same kind and amount as those he had received. In other words, it was the kind, nature and quantity of the things received that determined the kind, nature and quantity of the things owed. This was the primitive form of the real contract. Later on, it is true, the real contract was used in exchanges proper, in which the debtor owed not a thing equivalent to the one he had received, but an equivalent value. In this case, the thing played a small part. However, the use of the real contract for this purpose came relatively late; when it took this form, it was because the consensual contract was emerging. Thus, as we said about the Germans, until the appearance of the consensual contract, exchanges consisted of cash transactions in almost all cases. In fact, even in this case, the thing delivered was no less a source of the obligation and therefore affected the obligation. There was no need to wonder what one of the parties had meant to deliver, or what the other had wished to receive, since the delivery had been performed, since the thing was there, with its intrinsic value which determined the value owed by the debtor to the creditor. The object speaks for itself and decides. The role of the thing in the real contract is played by the words or the rites used in the solemn contract. In this case, it is the words used and the gesture performed that constitute the obligation; it is also these that define it. To ascertain what the promisor or debtor is required to give or do, we do not need to sound out his intent or that of the other party, but the formula that he has uttered. At any rate, that is where legal analysis must start. Since it is the words that have binding force, it is the words, too, that show the extent of the bonds created. And so, even in the last stage of Roman law, the contract by stipulation was subject to very strict interpretation. The intention of the parties, even when obvious, was of no effect if it was impossible to discern it in the words used (Accarias, *Précis du droit romain,* 213). It is because, once again, the formula has a value in itself, it has its own power, and this power could not depend on the intention of the contracting parties since, on the contrary, it is the formula which binds the parties. This is how a magic formula produces its effects, mechanically as it were and independently the intentions of those who might use it. If the latter know how to use it in a way that best fits their interests, so much the better for them. But the active power of the formula is not subject to their desires. For all these reasons, the good faith and intention of the contracting parties were hardly taken into account in real contracts and in solemn contracts. In Rome, it was only in the year 688 that the action in *dolo* was instituted, allowing the contracting party deceived by fraudulent manoeuvres to obtain redress for the injury caused.

However, once the consensual contract was born, this could no longer be the case. Indeed, the thing is no longer part of the contractual relationship, altering its nature. It is true that words are still used, at least in general; but these words no longer have any power in themselves since they are devoid of any religious dimension. Their only value is to express intentions and therefore it is the state of these intentions that determines the obligations contracted. Words in themselves no longer matter; they are only symbols to be interpreted, and what they expressed is the state of mind and the intention that inspired them. We said earlier that the expression 'to give one's word' is not quite metaphorical. There is indeed something that we give, that we alienate, that we forbid ourselves to alter. But strictly speaking, it is not the words uttered that are marked *ne varietur,* but the resolution they express. What I am giving to another is my firm intention to act in such or such a way: it is therefore this intent that we have to analyse to find out what I have given, that is, what I have undertaken to do. For the same reason, in order for a contract to exist, the contracting parties must intend it. Should the intention be lacking on either side, there can be no contract. For what one party is in fact giving is his intention of acting in a certain way, to transfer the ownership of a certain object; what the other is declaring is his intention to accept what is thus transferred to him. If the intention is lacking, nothing remains but the form of the contract, devoid of any positive content. There only remain meaningless words, therefore lacking any value. We do not for that matter have to specify the rules whereby the influence of the parties' intention on the contractual obligations is measured. It is enough to state the general principle and to show how the consensual contract had to be a *bona fide* contract and how it could not be *bona fide* unless it was consensual.

We can see how the consensual contract amounts to a revolutionary legal device. The paramount role of the consent or declaration of intention transformed the institution. It distinguishes itself by a whole set of clear-cut characteristics from the earlier forms of contracts from which it derives. By the mere fact that it is consensual, the contract is sanctioned, bilateral, and made in good faith. But that is not all. The principle on which this renewed institution is based also led to new developments, the causes and direction of which we now have to explain.

Consent may be given, depending on the circumstances, in many different ways and therefore may have different qualities which will cause its value and moral significance to vary. Once it was agreed that consent was the basis of the contract, it was natural that the public mind would distinguish the different forms that the consent might take, assess these forms, and determine their moral and legal impact accordingly.

The idea governing this evolution is that consent is only genuine, and only truly and absolutely binds the party who gives it, where it has been given freely. Anything that curtails the freedom of the contracting party reduces the binding force of the contract. Such a rule should not be confused with that requiring that the contract should be intentional, for I may very well have had the intention to contract as I have done, and yet have contracted only under duress. In this case, I do intend my undertaking; but I intend it because pressure has been placed on me. In this case, the consent is said to be vitiated, and as a consequence, the contract is null and void.

As natural as this idea may seem, it arose only very slowly and encountered many obstacles. Given that, for centuries, the binding force of the contract had been assumed to lie outside of the contracting parties (in the formula uttered, in the gesture made, or in the thing delivered), the value of the bond contracted could not be made to depend on what might have happened in the depths of the contracting parties' consciousness or on the circumstances in which their decision had been taken. It was not until the year 674, after the dictatorship of Scylla, that an action was created in Rome to allow those who had been constrained by threat to contract undertakings harmful to themselves, to obtain redress for the injury that had been caused to them. It was the spectacle of the disorder and abuses which took place in Rome under the reign of terror imposed by Scylla that suggested the idea. This action thus arose from exceptional circumstances but outlived them. It was given the name of *actio quod metus causa*. Its scope, by the way, was quite limited. The fear caused to a contracting party by a third party could lead to recision only where the object of the fear was an extraordinary evil of a kind to affect the strongest man. The only two evils considered to fit this requirement were death or physical torture. Later, with the softening of mores, the fear of unmerited servitude, a capital charge or an indecent assault were assimilated with the fear of death. But the fear of losing one's honour or fortune was never taken into account (Accarias, ibid., 1079).

In our contemporary law, the rule has been still further softened. The fear vitiating the contract no longer needs to be such that even a stoic would be affected by it. It is enough, as the maxim says (Art. 112) that it would move any reasonable man. The text of the code even adds that 'in this matter', we must take into account 'the age, sex and condition of the persons involved'. The duress at stake here is thus quite relative; in some cases, it may even be very slight. We have come a long way from the strict limitations of Roman law.

What is the origin of this legal precept, whose importance we shall explain later? It is commonly held that man is a free agent and therefore that the consent he gives can be ascribed to him only if it has been freely given. Here, we see ideas similar to those we shall find concerning responsibility. If, it is said, an act has not been committed by a criminal of his own will, this act does not come from him, and therefore he cannot be blamed for it. Similarly, in the case of the contract, there is a kind of responsibility that results from the promise I have made, for I am bound to perform certain acts as a consequence of this promise. But the party to whom the promise has been made cannot require of me that I fulfil it unless it is I myself who has made it. Now, if I am forced to do it by a third party, I am not in fact responsible, and therefore I cannot be bound by an undertaking that another has made, so to speak, through me. If the person who has forced me also happens to be the beneficiary of the contract, he finds himself, as it were, with no other guarantor than himself; that is to say, there is no longer any contract.

But the drawback of this explanation is that it supposes that a legal institution is only created to solve a metaphysical problem. Is man a free agent or not? This is a question which, in fact, has never had any impact on legislation and it is easy to understand why the law should not depend on it. Admittedly, we might believe that opinions on this controversial point may at times have contributed to determining the spirit and the letter of the law in one way or another, and that the law changes according to whether peoples believe in freedom or not. But the truth is that the public has never become conscious of this problem in its abstract form. There are hardly any societies that do not believe at the same time in something similar to what we call freedom, and in something analogous to determinism, without either of the two notions ever entirely excluding the other. From the birth of Christianity onwards, for example, we find at the same time the theory of predetermination by Providence and the theory whereby the faithful are themselves the source of their own faith and morality.

If indeed man is a free agent, he seems to be always able to refuse his consent if he wants; hence, why should he not bear the consequences of that consent? The fact is all the more surprising and inexplicable as, in the case we are examining, that is, contract, small acts of coercion are sometimes held to alter the consent. Yet no great fortitude is needed to resist them. We do not allow a man to kill another one to avoid losing money; rather, we make him liable for his act. However, nowadays we believe that the fear of an undeserved loss suffices to vitiate a contract and thus cancel the liability of the party who acts under duress. But the freedom and power to resist are the same in the two cases. Why is it that in the case described the act should be considered as deliberate and agreed upon, and in the other instance it should be of an entirely different nature? Lastly, there are many cases in which the fear is intense and leaves no room for choice, and the intention is therefore predetermined, but in which nonetheless the contract is valid. The tradesman who can only avoid the threat of bankruptcy by contracting a loan resorts to this means of salvation because he cannot do otherwise, and yet, if the lender has not taken unfair advantage of the situation, the contract is morally and legally valid.

It is therefore not the greater or lesser amount of freedom that matters: if the contracts imposed by direct or indirect constraint are not binding, it is not because of the state of the party's intention when he assented. Rather, it is because of the consequences that undertakings thus formed necessarily have on the contracting parties. Indeed, if the contracting party took the step that bound him only under an external constraint, or if his consent was forced out of him, it is because the consent was against his own interest and the just demands he might have under general principles of equity. The use of duress can have had no other purpose or result but that of forcing him to make over something that he did not want to, or do something he did not want to, or else to make over or do something under conditions he refused. Pain and suffering have thus been imposed on him, undeservedly so. Now, our feelings of sympathy for humans in general are hurt when suffering is undeservedly inflicted on someone. The only suffering we deem fair is a punishment and any punishment presupposes a guilty act. When an act harms one of our fellow creatures who has done nothing to diminish the natural sympathy we feel towards all humans, this act appears to us as immoral. We call it unjust. Now, an unjust act could not be sanctioned by law without contradiction. This is why any contract involving duress is void. It is not because the decisive cause of the undertaking is external to the individual making it. Rather, it is because this individual has suffered an unjustified injury. It is, in a word, because such a contract is unjust. Thus, the advent of the consensual contract, combined with the development of human feelings of sympathy, led to the idea that a contract was moral, and should be recognized and sanctioned by society, only if it was not just a means for exploiting one of the contracting parties – in a word, unless it was just.

However, it should be remembered that this principle was a new one. It is, in fact, a further transformation of the institution. Indeed, the true consensual contract entails simply that consent is the necessary but sufficient condition of the undertaking. We see now this new condition superimposed on the first which had gradually been becoming the essential condition of the contract. Now, it is not enough for the contract to be by consent, it has to be just and the manner in which the consent is given is merely the external criterion of the degree of fairness in the contract. The subjective state of mind of the contracting parties is no longer the only consideration: now it is the objective consequences of the undertakings that show their worth. In other words, just as the solemn contract gave birth to the consensual contract, so the latter gave birth to a new form of contract. It is the fair contract. We shall see in the next lecture how this new principle developed and how, in developing, it was to deeply change the present institution of ownership.

Just as the solemn contract and the real contract gave birth to the consensual contract, so the latter gave birth to a new form of contract. It is the fair contract, that is, an objectively fair contract. Its existence was proved by the rule whereby a contract is null and void when one of the contracting parties has given his consent only under obvious duress. Society refuses to sanction a declaration of intention that has been obtained by threat. Why is that? The argument that avoidance is due to the absence of the party's free will, as we have just seen, seems groundless. Are we taking the words 'free will' in the metaphysical sense? If so, if man is a free agent, he is free to resist all the pressures exerted against him; his freedom remains entire, whatever he is threatened with. Do we mean that a free act is a spontaneous act, and that the consent entails the spontaneity of the party that consents? How often do we consent, because we are forced by circumstances, constrained by them, without having a choice! And yet when it is things and not persons that place us under duress, the contract thus formed is binding. Under the pressure of illness, I feel myself forced to see a doctor who charges very high fees, I am just as constrained to pay them as if I had a gun at my head. We might give many other examples. There is always some constraint in acts we carry out, and in any consent we give, for they are never exactly in line with our desires. Contracts imply concessions and sacrifices made to avoid worse consequences. In this respect, there are only differences of degree in the ways in which contracts are formed.

The true reason we condemn a contract under duress is that it harms the contracting party who suffered the constraint. For it has forced him to yield what he did not want to, and it has forcibly wrested from him something that he owned. There has been some extortion. What the law refuses to sanction is an act which would make a man suffer undeservedly, that is, an unjust act. When the law does so, it is because our natural sympathy for our fellow-creatures abhors any suffering inflicted on a man, unless this man has previously committed an act that dilutes our sympathy for him and even turns it into the opposite feeling. When society considers a case of consent null and void, it is because such consent causes injury, and not because the party is not deemed to be the true cause of the consent he has given. And thus the validity of the contract becomes subordinated to the consequences it may have for the contracting party.

The injustices resulting from duress are, however, not the only ones that may be committed in the course of contractual relations. They are merely a sub-species. One person can persuade another to consent to utterly unjust transactions (for example, to provide things or services for a price lower than their value), by shrewdness and scheming, or by taking advantage of the other's weaker position. It is true that in each society and at every period of history there has always been a vague but strongly felt sense of the value of the various services and things that can be exchanged. Although the price of neither of these is subjected to public regulation, in each social group there will be a general opinion that fixes, at least roughly, their normal value. There is an average price that is considered the true price, the price that expresses the true value of the thing at a given moment. How this scale of values is arrived at is not our concern for the moment. Many different factors are involved in the building of this scale: a sense of the true utility of things and services, the labour they have cost, the relative ease or difficulty in procuring them, traditions and prejudices of all sorts, and so on. The fact remains (and this alone matters to us for now) that this scale is perfectly real and it is the benchmark by which the fairness of the exchange is judged. This normal price is, of course, only an ideal price; it very rarely coincides with the real price, which naturally varies with circumstances. There is no official quoted value that can apply to all individual cases. It is only a fixed point around which there must necessarily be oscillations in opposite directions, but these oscillations cannot go beyond a certain amplitude in any direction without appearing abnormal. We can even see that the more societies develop, the more this hierarchy of values becomes stable, regular and free from local conditions or particular circumstances, and takes on an objective form. When every town and almost every village had its own market, each locality set its own scale, its own tariff. These variations left far more room for private arrangements. This is why bargaining and individual prices are one of the characteristic features of small-scale trading and industry. However, the more we advance, the more prices are set internationally, through the system of stock exchanges, regulated markets covering entire continents. In olden times, under the system of local markets, in order to arrive at the price of an object there needed to be negotiations and a battle of wits. Today, we merely open the appropriate newspaper. We are also getting more and more used to the idea that the true prices of things exchanged, far from resulting from contracts, have been set beforehand.

This means that any contract that diverges form these prices too greatly must necessarily appear as unjust. An individual cannot exchange a thing for a price lower than its value without suffering an uncompensated and unjustified loss. It is as if as the amount unduly withheld were extorted from him by threat. It is because we think that it is this amount that he should have had, and, if he is despoiled of it without cause, our conscience pricks us, as mentioned earlier. The loss inflicted on him, if it is undeserved, makes us feel sympathy for him. It hardly matters that he does not resist the indirect duress suffered, or that he may even readily accept it. There is something about this exploitation of one man by another that offends us and rouses our indignation, even if it has been consented to by its victim or if it has not been inflicted under genuine duress. It is the same thing, of course, as if the exchange has been agreed at a price higher than the true value, for then it is the buyer who has been exploited. We see now that the notion of duress fades more and more into the background. A just contract is not simply any contract that is freely consented to (that is, without obvious constraint) but a contract by which things and services are exchanged at their true and normal value, in short, at the fair value.

Now, we cannot deny that such contracts seem immoral to us. For us to hold contracts as morally binding, we increasingly demand not only that they should be by consent, but also that they respect the rights of the contracting parties. The first of these rights is to provide goods or services only at a fair price. We disapprove of adhesion contracts, that is, contracts unduly favouring one of the contracting parties at the expense of the other. Therefore, we believe that the society is not bound to enforce it as fully as if it were a fair contract, since it is not equally binding. It is true that these moral judgments have so far remained just that and they have not yet greatly affected the law. The only contracts of this kind that we absolutely refuse to sanction are usurious contracts. In these contracts even the fair price, that is, the rate for lending money, has been fixed by law and it is forbidden to exceed it. For various reasons we need not examine, this particular form of abusive exploitation more swiftly led to stronger moral outrage, perhaps because in this case the exploitation seems more concrete and tangible. But leaving aside the usurious contract, all the regulations currently being introduced in industrial law, the purpose of which is to prevent the employer from abusing his power and paying his workers too little for their work – that is, payment that is far beneath their true value – bear witness to this. This is why there are proposals, justified or other- wise, to fix a statutory minimum wage. This shows that not every contract by consent, even when there was no actual duress, is held to be a valid and fair contract. In the absence of regulations for a minimum wage, there are now provisions in the codes of several European countries that require the employer to provide health, accident and old age insurance to his workers. These feelings also sparked our recent law on industrial accidents. It is one of the many means used by legislators to make labour contracts less unjust. Wages are not fixed, but the employer is obliged to guarantee certain specific advantages to his employees. There have been protests arguing that real privileges are being given to the worker. In one sense, it is true, but these privileges are meant to counterbalance in part the privileges enjoyed by the employer which allow him to undervalue the services provided by the worker at will. I will not examine here the issue of whether these provisions are as useful as they are deemed to be. It may be that they are not the best or even that they run counter to their purpose. It does not matter. It suffices to notice the moral aspirations that inspired them and whose reality they prove.

There are clear signs that this evolution has not come to an end, and that our demands will continue to grow. It is because the feeling of human sympathy that causes them will do likewise, and become more egalitarian as well. Suffering from all kinds of prejudice inherited from the past, we still tend to judge people from other social classes differently. We are more sympathetic to the suffering and undeserved hardship of a man of the upper classes with noble functions, than to that of people with inferior duties and labour. However, it looks as though our way of sympathizing with each of these will gradually even up: the suffering of one class will cease to seem more unbearable to us than the distress of the other, we will consider them as equal by the mere fact that both are instances of human suffering. Therefore we will take firm steps to ensure that the contractual system treats them equally. We will demand greater fairness in contracts. I do not mean that a day will come when this justice will be perfect, when there will be a perfect balance between the services exchanged. We would be right in saying that it is not fully possible. There are indeed services that are beyond any fair remuneration. Moreover, such a perfect equivalence can only be approximate. That being said, it is true that the balance of values today is already inadequate for our present idea of justice, and the more we advance, the more we will seek fairer solutions. Development is unending.

Now, the great obstacle it will encounter is the institution of inheritance. It is obvious that inheritance, by creating inequalities between men at birth that in no way reflect their worth or performances, distorts the entire contractual system from the start. What is the basic condition for guaranteeing the reciprocity of the services exchanged? It is this: in order to be capable of waging the 'battle' from which the contract arises and in the course of which the terms of the exchange are set, the contracting parties must stand as much as possible on an equal footing. Then, and only then, will there be neither victor nor vanquished, that is, things will be exchanged so as to be in balance and to be equal in value. What the one will receive will be equivalent to what he gives and vice versa. Should the contrary occur, the privileged contracting party could use his advantage to impose his will on the other and force him to yield the thing or service he offers at a price below its true value. If, for example, one party is making a contract to have enough to live on, whereas the other is doing it to improve his standard of living, it is obvious that the resistance and strength of the latter will far exceed that of the former, by the mere fact that he can refuse to continue negotiating if he fails to get the terms he wants. The other cannot do so. He therefore has to yield, and be subjected to the rules laid down for him. Now, the institution of inheritance means that men are born either rich or poor, that is, there are two main classes in society, along with various intermediate classes. The first party has to sell his services, at whatever price, to the other in order to have enough to live on, the other can do without these services because he has his own resources – although these resources do not consist of services rendered by those who enjoy them. Therefore, as long as this marked division exists in society, more or less fortunate expedients may lessen the unfairness of contracts; but in principle, the system will continue to function in conditions which will not allow it to be just. Adhesion contracts can be formed in other conditions; but in itself, the system of contracts is always leonine when it comes to the relationship between rich and poor. It is the usual way of assessing the services of those deprived of wealth that seems unjust, because these services are assessed under conditions that do not allow their true social value to be measured. Inherited fortune distorts the balance. It is against this unjust method of evaluation and against the society that allows it that our conscience increasingly protests. No doubt it was accepted unprotestingly over the centuries, because there was less need for equality. However, it is too patently in contradiction with today's morality.

We begin to discern how important the advent of what we have called the fair contract was in history, and what widespread repercussions this concept was bound to have. The institution of ownership was transformed in its entirety, since it would mean the death-knell for one of the main sources of acquisition, inheritance. But the development of contract law does not affect the right of property only in this indirect and negative way: that right is affected directly. We have just said that justice required that the services rendered and exchanged should not be paid below their true price. But this principle entails another one, which is its corollary, stating that any value received must correspond to a service rendered. It is indeed obvious that insofar as there is no such equivalence, the favoured individual can only have obtained the excess value he enjoys by taking it from the other party's share. Hence this principle: the distribution of things among individuals can be just only insofar as it is proportionate to the social worth of each. An individual's property should be the counterpart of the services he has rendered to the society. Nothing in this principle offends the feelings of human sympathy that are at the root of this branch of morals. It is because the intensity of these feelings tends to vary according to the social merit of each individual. We have more sympathy for those who serve the collectivity better; we are better disposed towards them, and therefore we are not inclined to protest if they are better treated (with certain reservations we shall formulate later on). Moreover, it is in the best interests of society that property be distributed thus, because it is important for society that things be in the hands of the most capable.

Thus, the principle that is the basis of fair contracts expands its influence beyond contract law and is becoming the basis of property law. In the current state of things, the primary distribution of property is made according to birth (inheritance); and thenceforth the property originally distributed in this way is exchanged by contracts. But these contracts, inevitably, are in part unjust due to the structural inequality between the contracting parties because of the institution of inheritance. This intrinsic injustice in the right of ownership can only be eliminated if the only economic inequalities dividing men are those resulting from the unequal services they render. That is how the development of contract law has led to a complete overhaul of the morals governing ownership. But close attention should be paid to the way in which we summarily formulate this principle common to property law and contract law. That is not to say that property results from labour, as if there were a kind of logical necessity for the thing to be attributed to the person who worked to make it, as if labour and property were synonyms. The link between the thing and the person, as we said, is not a logical one; there is nothing in labour that by definition entails that the thing this labour applies to belongs to the workman. We have shown the complete impossibility of such a deduction. It is the society that synthesizes these heterogeneous terms, property and labour; it is the society that decides, allocates and distributes according to its feelings for the individual and the way it assesses the value of his services. And since this allocation can be made according to very different principles, it follows that the right of property is in no way something defined once and for all, a kind of immutable concept. On the contrary, it is something that is likely to evolve indefinitely. Even the abovementioned principle can vary more or less, and is therefore capable of development. (We shall return to this point.) At the same time, this is how we avoided the mistakes of the economists and the socialists, when they amalgamated labour and property. In doing so, they gave too much importance to the quantity of labour and not enough to its quality. However, according to what we have just said, it is not the amount of labour put into a thing that gives it value; it is the value assigned to this thing by the society, and this assignment depends not so much on the amount of energy put in, as on the useful effects it produces, or at least those are that are felt by the collectivity, for there is here a subjective factor which is impossible to eliminate. An idea of genius, conceived effortlessly and with pleasure, has greater value and merit than years of manual labour.

Given that this principle, although it is now engraved in the moral consciousness of civilized peoples, is still not formally acknowledged by the law, it raises a practical question. What reform will make it a reality in law? A first reform is possible as of now and almost without transition. It is the abolition of intestate succession, and above all, of the mandatory succession provided for in our Code of Civil Law in the case of direct descent. We have seen moreover that intestate succession, a vestige of the ancient right of family joint ownership, is now archaic and devoid of rationale. It no longer corresponds to anything in our customs and could easily be abolished without troubling the moral structure of our societies in any way. The question may seem more delicate when it comes to testamentary inheritance. It is not because the latter is more easily reconciled with the principle we have just set out. It is because it goes against the spirit of justice just as much as the intestate succession and it creates the same inequalities. Today, we no longer tolerate that titles, dignities that we may have acquired, or offices that we may have held, should be bequeathed. Why, then, should property be transferable? The social position that we have reached is at least as much the result of our work as of our fortune. If the law forbids our disposing of the first, why should it be any different with the second? Such a restriction on the right to dispose of our property in no way undermines the concept of individual property; quite the contrary. It is because individual property is property that begins and ends with the individual. It is rather hereditary transmission, testamentary or otherwise, which runs counter to the spirit of individualism. There are no real difficulties on this matter, except when it comes to testamentary inheritance in the case of direct descent. Here, a kind of conflict arises between our sense of justice and certain family customs that are extremely deep-rooted. It is obvious that today, the idea that we could be prevented from leaving our possessions to our children would be strongly resisted. It is because we work to ensure their happiness as much as ours. However we may think this because of the current structure of ownership. Succession is hereditary and as a result, the economic conditions of individuals are unequal from the very beginning, when they enter life in society. In those circumstances, we seek to make this inequality as advantageous as possible for the people we love best; sometimes, we may even want to weigh the balance in their favour. Hence our concern to work for them. But if equality were the rule, we would feel this need much less, for it would no longer be perilous for them to face life with no other resources but their own. This danger is solely due to the fact that, in the present state of things, certain people benefit from these initial advantages, thus placing the people who do not have them in a state of obvious inferiority. Indeed, it is possible that there will always be remnants of the right to will property. Ancient institutions never disappear entirely, they only recede into the background and die out progressively. The institution of inheritance has played too significant a role in history for it to be possible to suppose that nothing of it should survive. However, only weakened forms will survive. We may imagine for instance that every head of a family would be allowed to leave his children distinct shares of his patrimony. The inequalities thus remaining would be slight enough not to affect the application of contract law seriously.

Moreover, it is impossible today to make any accurate forecast on this matter, for there is a missing element in our knowledge. Where would the wealth let loose, so to speak, by each generation, go when they die? When there are no longer any heirs, by birth or by right, who would then inherit? The State? Anyone can see that it is impossible to concentrate such huge resources in hands already so improvident and wasteful. Or perhaps, it should distribute these things among individuals, or at least certain things, such as those essential to labour (the land, for instance). For instance we can imagine some sort of public auction whereby these kinds of goods would be given to the highest bidder. However, it is clear that the State is too distant from things and individuals to be able to perform such huge and complex tasks with any success. To do this, there should be secondary groups, smaller and closer to the ground. It is difficult to imagine anyone other than professional groups being suited to the task. They are capable of managing every individual type of interests and spread throughout the country; they would also be able to take into account the local differences and circumstances. In the economic sphere, they would be perfectly suited to becoming the heirs of the family. If the family has hitherto been best suited to ensure the stability of economic life, it is because it is a small group in direct touch with people and things, and it was truly enduring. But today this stability no longer exists. The family is continually falling apart, it is only transient, it exists only intermittently. It no longer has sufficient power to link one generation to another economically. But, on the other hand, only a secondary unit, of limited size, can replace it. It can and should be larger than the family because the economic interests themselves have gained importance, and are sometimes scattered all over the country. But it is impossible for any central unit to be present and active everywhere at the same time. All these points, therefore, force us to opt for professional groups. Besides these practical consequences, the study of contract law leads us to an important theoretical point. In the branch of ethics we have just been examining – that, is, human morality, we usually distinguish between two very different categories of duty between which we see a break in continuity: the first ones, duties of justice, and the others, duties of charity. They seem to stem from completely different ideas and feelings. Again, within the category of justice, a further distinction is made, between commutative and retributive justice. The latter is the one that rules or ought to rule exchanges, pursuant to which we ought always to receive a fair price for what we give; the former pertains to the way laws, duties and rank are allocated and apportioned by the society among its members. Now, the consequence of this is that there are only differences of degree between these different layers of morality, and that they correspond to one and the same collective consciousness and to one and the same collective feeling considered at different stages of its development.

First, as far as distributive and retributive justice are concerned, we have seen that they mutually condition and involve each other. For exchanges to be fair, they have to be made according to a fair distribution; and, even if it was initially made pursuant to all the rules of fairness, this sharing out of things would of course still not remain fair if exchanges could be contracted in unfair circumstances. Both are the legal consequence of the same moral sentiment, that is, the feeling of sympathy that man has for man, but considered in both cases from two different angles. On the one hand, an individual should not give more than he receives or render services not paid at their true value. On the other, there should be no social inequalities among men other than those reflecting their own unequal social value. In a word, both forms of this sentiment tend to erase and prevent social acceptance of any physical or material inequalities, or those due to the lottery of birth or to family circumstances, so that only inequalities of merit remain.

As far as justice alone is concerned, however, these inequalities still survive. Now, in terms of human sympathy, even these inequalities cannot be justified. For it is man as a human being that we love and should love, and not as a scientist of genius or as a skilled industrial owner, etc. Ultimately, are not those inequalities of merit fortuitous, too? Are they not inequalities inherited at birth, that it is unjust to make men bear responsibility for? It does not seem fair to us that a man should be better treated in society than another because he was born into such or such wealthy or dignified family. But is it fairer that a man should be better treated in society because he was born of a father of higher intelligence, or in an environment of higher morality? Here is the point where the realm of charity begins. Charity is the sense of human sympathy that disregards even these last forms of inequality, effacing and denying all particular merit in this final form of hereditary succession – intellectual inheritance. In a word, it is justice at its apex. Charity is where society manages to overcome nature completely, imposing its laws on it, and replacing the natural physical inequality of things with moral equality. However, this sense of human sympathy can reach this degree of intensity only in certain higher consciences. There remain, on average, consciences that are too weak to be able to reach the end of their logical development. We have not yet reached the point where man loves all his fellow-creatures as brothers, whatever their intellect, their reasoning or their moral worth. Nor have we reached the point where man has succeeded in shedding his egotism so that he no longer needs to give a temporary value to merit (a value that has a tendency to shrink) in order to stimulate sympathy and to contain egotism. This is what makes complete egalitarianism impossible today. On the other hand, there is no doubt that the feelings of human fraternity are increasingly intense, and that the best among us are capable of working without expecting an exact remuneration for their sufferings and services. This is why we increasingly seek to alleviate and reduce the effects of an overly rigorous distributive and commutative justice – a justice which in reality is always incomplete. And this is why, the more we advance, the more charity becomes [illegible] and, so it ceases to be a kind of superogatory, or optional, duty, and becomes a strict obligation that gives birth to new institutions.

References

Barnes, J.A. 1966. 'Durkheim's *Division of Labour in Society*', *Man* I: 158–75.

Bayet, Albert 1925. *Le Suicide et la morale* Paris: Alcan.

Baxi, Upendra 1974. 'Durkheim and Legal Evolution: Some Problems of Disproof' Comment. *Law and Society Review* 8(4): 645–52.

Becker, Howard S. 1963. *Outsiders: Studies in the Sociology of Deviance* Glencoe, IL: Free Press.

Becker, Howard S. 1974. 'Labelling Theory Reconsidered', in P. Rock and M. MacIntosh (eds) *Deviance and Social Control* London: Tavistock.

Bohannan, Paul 1957. *Justice and Judgment Among the Tiv* London: Oxford University Press.

Bouglé, C. 1907. 'Note sur *l 'Année sociologique*', appendix to his *Qu'est-ce que la sociologie?* Paris: Alcan.

Calavita, Kitty, Dimento, Joseph, Geis, Gilbert and Forti, Gabrio 1991. 'Dam Disasters and Durkheim: An Analysis of the Theme of Repressive and Restitutive Law', *International Journal of the Sociology of Law* 19: 407–26.

Candea, Matei (ed.) 2010. *The Social after Gabriel Tarde: Debates and Assessments* London: Routledge.

Cartwright, B.C., and Schwartz, R.D. 1973. 'The Invocation of Legal Norms: An Empirical Investigation of Durkheim and Weber', *American Sociological Review* 38(3): 340–54.

Chazel, François 1991. 'Emile Durkheim et l'élaboration d'un "programme de recherche" en sociologie du droit.' Pp. 27–38 in *Normes juridiques et régulation sociale*, ed. F. Chazel and J. Commaille. Paris: Librairie générale de droit et de jurisprudence.

Cicourel, Aaron 1967. *The Social Organization of Juvenile Justice* New York: Wiley.

Clarke, Michael 1976. 'Durkheim's Sociology of Law', *British Journal of Law and Society* 3: 246–55.

Clifford-Vaughan, Michalina, and Scotford-Morton, Margaret 1967. 'Legal Norms and Social Order: Petrazycki, Pareto, Durkheim', *British Journal of Sociology* 18: 269–77.

Cochez, Caroline 2004. 'Le droit dans *l'Année sociologique* (1896–1925): Contribution à l'étude de la place du droit dans les premiers temps de l'école durkheimienne' Master's Thesis, Université de Lille, France.

Cohen, Stanley and Scull, Andrew (eds) 1983. *Social Control and the State: Historical and Comparative Essays* Oxford: Martin Robertson.

Corning, P.A. 1982.'Durkheim and Spencer', *British Journal of Sociology* 33 reprinted in Offer (ed.) 2000, vol. 2: 307–29.

Coser, Lewis 1960. 'Durkheim's Conservatism and Its Implications for His Sociological Theory', in Kurt Wolff (ed.) *Essays on Sociology and Philosophy by Emile Durkheim et al.* New York: Harper: 211–32.

Cotterrell, Roger 1977. 'Durkheim on Legal Development and Social Solidarity', *British Journal of Law and Society* 4: 241–52.

Cotterrell, Roger 1991. 'The Durkheimian Tradition in the Sociology of Law', *Law and Society Review* 25.4: 923–45.

Cotterrell, Roger 1997. *Law's Community: Legal Theory in Sociological Perspective* New York: Oxford University Press.

Cotterrell, Roger 1999. *Emile Durkheim: Law in a Moral Domain* Edinburgh: University of Edinburgh Press.

Cotterrell, Roger 2010. 'Justice, Dignity, Torture, Headscarves: Can Durkheim's Sociology clarify Legal Values?', *Social and Legal Studies* 20: 3–20.

Davy, Georges 1920. 'Emile Durkhiem: l'œuvre', *Revue de métaphysique et de morale* 27: 71–112.

Davy, Georges 1922. *La Foi jurée: étude sociologique du problème du contrat* Paris: Alcan.

Deflem, Mathieu 2008. *Sociology of Law: Visions of a Scholarly Tradition.* Cambridge: Cambridge University Press.

Delprat, G. 1900. 'L'Enseignement sociologique à l'Université de Bordeaux', *Revue philomatique de Bordeaux et du Sud-Ouest 3ᵉ année*, August: 357.

Devlin, Lord Patrick 1965. *The Enforcement of Morals* London: Oxford University Press.

Diamond, A.S. 1971. *Primitive Law, Past and Present* London: Methuen.

Didry, Claude. 2000. 'La réforme des groupements professionnels comme expression de la conception durkheimienne de l'État', *Revue française de sociologie* 41(3): 513–38.

Douglas, J.D. 1966. *The Social Meanings of Suicide* Princeton: Princeton University Press.

Dowbiggin, Ian 1991. *Inheriting Madness* Berkeley: University of California Press.

Dubow, Fred 1974. 'Nation Building and the Imposition of Criminal Law', unpublished paper presented to the Annual Meeting of the American Sociological Association, Montreal, Canada.

Durkheim, Emile 1886. 'Les études de science sociale', *Revue philosophique* xxii: 61–80.

Durkheim, Emile 1888a. 'Cours de science sociale: leçon d'ouverture', *Revue internationale de l'enseignement* xv, 1888: 23–48.

Durkheim, Emile 1888b. 'Introduction à la sociologie de la famille', *Annales de la Faculté des Lettres de Bordeaux*: 257–81.

Durkheim, Emile 1892. *Quid Secundatus Politicae scientae Instituendae Contulerit* Bordeaux: Gounouilhou.

Durkheim, Emile 1893. *De la division du travail social: étude sur l'organisation des sociétés supérieures* Paris: Alcan.

Durkheim, Emile 1893 Review of Richard's 'Essay on the Origin of the Idea of Law' ('Essai sur L'origine de L'idée de droit') in *Revue philosophique* 35 (1893), pp. 290–6.

Durkheim, Emile 1895 'Criminality and Social Health' ('Crime et santé sociale'), *Revue philosophique* 39 (1895), pp. 518–23.

Durkheim, Emile 1895. *Les règles de la méthode sociologique* Paris: Alcan.

Durkheim, Emile 1897. *Le suicide: étude de sociologie* Paris: Alcan.

Durkheim, Emile 1898. 'Individualism and the Intellectuals' ('L'Individualisme et les intellectuels'), *Revue bleue*, 4th series 10 (1898) pp. 7–13.

Durkheim, Emile 1898. 'Préface', *L'Année sociologique* 1: i–vii.

Durkheim, Emile 1899. 'Préface', *L'Année sociologique* 2: i–vi.

Durkheim, Emile 1900. Review of 'The Historical Development of Legal Constraint' ('Das Zwangsmoment im Recht in entwicklungsgeshichtlicher Bedeutung') by Neukamp, *L'Année sociologique*, vol. 3 (1900), pp. 324–5.

Durkheim, Emile 1900. 'La sociologie en France au XIXe siècle', *Revue bleue* 12: 609–13 and 647–52.

Durkheim, Emile 1901a. 'Sociology of Crime and of Moral Statistics' ('Sociologie criminelle et statistique morale'), *L'Année sociologique*, vol. 4 (1901), pp. 433–6.

Durkheim, Emile 1901b. 'Two Laws of Penal Evolution' ('Deux lois de l'évolution pénale'), *L'Année sociologique* 4 (1901), pp. 65–95.

Durkheim, Emile 1904a. Review of Lévy-Bruhl's *Morality and the Science of Morals* (*La Morale et la science des mœurs*) in *L'Année sociologique*, vol. 7 (1904), pp. 380–4.

Durkheim, Emile 1904b. Review of Kulischer's 'Research on Primitive Penal Law' ('Untersuchungen über das primitive Strafrecht'), *Zeitschrift für vergleichende Recluswissenschaft*, XVI (1904) Bd., 1–11., pp. 1–22. In *L'Année sociologique*, 8, pp. 460–3.

Durkheim, Emile 1910. 'Moral and Juridical Systems' ('Systèmes juridiques et moraux') in *L'Année sociologique*, vol. 11 (1910), pp. 286–8.

Durkheim, Emile 1912. *Les Formes élémentaires de la vie religieuse* Paris: Alcan.

Durkheim, Emile 1913. Review of Lévy-Bruhl, *Les fonctions mentales dans les sociétiés inférieures* and Durkheim, *Les formes élémentaires de la vie religieuse*, *L'Année sociologique* 12:33–37.

Durkheim, Emile 1950. *Leçons de sociologie: physique des moeurs et du droit.* Istanbul: L'Université d'Istanbul, 'Publications de l'Université, Faculté du Droit no. 111 and Paris: Presses Universitaires de France: 1950.

Durkheim, Emile 1951. *Suicide : A Study in Sociology* translated by J.A. Spaulding and G. Simpson and edited with an Introduction by G. Simpson. Glencoe, IL: Free Press, and London: Routledge & Kegan Paul.

Durkheim, Emile 1957. *Professional Ethics and Civic Morals* translated by Cornelia Brookfield. London: Routledge & Kegan Paul.

Durkheim, Emile 1960. *Montesquieu and Rousseau: Forerunners of Sociology* translated by R. Mannheim. Ann Arbor: University of Michigan Press.

Durkheim, Emile 1961. *Moral Education: A Study in the Theory and Application of the Sociology of Education* translated by Everett K. Wilson and Herman Schnurer, and edited by Everett K. Wilson. New York: Free Press (originally published 1925).

Durkheim, Emile 1963. *Primitive Classification* London: Cohen and West/Chicago: University of Chicago Press (originally published 1903).

Durkheim, Emile 1974. *Sociology and Philosophy* translated by D. F. Pocock with an introduction by J. G. Peristiany including the text of 'The Life and Work of Emile Durkheim' by Talcott Parsons. New York: Free Press.

Durkheim, Emile 1987. 'Sociologie et sciences sociales', reprinted in Durkheim, *La science sociale et l'action* ed. J.C. Filloux, second edition, Paris: Presses Universitaires de France.

Durkheim, Emile 1995 *The Elementary Forms of Religious Life* (1912) translated by Karen E. Fields New York: Free Press.

Durkheim, Emile 2008. 'Anti-Semitism and Crisis', (trans. Chad Goldberg), *Sociological Theory* 26: 321–3 (originally published 1899).

Durkheim, Emile 2013a *The Division of Labour in Society*, Steven Lukes (ed) Basingstoke, Palgrave Macmillan (second edition, originally published 1902).

Durkheim, Emile 2013b *The Rules of Sociological Method and Selected Texts on Sociology and its Method* Steven Lukes (ed.) Basingstoke, Palgrave Macmillan (second edition, originally published 1901).

Durkheim, Emile and Fauconnet, Paul 1903. 'Note sur les systèmes juridiques', *Année sociologique* 6: 305.

Erikson, Kai 1966. *Wayward Puritans* New York: John Wiley.

Fauconnet, Paul 1920. *La responsabilité : étude sociologique* Paris: Alcan.

Foucault, Michel 1965. *Madness and Civilization* New York: Pantheon.

Foucault, Michel 1977. *Discipline and Punish: The Birth of the Prison* London: Allen Lane/New York: Pantheon.

Garland, David 1983. 'Durkheim's Theory of Punishment: A Critique', in D. Garland and P. Young (eds) *The Power to Punish: Contemporary Penality and Social Analysis* London: Heinemann: 37–61.

Garland, David 1990. *Punishment and Modern Society: A Study in Social Theory* Chicago: University of Chicago Press.

Garland, David 1991a. 'Sociological Perspectives on Punishment', *Crime and Justice* 14: 115–65.

Garland, David 1991b. 'The Rationalization of Punishment', in Heikki Pihlajamäki (ed.) *Theatres of Power: Social Control and Criminality in Historical Perspective* Helsinki: Matthias Calonius Society.

Garland, David 2001. *The Culture of Control: Crime and Social Order in Contemporary Society* Chicago: University of Chicago Press.

Garland, David 2006. 'Concepts of Culture in the Sociology of Punishment', *Theoretical Criminology* 10, 4: 419–47.

Gluckman, Max 1955. *The Judicial Process Among the Barotse of Northern Rhodesia* Glencoe: Free Press.

Harcourt, Bernard 2011. *The Illusion of Free Markets: Punishment and the Myth of Natural Order* Cambridge, MA and London: Harvard University Press.

Hart, H.L.A. 1955. 'Are There Any Natural Rights?', *Philosophical Review* 64: 175–91.

Hart, H.L.A. 1961. *The Concept of Law* Oxford: Oxford University Press.

Hart, H.L.A. 1968. 'Social Solidarity and the Enforcement of Morality', *University of Chicago Law Review* 35: 1–13.

Hay, Douglas 1975. 'Property, Authority and the Criminal Law', in D. Hay *et al.* *Albion's Fatal Tree* New York: Pantheon: 17–63.

Hay, Douglas, Linebaugh, Peter, Rule, J.G., Thompson, E.P. and Cal Winslow 1975. *Albion's Fatal Tree: Crime and Society in Eighteenth Century England* Harmondsworth: Penguin.

Hayek, Friedrich A. 1978. *New Studies in Philosophy, Economics and the History of Ideas* London: Routledge.

Hoebel, E.A. 1954. *The Law of Primitive Man* Cambridge: Harvard University Press.

Hunt, A. 1978. *The Sociological Movement in Law* Philadelphia: Temple University Press.

Huvelin, Paul 1907. 'Magie et droit individuel', *Année sociologique* 10: 1–47.

Ignatieff, Michael 1978. *A Just Measure of Pain: The Penitentiary and the Industrial Revolution* New York: Pantheon.

Ingold, T. 1986. *Evolution and Social Life* Cambridge: Cambridge University Press.

Joas, Hans 1993. 'Durkheim's Intellectual Development: The Problem of the Emergence of New Morality and New Institutions as a Leitmotif in Durkheim's Oeuvre', pp. 229–45 in S. P. Turner (ed.), *Emile Durkheim: Sociologist and Moralist* London: Routledge.

Joas, Hans 2008. 'Punishment and Respect: The Sacralization of the Person and its Endangerment', *Journal of Classical Sociology* 8: 159–77.

Jones, T.A. 1981. 'Durkheim Deviance and Development: Opportunities Lost and Regained', *Social Forces* 59: 1009–24.

Lanza-Kaduce, Lonn, Krohn, Marvin D., Radosevich, Marcia and Akers, Ronald L. 1979. 'Law and Durkheimian Order: An Empirical Examination of the Convergence of Legal and Social Definitions of Law', pp. 41–61 in *Structure, Law, and Power: Essays in the Sociology of Law*, eds P. J. Brantingham and J. M. Kress. Beverly Hills: Sage Publications.

Lemert, Edwin 1951. *Social Pathology* New York: McGraw-Hill.

Lemert, Edwin 1967. *Human Deviance, Social Problems, and Social Control* Englewood Cliffs: Prentice Hall.

Lenman, B. and Parker, G. 1980. 'The State, the Community, and the Criminal Law in Early Modern Europe', in V.A.C. Gatrell, B. Lenman and G. Parker eds *Crime and the Law: The Social History of Crime in Western Europe Since 1500* London: Europa.

Lévy, E. 1899. *Responsabilité et contrat* Paris: Librairie Cotillon.

Lévy-Bruhl, H. 1961. *Sociologie du droit* Paris: Presses Universitaires de France.

Linebaugh, Peter 1975. 'The Tyburn Riot against the Surgeons', in D. Hay *et al. Albion's Fatal Tree* New York: Pantheon: 65–117.

Lukes, Steven *Emile Durkheim: His Life and Work* first published by Harper & Row, New York 1972, by Allen Lane in 1973 and by Peregrine Books 1975.

Lukes, Steven 2006. 'Liberal Democratic Torture', *British Journal of Political Science* 36: 1–16.

Lukes, Steven and Prabhat, Devyani 2012. 'Durkheim on Law and Morality: The Disintegration Thesis', *Journal of Classical Sociology* 12, 3–4: 363–83.

Maine, H.S. 1919. *Ancient Law* 10th edn. London: John Murray.

Malinowski, Bronislaw 1922. *Argonauts of the Western Pacific* London: Routledge.

Malinowski, Bronislaw 1966. *Crime and Custom in Savage Society* Totowa: Littlefield Adams.

Martinson, Robert 1974. 'What Works: Questions and Answers about Prison Reform', *The Public Interest* 35, Spring: 22–54.

Matza, David 1969. *Becoming Deviant* Englewood Cliffs: Prentice Hall.

Mauss, Marcel 1896. 'La religion et les origines du droit pénal', *Revue de l'histoire des religions* 34: 269–95 and 35: 31–60, reprinted in M. Mauss, *Œuvres* vol. 2, ed. V. Karady. Paris: Editions de Minuit, 1969: 651–98.

Mauss, Marcel 1925. 'In memoriam: l'oeuvre inédite de Durkheim et de ses collab-oratueurs', *L'Année sociologique*, new series, 1: 7–29.

Merton, Robert K. 1934. 'Durkheim's Division of Labor in Society', *American Journal of Sociology* 40(3): 319–28.

Mills, C. Wright 1959. *The Sociological Imagination* New York: Oxford University Press.

Moberly, Sir Walter 1968. *The Ethics of Punishment* London: Faber & Faber.

Morel, B.A.1857. *Traité des dégénérescences physique, intellectuelles, et morales de l'espèce humaine* Paris: Masson.

Moyn, Samuel 2010. *The Last Utopia: Human Rights in History.* Cambridge: Harvard University Press.

Needham, Rodney 1963. 'Introduction', to Emile Durkheim, *Primitive Classification* London: Cohen and West/Chicago: University of Chicago Press.

Nye, Robert 1984. *Crime, Madness, and Politics in Modern France* Princeton: Princeton University Press.

Offer J. (ed.) 2000. *Herbert Spencer: Critical Assessments* 4 vols. London and New York: Routledge.

Offer, J. 2010. *Herbert Spencer and Social Theory* Basingstoke and New York: Palgrave Macmillan.

Parsons, Talcott 1937. *The Structure of Social Action* Second edition 1949. New York: McGraw Hill.

Pearce, Frank 1989. *The Radical Durkheim* London: Unwin Hyman.

Perrin, R. 1995. 'Durkheim's *Division of Labour* and the shadow of Herbert Spencer', *Sociological Quarterly* 36 reprinted in Offer (ed.) 2000 vol 2: 339–60.

Prosser, Tony 2006. 'Regulation and Social Solidarity', *Journal of Law and Society* 33(3): 364–87.

Rothman, David 1974. 'Prisons: The Failure Model', *The Nation* 21 December.

Scheff, Thomas 1966. *Being Mentally Ill: A Sociological Theory* Chicago: Aldine.

Schwartz, R.D. 1974. 'Legal Evolution and the Durkheim Hypothesis: A Reply to Professor Baxi', *Law and Society Review* 8(4): 653–68.

Schwartz, R.D. and Miller, J.C. 1964. 'Legal Evolution and Societal Complexity', *American Journal of Sociology* 70: 159–69.

Searle, John R. 1997. *The Construction of Social Reality* New York: Free Press.

Searle, John R. 2010. *Making the Social World: The Structure of Human Civilization* New York: Oxford University Press.

Serafimova, Maria, Hunt, Stephen, Marinov, Mario, with Vladov, Vladimir, Consulting editor and translation from Bulgarian, 2009. *Sociology and Law: The 150th Anniversary of Emile Durkheim (1858–1917).* Newcastle upon Tyne: Cambridge Scholars Publishing.

Sheleff, L. S. 1975. 'From Restitutive to Repressive Law: Durkheim's *The Division of Labour in Society* Revisited', *Archives européennes de sociologie (European Journal of Sociology)* 16: 15–45.

Sheleff, L. S. 1997. *Social Cohesion and Legal Coercion: A Critique of Weber, Durkheim and Marx* Amsterdam: Rodopi.

Skolnick, Jerome 1966. *Justice Without Trial* New York: John Wiley.

Skrentny, John 2004. *The Minority Rights Revolution* Cambridge: Harvard University Press.

Smith, G.H. 1981. 'Herbert Spencer's theory of causation', *Journal of Libertarian Studies* 5 reprinted in Offer (ed.). 2000 vol 2: 384–425.

Smith, Philip 2003. 'Narrating the Guillotine: Punishment Technology as Myth and Symbol', *Theory, Culture and Society* 20(5): 27–51.

Spitzer, Steven 1975. 'Punishment and Social Organization: A Study of Durkheim's Theory of Penal Evolution', *Law and Society Review* 9: 613–38.

Spitzer, Steven and Scull, Andrew 1977. 'Social Control in Historical Perspective: From Private to Public Responses to Crime', in David Greenberg (ed.) *Corrections and Punishment* Beverly Hills: Sage.

Stone, Lawrence 1987. *The Past and Present Revisited* London: Routledge & Kegan Paul.

Sudnow, David 1965. 'Normal Crimes: Sociological Features of the Penal Code in a Public Defender's Office', *Social Problems* 255–76.

Tarde, Gabriel 1895. 'Criminality and Social Health' ('Criminalité et santé sociale') *Revue philosophique* 39: 148–62.

Tarde, Gabriel 1898. *Études de psychologie sociale* Paris: Giard et Brière.

Taylor, Ian, Walton, Paul and Young, Jock 1973. *The New Criminology* London: Routledge & Kegan Paul.

Thompson, E.P. 1975. *Whigs and Hunters: The Origin of the Black Act* New York: Pantheon.

Thompson, K. 1985 *Readings from Emile Durkheim* London: Tavistock.

Tiryakian, Edward A. 1964. 'Durkheim's "Two Laws of Penal Evolution"', *Journal for the Scientific Study of Religion* 3(2): 261–6.

Traugott, Mark 1978. 'Introduction' to *Emile Durkheim on Institutional Analysis* Chicago: University of Chicago Press.

Trubeck, David 1972. 'Max Weber on Law and the Rise of Capitalism', *Wisconsin Law Review* 3: 720–53.

Turkel, Gerald 1979. 'Testing Durkheim: Some Theoretical Considerations', *Law and Society Review* 13: 721–38.

Veitch, Kenneth 2010. 'Social Solidarity and the Power of Contract', *Journal of Law and Society* 38, 2: 189–214.

Vogt, W. Paul 1983. 'Obligation and Right: The Durkheimians and the Sociology of Law', in P. Besnard (ed.) *The Sociological Domain: The Durkheimians and the Founding of French Sociology* Cambridge: Cambridge University Press.

Vogt, W. Paul 1993. 'Durkheim's Sociology of Law: Morality and the Cult of the Individual', pp. 71–94 in *Emile Durkheim: Sociologist and Moralist*, ed. S. P. Turner. London: Routledge.

Wacquant, Loïc 2009a. *Punishing the Poor: The Neoliberal Government of Social Insecurity* Durham: Duke University Press.

Wacquant, Loïc 2009b. *Prisons of Poverty* Minneapolis: University of Minnesota Press.

Wacquant, Loïc forthcoming. *Deadly Symbiosis: Race and the Rise of the Penal State* Cambridge: Polity Press.

Weber, Max 1966. *Max Weber on Law in Economy and Society* Max Rheinstein (ed.) Cambridge: Harvard University Press.

Weber, Max 1978. *Economy and Society* G. Roth and C. Wittich (eds) Berkeley: University of California Press.

Wimberley, Howard 1973. 'Legal Evolution: One Further Step', *American Journal of Sociology* 79(1): 78–83.

Zafirovski, M.Z. 2000. 'Spencer is Dead, Long Live Spencer: Individualism, Holism and the Problem of Norms' *British Journal of Sociology* 51 (3): 553–79.

Index

Notes: **bold type** = extended discussion or term emphasised in text; n = endnote or footnote; t = table.